Tim Hartman's *Kwame Bediako: African Theology*
theological commentary on the life and work of c
twentieth-century theologians. It is a commendab
in the contours and trajectories of world Christiaı
not immortalize, the huge contributions that Kwame Bediako made to our understanding of the intersection between the church in Africa and world Christianity. We
simply cannot talk about Christianity as a non-Western religion without Bediako's life
and work, from his conversion from atheism to Christianity, and subsequently, to the
establishment of the Akrofi-Christaller Institute of Theology, Mission and Culture.
Hartman offers us an insightful and holistic engagement with Bediako's theological legacy that students, scholars, and ordinary Christians will all find very helpful
in understanding Bediako, who brought together in his person what it means to be
a conservative evangelical Christian, an African, and an astute theologian, without
undermining any of those identities.

J. Kwabena Asamoah-Gyadu, PhD FGA
Baëta-Grau Professor of Contemporary African Christianity and Pentecostal Theology,
President, Trinity Theological Seminary, Legon, Ghana

It has been my observation through the years that the more helpful interpreters of
Kwame Bediako have been those who have drawn on a significant number of his works,
published or otherwise. The merit of this book is that it identifies succinctly key themes
in Bediako's writings and demonstrates exposure to an extensive range of material,
making for a more illuminating analysis and a helpful navigation of criticisms that
have been levelled against Bediako's ideas. At the same time, the self-acknowledged
Westerner's perspective points to the potential value of Bediako's insights for Christian
self-understanding and theological innovation in the West.

Gillian Mary Bediako, PhD
Deputy Rector, Akrofi-Christaller Institute of Theology, Mission and Culture,
Akropong-Akuapem, Ghana

Tim Hartman has written a brilliant book interrogating Kwame Bediako's theology of
culture, identity, and history in light of Bediako's use of patristics and twentieth-century
African theology. Hartman invites readers to think with Bediako and his interlocutors,
and the result is an illuminating theological exposé and debate on the Christocentric
focus of an iconic African theologian of the twenty-first century – one who joined his
ancestors much too soon.

Elias Kifon Bongmba, PhD
Harry and Hazel Chavanne Chair in Christian Theology,
Chair, Department of Religion, Rice University, Houston, Texas, USA
Executive Editor, *The Journal of Religion in Africa*

If we are to take seriously the theological implications of world Christianity, there is no better person to begin consulting than Kwame Bediako. His thoughtful considerations about indigenous and Christian identity, the translatability of the gospel, the (dis)continuities between historic and local expressions of Christianity, and the contextual relevance of theology, resonate deeply with the concerns of today's Christians in so many parts of the world. Tim Hartman has done us a tremendous service by composing this meticulous and readable primer to the foremost theologian produced by Africa in the late twentieth century.

Alexander Chow, PhD
Senior Lecturer in Theology and World Christianity,
Co-Director, Centre for the Study of World Christianity,
School of Divinity, University of Edinburgh, UK

This book reflects upon numerous important African theological contributions to world Christianity. First, it offers a comprehensive and textured theological engagement with the person and work of one of Africa's most important contemporary theologians, Kwame Bediako. In doing so, Tim Hartman provides a superb engagement with Bediako's work, making it accessible to a much wider theological audience. Second, this book helps African Christian theologians to access a rich and important source of African contextual theology. I highly recommend this book to anyone who wishes to understand the contribution of contemporary African Christian theology in the shaping of world Christianity.

Dion A. Forster, PhD
Director of the Beyers Naudé Centre for Public Theology,
University of Stellenbosch, South Africa

As a theologian from Asia, I welcome Hartman's invitation to learn from Bediako's significant theological legacy. This book affirms and strengthens the collective non-Western contribution to Christian theology that has received inadequate attention. Hartman models a critical and constructive engagement with Bediako's theological methods and conclusions. For example, as one interested in the church's role in the public space, I was challenged to review the theological decisions needed while reflecting on a theology of "nondominating power." This is relevant when we are increasingly aware of living in a religiously pluralistic world threatened by forces promoting religious hegemony. Hartman helpfully sheds light on Bediako's turn to Christ's notion of power: "the power of forgiveness over retaliation, of suffering over violence, of love over hostility, of humble service over domination" (pg. 118).

The gaps and critiques of Bediako's theological contributions or omissions are not overlooked. In our *learning from* and *thinking with* Bediako and Christians from Africa, I am inspired to join Hartman and theologians around the world on a theologically reflexive journey where our "theological assumptions and beliefs will be remade in the process" (pg. 128). Bediako proposed a theological revolution; Hartman's overview of Bediako's thought invites us to join this quiet revolution with humility and courage.

Rev. Sivin Kit, PhD
Program Executive for Public Theology and Interreligious Relations,
Theology for Transformation/Action for Justice,
Department for Theology, Mission and Justice,
The Lutheran World Federation

This is an astonishing, exciting, and important book, because it uses the work of Kwame Bediako, confirming that theology *is* biography. Tim Hartman describes the work of Bediako in an illuminating manner and has been able to weave into it the work of other scholars including their critiques on Bediako's works. Hartman locates the theology of Bediako in his personal relationship with Christ and shows how that identity in Christ provided Bediako with the tools to navigate the tensions of Christian identity in his own culture. To use the words of Bediako himself, "theology is God's encounter with a person in and with his/her particular and peculiar identity. Identity is essentially the partner and interlocutor of vibrant theology." This is a way of doing theology that is genuine and contextual not a pre-fabricated construct from somewhere else. This book demonstrates how Bediako has shown from his work and life that it is possible to be truly African and truly Christian.

Esther Mombo, PhD
Lecturer, St. Paul's University, Limuru, Kenya

In this deeply engaging and accessible book, Tim Hartman offers a comprehensive and critical engagement with the scholarship of Kwame Bediako. Thoroughly reflexive throughout of his positioning as a white North American, Hartman's engagement is neither patronizingly hagiographical nor prudently uncritical. While Bediako himself did not characterize his own work as "decolonial," in many ways the account that Hartman offers suggests that Bediako may have inadvertently provided discernible direction to the "decolonial turn" that is gaining increasing scholarly and popular traction. If anything, Bediako's work, as it is presented here, should be considered as part of the genealogy of decolonial knowledge production. This is essential reading for scholars and students wanting to understand how Bediako's work theologically repositions power and resistance, beyond Western modernity, by reclaiming epistemologies and theologies that are distinctly African.

Sarojini Nadar, PhD
Director, Desmond Tutu Centre for Religion and Social Justice

Kwame Bediako: African Theology for a World Christianity is a cogent summary of Kwame Bediako's thought which also considers the views of his critics. It ably weaves together Bediako's views and captures the themes that were dear to him. The book preserves the freshness and enduring nature of Bediako's ideas to the glory of God and the service of the global church.

Indeed, Bediako always maintained that the shift in the center of gravity of Christianity to the southern continents, especially Africa, was not to be a basis for any triumphalism on the part of Africans but rather an opportunity for service to the global church. This book helps to advance that service, especially to the church in the West. It should be required reading not only for accessing Bediako's thought but also for an initial appreciation of one major African theologian's contribution to world Christianity. Tim Hartman thus achieves the twin aims that he set out in his preface.

Benhardt Yemo Quarshie, PhD
Rector, Akrofi-Christaller Institute of Theology, Mission and Culture,
Akropong-Akuapem, Ghana

The Ghanaian Presbyterian theologian Kwame Bediako was at the same time profoundly African in his cultural perspectives and profoundly evangelical in his theological convictions. That combination, though not unique, is all too rare in academic writing, and Tim Hartman's book is a valuable exposition of why and how Bediako held these two allegiances together. Hartman responds carefully to the criticisms that other African theologians have levelled against Bediako. This book also forms a powerful call to evangelical Christians in the West to heed the serious challenge that Bediako's writings pose to their false assumptions that their own understanding of the faith is somehow free of cultural distortions.

Brian Stanley, PhD
Professor of World Christianity,
School of Divinity, University of Edinburgh, UK

Kwame Bediako

Langham
GLOBAL LIBRARY

Kwame Bediako

African Theology for a World Christianity

Tim Hartman

Langham
GLOBAL LIBRARY

© 2021 Tim Hartman

Published 2021 by Langham Global Library
An imprint of Langham Publishing
www.langhampublishing.org

Langham Publishing and its imprints are a ministry of Langham Partnership

Langham Partnership
PO Box 296, Carlisle, Cumbria, CA3 9WZ, UK
www.langham.org

ISBNs:
978-1-83973-073-3 Print
978-1-83973-489-2 ePub
978-1-83973-490-8 Mobi
978-1-83973-491-5 PDF

Published in the USA and Canada by Fortress Press

British Library Cataloguing-in-Publication Data
A catalogue record for this book is available from the British Library

ISBN: 978-1-83973-073-3

Cover & Book Design: projectluz.com

In memory of Manasseh Kwame Dakwa Bediako –
may your deep theological wisdom
and love of Jesus Christ
continue to shape the Christian faith of the twenty-first century.

Contents

Acknowledgements

Kwame Bediako passed away four years before I started reading his writings. I have tried to compensate for not getting to know him personally by reading everything he published, visiting Ghana five times in the last eight years, and talking to as many people as possible who knew him. My learning was given invaluable aid by Dr. Gillian Mary Bediako, Kwame's widow, without whose support and generous sharing of unpublished documents this book could not have been written. I am grateful for her patience with the many questions from this white North American who was eager to learn about her late husband. With her blessing, the staff of the Akrofi-Christaller Institute opened their library and accommodations to me. I am especially grateful to B. Y. Quarshie, Ben Asiedu, Abraham Ng'ang'a Waigi, Philip Laryea, Rudolf Gaisie, and Femi Adeleye for their kindnesses and advice shared with me. The insight and encouragement from Kwabena Asamoah-Gyadu, Mercy Oduyoye, and John Azumah, and video footage from James Ault gave me a broader understanding and deeper appreciation for Bediako and his writings.

I wrote this book during a sabbatical from Columbia Theological Seminary that was extended by a generous Sabbatical Grant for Researchers from the Louisville Institute. Thank you to Kelly Campbell and her staff at the John Bulow Campbell Library – Erica Durham, Tammy Johnson, Mary Martha Riviere, and especially Griselda Lartey, who responded to my numerous requests with patience and wisdom – and to Martha Moore-Keish for covering for me while I was away from teaching and for her comments on the introduction and conclusion; to student research assistants Hannah Trawick, Kathy Saxbury, and Caitlin Hubler. Thank you to Tom Petty who translated portions of Bediako's French master's thesis and first doctorate, and to Dave Rohrer who gave vital feedback on the manuscript through his pastoral eyes. Thank you to Pieter Kwant and Luke Lewis of Langham Publishing for their persistence and flexibility, and to Carey Newman at Fortress Press for his passion for this project.

One of the privileges of the extended sabbatical was the opportunity to live with my family in Cape Town, South Africa, while I served as a visiting scholar at the Desmond Tutu Centre for Religion and Social Justice at the University of the Western Cape. The generative conversations with colleagues, especially Teddy Sakupapa's insistence on a chapter about politics, the proximity to many African theologians, and the blessing of René August's friendship, were deep gifts. Additional research was partially supported by the Desmond Tutu Chair in Religion and Social Justice, Sarojini Nadar, under the auspices of the National Research Foundation of South Africa (Grant number: 118854). Of course, I acknowledge that the opinions, findings, and conclusions expressed in this book are mine alone, and the NRF, the Akrofi-Christaller Institute, the Louisville Institute, and no other person or entity accepts any liability whatsoever for my views.

Thank you to my wife and children for joining me on this grand adventure. For sending me off, welcoming me home, and joining me on my sabbatical travels. May we continue to live out what we have learned from Kwame Bediako and African Christian thought. For me, Bediako has served as an apostle to the West, though he would not describe himself that way. My hope is that this book will encourage readers, Africans and non-Africans, to learn from Bediako for themselves, and to allow him to shape their theological thinking as he has mine.

Preface

Kwame Bediako's writings first drew me in through his engagement with questions of identity, gospel, and culture that I found so similar to questions I was asking as a theologian and pastor. Both Bediako's methods and his content offered me significant insights into how to better understand the disconnects that I felt between much of the teachings of contemporary North American Christianity and the prevailing cultural questions of the early twenty-first century. In my experience, contemporary theology – particularly of the more "popular" varieties – is an extended exercise in talking to ourselves. There is an insularity to the conversations as well as significant anxiety about why young people are not coming to church, or how to talk with people of non-Christian religions, or how to be Christian in an increasingly secular age. My nascent intuition noted that while many authors sense that what they are writing is not making the difference they intend or hope for, they do not know how to get outside the theological bubble that had formed and nurtured them. Kwame Bediako offers a breath of fresh air.

Bediako presses readers to interrogate their own theological convictions. Reflecting on Christian identity in light of cultural presuppositions, Bediako asks what it means to be African and Christian after the shortcomings of colonialism. Amid today's increasing secularization and intensifying globalization, Christians in Europe and North America must ask what it means to be Christian after Christendom when Christians no longer possess political power nor dominate the cultural narratives. Many Western Christians are not prepared to answer contemporary questions about Christian identity, the relationship between gospel and culture, religious pluralism, and, most simply, what is the gospel? Learning from someone who has thought through these issues can be extremely helpful. Through an in-depth study of a single African theologian, misleading stereotypes of Africans and African Christians may be overcome. Reading a theologian such as Bediako offers Western Christians a wider canon of resources than have previously been employed by most Western theologians. Bediako analyzed Western thought and theology from the perspective of an informed outsider. His writings present an opportunity for Western Christians to emulate the alternative theological foundation of his theology.

Bediako's work exposes how syncretistic Western theology can be while also offering concrete suggestions for the future of Western theology. For Christians who believe that their theology is self-evident, or without context, Bediako's work names some of the cultural blinders that are endemic to Western theology. For Christians who seek to safely maintain their theological views by labeling the views of others with a modifier such as feminist theology, liberation theology, or Asian-American theology, Bediako offers a mirror. His writings expand the ways that cultural understandings – whether Western, or African, or any other culture – and the gospel of Jesus Christ can be unconsciously confused.

Implicit in my overview of Bediako's thought is the reality that I am an outsider to Bediako's world. I am not African, and I never had the opportunity to meet him. I am a white male of European descent born and raised in the United States. While my intent is to offer this book as an introduction to Bediako's thought in a manner that is faithful to his entire corpus, I am aware that my selections of what is significant are shaped by my own biases. This book is a theological introduction rather than a biography. My focus is primarily on Bediako's ideas rather than on his life. Hopefully a biography of Bediako will soon be written, possibly by a Ghanaian. My hope is that this book will function in two ways. First, as a clear, straightforward, objective as possible introduction to Bediako's ideas and contributions to Christian thought. This first angle will be useful for a wide audience from around the world who simply want to know what Bediako has said, or want to learn something about African theology, or have never read an African theologian before. Toward this end, each chapter will offer a list of suggestions for further reading from Bediako's writings. Second, especially for readers unfamiliar with Christian theologies that have originated from the African context, this book will paint a clear picture of how Bediako – as an African theologian – understands Christian thought and challenges myopic theological understandings by offering alternative ways of understanding the Christian faith. My hope is that theological understandings will be broadened and that unhelpful, oppressive, and misguided theological understandings would be dropped.

For those new to Bediako, his volume of collected essays entitled *Jesus and the Gospel in Africa* is the best place to start because of its accessibility, affordability, and range of content.[1] *Jesus and the Gospel in Africa* offers a number of Bediako's essays and book excerpts and includes Bediako's best-known essay, "Jesus in African Culture: A Ghanaian Perspective," as well as

---

1. Kwame Bediako, *Jesus and the Gospel in Africa* (Maryknoll, NY: Orbis Books, 2004).

selections from his two monographs, *Theology and Identity: The Impact of Culture upon Christian Thought in the Second Century and Modern Africa* and *Christianity in Africa: The Renewal of a Non-Western Religion.*[2] For readers who have already read Bediako's three books, the next step is to consult the Further Reading of Kwame Bediako lists at the end of each chapter. At this time, Bediako's articles and lectures from 2000 until his death in 2008 have not yet been compiled into a published volume.

Bediako offers both critique and a call to action. North American Christians must interrogate their own theological assumptions and begin the process of learning from those outside the West.[3] With growing attention on Christianity in the global South, scholars, theological educators, and other Christians can learn from Bediako's belief that African Christianity is a laboratory for theological innovation that can benefit the whole world.

---

2. Kwame Bediako, *Theology and Identity: The Impact of Culture upon Christian Thought in the Second Century and Modern Africa* (Oxford: Regnum, 1992); *Christianity in Africa: The Renewal of a Non-Western Religion* (Edinburgh: Edinburgh University Press, 1995).

3. Though Bediako shaped the field of African Christian thought, his work is not unique. His thought builds on the work of John Mbiti, Bolaji Idowu, Andrew Walls, Lamin Sanneh, and others while offering what would later be called a contextual theology with some similarities (and stark differences) in approach to Stanley Samartha, Lesslie Newbigin, and even Douglas John Hall.

Introduction

Kwame Bediako was an accomplished theologian, a provocative orator, and a passionate teacher. His intellect and personality came together in the classroom at the Akrofi-Christaller Institute of Theology, Mission, and Culture in Akropong-Akuapem, Ghana. He begins a 2006 class by stating, "We need to set things a bit in context as we [just] prayed about turning the world upside-down." To make his point, Bediako posts a map from the early twentieth century and says, "This map of the world's religions and missions is now outdated." The map used colors to indicate the prominence of a given religion in a certain region. Europe and North America are colored pink indicating the large number of Christians. Africa, Asia, and South America are colored grey indicating non-Christians, or heathens. Bediako continues, "You see the pink shading shows where the Christians are, but that is *where they were*. And the darker shading shows where the non-Christians are." He then gestures at the map to show and emphasize the significance of his points: "If we were to remake this map at the end of the twentieth century, we would shade this pink along here [the lands south of the equator] and shade the other colors and the heathen colors here [North America and Europe]." After a pause, Bediako reflects on the significance of the changes in the world Christian population during the twentieth century: "That there should be in our own time such a radical shift in the center of gravity. No one saw it coming."[1]

The Edinburgh Missionary Conference of 1910 had ushered in the so-called "Christian Century" by concluding that Africa had nothing to offer religiously.[2] The expectation was that Africans (as well as Asians) would grow into Christians who understood themselves and the world from a distinctly European point of view. As European influence continued to grow through colonial structures in the early twentieth-century, Western Christianity was expected to flourish as well. The goal was for Africans and others to become little Christs and little Europeans. To the great surprise of many, the Christian

---

1. *African Christianity Rising*, film directed by James Ault (Northampton, MA: James Ault Productions, 2013). See "Kwame Bediako – pieces of his life story," 26 May 2013, https://www.youtube.com/watch?v=kqMdQr_n8j8, and http://jamesault.com/documentaries/africa-project/.

2. For more on the Edinburgh Missionary Conference of 1910, see Brian Stanley, *The World Missionary Conference, Edinburgh 1910* (Grand Rapids: Eerdmans, 2009).

faith only began to grow in Africa *after* the missionaries left and colonization had formally ended.

While Christianity has been receding in the West, both in terms of influence and numbers of adherents, Christianity has been growing exponentially in the global South. In 1910, 66 percent of Christians worldwide lived in Europe and North America. In 2010, 61 percent of Christians lived in the global South, and 63 percent of Africans are Christians.[3] While the number of Christians worldwide has quadrupled over the last century to 2.2 billion, the proportion of the world population that is Christian has remained constant at about one-third. Yet in a dramatic change few saw coming, there are now nearly twice as many Christians in the global South than the global North.

Bediako believed that these demographic shifts necessitated theological shifts. He continued his 2006 class asking, with a vision for the future, if "the church of the next century will be deeply affected and shaped by what will have happened in the minds and the lives and testimony of Christians where the Christians *now are?*"[4] This shift in the center of gravity formed the basis for Bediako's life work on Christian identity, the infinite translatability of the gospel of Jesus Christ, Christianity as a non-Western religion, and the impact of African Christianity on the wider world. However, his main interest was not primarily sociological but theological. Bediako's interest in the statistics of religious adherence came from his belief that God is at work in each individual, especially Africans.

Maintaining the status quo of the Christian faith and Christian theological reflection was not a possibility for Bediako. The tremendous, unexpected growth of Christianity in Africa that took place after the European missionaries left must change how Christians think about God and their faith. In his 2006 classroom, Bediako moved from demographic observation to theological provocation in his conclusion: "Then the question arises: what is the nature of our Christianity?"[5] The significant growth of the Christian faith outside of Europe and North America during the last half century demonstrates that Christianity is not simply a Western phenomenon. What *is* the nature of our Christianity?

In many ways, Bediako's theological project is quite audacious, so much so that his methods might offend some theologians trained in the Western

---

3. "Global Christianity: A Report on the Size and Distribution of the World's Christian Population," Pew Research Center, 19 December 2011.

4. Ault, *African Christianity Rising.*

5. Ault.

academy. In short, Bediako believed that Western culture had corrupted the Christian faith. As soon as Emperor Constantine had yoked political power with the Christian faith in the fourth century, Christianity became poisoned.[6] In Bediako's first book, *Theology and Identity*, he compares four Greco-Roman theologians with four twentieth-century African theologians. Bediako's explicit claim is that the most helpful and necessary starting points for the work on identity and questions of gospel and culture in African Christian thought in the mid-twentieth century lay in the earliest Christian theologians. His implicit claim is that there are no theologians worth reading between the years 450 and 1950! All of the Christian theologians in that entire millennium and a half were compromised by their access to power and privilege. As a result, everyone after Augustine, from Aquinas to Calvin to Wesley to Barth, were of little use for Bediako's project of decolonizing the African Christian mind. All of these theologians were *Western*, indelibly shaped by Western culture and Western readings of the Bible. They were part of the story of Western Christianity that Africans can learn from but should not be taken as normative. For Bediako, the assumptions of Western Christianity led to the horrors of colonization in Africa and around the globe. Any Christianity that was going to be truly African would have to emerge from outside of Western Christianity, not within it. Bediako explicitly sought a different canon of resources to expand the Christian theological imagination. His theology presents an alternate, non-Western foundation for theological reflection.

Bediako knew well what he was rejecting. Schooled in the finest missionary schools in the Gold Coast (later Ghana), he earned two European doctorates: the first in Francophone literature from the University of Bordeaux, and the second in patristic theology from the University of Aberdeen. His rejection of Western theology was informed and intentional, though imprints of Western thought did leave their marks upon his theology. He drew upon the resources of the early church to articulate an understanding of African Christian identity. In doing so, he blazed a path for others toward an understanding of world Christianity that is not dominated by Western Christianity.

Reading Bediako challenges the established set of theological questions that belong to Western Christianity and helps readers put on some new lenses. Thus readers of Bediako may come to understand themselves differently, their churches differently, Europe and Africa differently, the Christian faith differently, and the Bible differently. Bediako believed that everyone encounters

---

6. See Tim Hartman, *Theology after Colonization: Bediako, Barth, and the Future of Theological Reflection* (South Bend, IN: University of Notre Dame Press, 2020), 3–34.

the Bible and the Christian faith wearing cultural blinkers (or blinders). Many Western Christians in particular are blissfully unaware of these blinkers and the damage that cultural blindness causes them spiritually and theologically. Reading Bediako may help Western Christians to identify, name, and work to lessen the harmful effects of the cultural blinkers that they unconsciously wear. This process can be awkward and uncomfortable for Westerners who have never noticed that their perspectives on the Bible and the Christian faith are culturally inflected and not simply shared by everyone in all times and places as *the truth*.

For African Christians and other Christians in the non-Western world, reading Bediako can affirm the value of their insights and perspectives on the Bible and matters of Christian faith and identity. After centuries of being taught to reject their own cultural perspective in favor of the correct (i.e. the *Western*) perspective, Bediako offers an alternative path for nurturing indigenous understanding of the Christian faith. Further, Bediako affirms these non-Western versions of the Christian faith as more authentic to the Scriptures of the Old and New Testaments than Western Christianity. Bediako's non-Western theology can be liberating. For some that freedom may be overwhelming.

As the reign of Western Christianity wanes across the globe – from the end of European colonization to the rise of secularity in Europe and North America – voices such as Bediako's are vital resources for both those who have benefited from Western Christianity's cozy relationship with political power and those who have suffered from that partnership.

Bediako's three books and over seventy-five articles and book chapters raise and address questions of identity, gospel and culture, how to read the Bible including issues of translation, how to understand history, the role of context in theological reflection, and what it means to be a Christian in contemporary society, including questions of politics, democracy, and religious pluralism. Then toward the end of his life, Bediako offered some tantalizing glimpses of how he thought Christian theology should be remade in light of the insights of African Christian thought.

1

Identity

"In Becoming Christian, I Was Becoming African Again"

Bediako's theology is deeply personal. His theology of Christian identity grew out of his own life experiences and spiritual journey. Manasseh Kwame Dakwa Bediako (1945–2008) had a simple upbringing with nine brothers and sisters in Tesano on the north side of Ghana's capital city, Accra, the second child and first son of a police inspector. His first name was given because he was the son of Ephraim Nkansah Bediako, and Genesis 48 records the names of Joseph's sons as Ephraim and Manasseh. His second name is the traditional Ghanaian name for a baby boy born on Saturday, and his third name honors his paternal grandfather, Dakwa, who taught the Christian faith alongside European missionaries.[1] Kwame Bediako was raised as a nominal church attender and also taught the traditional customs and religious beliefs of the Akan people of Ghana.[2]

---

1. Bediako's grandfather was a catechist with the Basel Mission. For more on the work of the Basel Mission in the Gold Coast (later Ghana), see Yaw Danso, *The Basel Mission in Anum 1863–1918* (Osu, Ghana: Heritage, 2013); and Jon Miller, *Missionary Zeal and Institutional Control: Organizational Contradictions in the Basel Mission on the Gold Coast, 1828–1917* (Grand Rapids: Eerdmans, 2003).

2. For helpful secondary literature on Kwame Bediako, I highly recommend Sara Fretheim, *Kwame Bediako and African Christian Scholarship: Emerging Religious Discourse in Twentieth-Century Ghana* (Eugene, OR: Pickwick, 2018); and Bernhard Dinkelaker, *How Is Jesus Christ Lord? Reading Kwame Bediako from a Postcolonial and Intercontextual Perspective* (Bern: Peter Lang, 2017).

Trained in Western Thought

After primary school, Bediako gained entrance to the prestigious Mfantsipim School in Cape Coast which had been started by Methodist missionaries from England.[3] There he "distinguished himself not only academically, but also as an outstanding School (Head) Prefect, nicknamed 'Joe Noir,' loved and respected by all the boys, despite his being a strong disciplinarian."[4] Bediako took his A-Levels in English literature, French, and Latin, and in these ways was an ideal colonial subject, gaining a strong European education. His classmates remembered him as "among the best in our group of very fine scholars . . . the quintessential black man" who "excelled" at English oratory.[5] They "thought he was better cut for the legal profession" and were later shocked that he had become a preacher and theologian.[6] Their surprise was well-founded.

Bediako did his best to internalize Western ways of thinking. Religiously, his commitment to European thought led him to "a phase of self-conscious atheism" during his undergraduate years at the University of Ghana, Legon, 1965–69.[7] His intellect and passion for learning gave him a clear and successful career path. Upon graduating with an honors degree in French studies, Bediako was awarded a scholarship from the French government for post-graduate study at L'université de Bordeaux III. The University of Ghana offered him additional money with the condition that he return to join their faculty when his doctorate was completed.[8] Bediako's "sudden and surprising conversion to Christ"[9] in the summer of 1970 radically altered the course of his life, leaving him and others wondering "what had happened."[10]

---

3. Kofi Annan, later Secretary General of the United Nations and recipient of the Nobel Peace Prize in 2001, was Bediako's senior by a few years at Mfantsipim. Hans Visser and Gillian Mary Bediako, "Introduction," *Jesus and the Gospel in Africa*, (Maryknoll, NY: Orbis, 2004), xi.

4. "Call to Glory," Funeral program for Kwame Bediako, 3 July 2008.

5. "Tribute to the late Rev Professor Kwame Bediako by Mfantsipim Old Boys Association, Class of '63," "Call to Glory," 23.

6. "Call to Glory," 23.

7. Kwame Bediako and Gillian Bediako, "'Ebenezer, this is how far the Lord has helped us': Reflections on the Institutional Itinerary of the Akrofi-Christaller Memorial Centre for Mission Research and Applied Theology (1974–2005)," unpublished handbook, Akropong-Akuapem: ACI, 2005, 4.

8. "Call to Glory," 19.

9. Bediako and Bediako, "Ebenezer," 4.

10. Bediako and Bediako, 4.

The Limits of Western Thought

Bediako's academic progress halted the summer after his first year of graduate school. His personal anguish gave him writer's block, and he struggled to write his master's thesis on Francophone literature. Seeking inspiration one August day, he decided to take a shower to clear his mind. However before he opened the faucet, his feet were wet with his tears. Bediako described the moment:

> It was in the summer, the summer of '70. I came to a point in my life. I had done well academically. Everything was great for me; I was studying Modern Languages. Yet, there was this pit of futility within, which caused me to begin to review my life. Suddenly it occurred to me that I had come to a dead end. And I think I remember saying something to this effect: "God, I am tired. Take my life." Now I did not pray; I did not know what god I was talking to. Instead, what happened was: I did not fall, I literally crumpled under the shower. I did not turn on the tap, yet I felt a drop on my foot. It was a tear. I did not realize that. "Take my life," I had said. Yet, somehow, I felt flooding into me a newness of life. Quickly I got up, had my shower, went back to my room. And, I had never done this ever before, I spent half of that night in prayer.[11]

Bediako's writer's block opened up a more personal, existential crisis. Living his life as an African in Europe, studying the works of a Congolese poet living in Paris who wrote in French, staunchly arguing against Christians in Bordeaux about the implausibility of their beliefs, all had left Bediako with a "pit of futility within." The isolation and loneliness of living on his own, far from home, facing the possibility of academic failure, wore Bediako out. He was tired in body, mind, and soul. When he cried out, "God, I am tired. Take my life," tears fell from his eyes and a new spirit filled him.

Bediako's conversion became a defining event in his life, even if it took him a number of years to comprehend what had happened to him. In Bediako's last public address, he reflected upon that night, naming its significance as

> my personal Damascus road experience in Bordeaux, France, and my transition from atheism through my exposure to Western culture, my passing through the gates of French intellectual culture, a transition into an awareness of the living Christ and the realization that the pursuit of the intellectual life without reference

---

11. In Ault, *African Christianity Rising*: see "Kwame Bediako – pieces of his life-story" (26 May 2013): https://www.youtube.com/watch?v=kqMdQr_n8j8.

to the living God and the living Christ is futile. And as I reflected
on what was happening to me it occurred to me that in becoming
Christian, I was becoming African again.[12]

Bediako's conversion from atheism to Christianity opened up a way for him to
be spiritual again. Bediako sensed a deep connection between his conversion
to Christianity and his rediscovery of his African identity. As he put it,

in becoming Christian . . . I discovered I was becoming African
again. I was recovering my sense of the spirituality of life. I was
recovering my sense of the nearness of the living God. I was
recovering my African sense of the wholeness of life. I find in
becoming Christian, I am being more African than I think I was.
I am being more, who I am.[13]

The spiritual and the intellectual were deeply intertwined for Bediako. He
sought integration between who he was and what he believed. For years, he
had minimized his African heritage in favor of drinking deeply from the well
of European thought.

While many Africans had been introduced to Jesus Christ by Europeans
and become Christians, Bediako's encounters with European thought had
the opposite effect. He reflected upon the impact of Western thought on his
spiritual journey, writing,

Curiously, my increasing exposure to Western intellectual culture,
particularly through my French Studies, had not led me to find
Christ; instead, it made me an atheist who thought that God
was irrelevant to my intellectual development. In becoming
a Christian, and in finding how central God is in all life, I was
very conscious that I was recovering my African identity and the
spiritual view of life.[14]

The spiritual-theological claim of being a Christian allowed Bediako to embrace
his African-ness in a new way. For Bediako, the centrality of God in all of life –
that is expressed in Christian thought – is more similar to the African spiritual
view of life than to European thought. Bediako's journey had taught him that
one could be "Western" without God or religion. Yet for him, to be African was

---

12. Kwame Bediako, "Andrew F. Walls as Mentor," in *Understanding World Christianity: The Vision and Work of Andrew F. Walls*, ed. William R. Burrows, Mark R. Gornik, and Janice A. McLean (Maryknoll, NY: Orbis, 2011), 8.

13. In Ault, *African Christianity Rising*. See "Kwame Bediako – Pieces of His Life-Story."

14. Bediako and Bediako, "Ebenezer," 4.

to be "incurably religious."[15] As Bediako grew into increasing consciousness of having become an *African* Christian, his lifelong theological quest became to articulate this question of identity for himself and other Africans.

"Living at Two Levels"

Bediako sought to prevent and counteract the experience of many African Christians of "living at two levels," feeling homeless, half African and half European, while never feeling that they properly belonged to either group.[16] As a result of the condemnation of African spirituality by colonial missionaries, some African Christians were unable to see how to integrate or reconcile their African cultural heritage with their Christian beliefs; they simply held them both simultaneously and separately, living a bifurcated existence. Bediako grew up in a nominally Presbyterian family, yet when he left for France, his father visited a traditional shrine to ask for protection for his son while he was away. Upon Bediako's return to Ghana seven years later, his father proposed thanking the shrine-spirit for Bediako's safe return. Bediako declined and explained that he had come to understand that Jesus Christ protected him and protected his father as well.[17] Bediako's lifelong calling became helping African Christians to understand their identity in Jesus Christ as Africans.

Bediako wanted African Christians to feel that they were authentic Africans and true Christians. He laid the blame for this situation with the churches and their theology, not with individual Africans. "Up to now," he wrote, "our churches have tended to . . . present the Gospel as though it was concerned with an entirely different compartment of life, unrelated to traditional religious piety." The result has been that many people do not see any connection between "the Jesus of the Church's preaching" and "the terrors and fears that they experience in their traditional worldview." What Bediako longed for was the proclamation of the churches to show how "God in the Lord Jesus Christ [is] speaking immediately to us in our particular circumstances, in a way

---

15. The original quotation, "Africans have been called incurably religious," comes from Geoffrey Parrinder, *Religion in Africa* (Harmondsworth: Penguin, 1969), 235. Parrinder's claim has been deeply contested. See Jan Platvoet and Henk van Rinsum, "Is Africa Incurably Religious?: Confessing and Contesting an Invention," *Exchange* 32, no. 2 (2003), 123–53; and Kehinde Olabimtan, "'Is Africa Incurably Religious?' II: A Response to Jan Platvoet and Henk van Rinsum," *Exchange* 32, no. 4 (2003), 322–39. When he wrote his response, Olabimtan was on the staff of the Akrofi-Christaller Centre where Bediako was the founder and director.

16. Bediako, "Jesus in African Culture," in *Jesus and the Gospel in Africa*, 23.

17. Hans Visser and Gillian Mary Bediako, "Introduction," in *Jesus and the Gospel in Africa*, xi-xii.

that assures us that we can be authentic Africans and true Christians."[18] The question facing Bediako was whether or not it is possible to be both African and Christian, and if so, how such a combination might be possible.

Part of the problem for some African Christians is that they are uncertain about who they are: Africans? Christians? that is, Europeans baptized with a "Christian name"? Somehow both Africans *and* Christians?[19] The impact of Western colonization and Christianization on Africans "produce[d] an identity crisis . . . in a variety of forms . . . [including] on the place and role of Christianity in African life."[20] The tactics of the European missionaries gave the impression that the gospel of Jesus Christ must be wrapped in Western European packaging and conceived in Western European theological categories. This colonial approach prompted questions such as "Must we become other than African in order to be truly Christian?"[21] One particular example is requiring a baby girl to be baptized with a so-called Christian name, such as Charlotte, in place of the name Afua, given to baby girls born on a Friday in Ghana. Charlotte is not a name found in the Bible, and as such is not more Christian than Afua; however, it certainly is more European.[22]

In Bediako's analysis, a loss of memory crippled Africans' search for identity. Africans had lost the memory of their religious past: "For theological memory is integral to identity; without memory we have no past, and having no past, our identity itself is lost."[23] His early work sought to articulate African Christian identity by naming how their identity is *already* present and does not need to be created.

---

18. Bediako, "Jesus in African Culture," 23.

19. Questions of identity are not unique to African Christians in the mid to late twentieth century. As formal colonialism ended, many people of African descent were asking similar questions. Aimé Césaire of Martinique, the founder of the négritude movement, asked: "Who and what are we? A most worthy question!" while reflecting particularly on the disorienting displacement of slavery and the middle passage. See Aimé Césaire, *Notebook of a Return to the Native Land*, ed. and trans. Clayton Eshleman and Annette Smith (Middletown, CT: Wesleyan University Press, 2001), 18; translated from the French 1939 edition, *Cahier d'un retour au pays natal*.

20. Kwame Bediako, *Christianity in Africa: The Renewal of a Non-Western Religion* (Edinburgh: Edinburgh University Press, 1995), 76.

21. Diane B. Stinton, *Jesus of Africa: Voices of Contemporary African Christology* (Maryknoll, NY: Orbis, 2004), 11.

22. For more on differences between African names and Christian names, see Benson Ohihon Igboin, "An African Religious Discourse on Names and Identity," *Filosofia Theoretica: Journal of African Philosophy, Culture and Religions* 3, no. 1 (January–June, 2014): 26–40.

23. Bediako, *Theology and Identity*, 237.

The significance of Bediako's focus on and articulation of African Christian identity is noteworthy in part because of the criticism he has received from other African theologians. South African theologian Tinyiko Maluleke affirms the importance of Bediako's work in stating, "that it is no longer necessary for the African Christian to regard her *Christianness* as something foreign and exterior to who she is. Rather, accepting her Christianness as an essential part of who she is, the African Christian must go on and assert a presence on the African social scene."[24] However, Maluleke asserts that his "suspicion is that things are not as simple as Bediako . . . [made] them out to be."[25] David Kirwa Tarus and Stephanie Lowery fear that "Bediako does not adequately deal with the way these communal identities often conflict with each other within the larger African identity, complicating the issue of Christian identity in Africa."[26] African Christian identity is a combination of African beliefs and Christian beliefs.

Bediako understood part of the colonial project as interjecting a substitute past into the African past. Colonialism "threatened to deny African Christians their own past and sought instead to give them a past which could not in any real sense become fully theirs."[27] In the experience of colonialism, Africans were given not only a religious system that was foreign to them, but an entire religious and cultural history that was imported. Students were required to learn things that had no relevance to them. The result of this colonial education was that Africans, like other colonized peoples, "know more, even today, about English kings and queens than they do about our own national heroes, our own slave rebels – the people who helped build and to destroy our society."[28] Colonized peoples were taught to reject their native cultures and languages and to embrace European cultures, languages, and God.

In Bediako's terms, Africans were forced to swap their own experiences for those of Europeans, even to experience God in the way prescribed by Europeans. The overriding assumption of the colonial project was that the Christian faith and Christian theology transcend culture. This uninterrogated

24. Tinyiko Sam Maluleke, "Identity and Integrity in African Theology: A Critical Analysis," *Religion and Theology* 8, no. 1 (2001): 38.

25. Maluleke, "Identity and Integrity," 38.

26. David Kirwa Tarus and Stephanie Lowery, "African Theologies of Identity and Community: The Contributions of John Mbiti, Jesse Mugambi, Vincent Mulago, and Kwame Bediako," *Open Theology* (2017): 314.

27. Bediako, *Theology and Identity*, 237. See also Bediako, *Jesus and the Gospel in Africa*, 53.

28. Kamau Brathwaite, "History of the Voice," in *Roots: Essays in Caribbean Literature* (Ann Arbor: University of Michigan Press, 1993), 263.

assumption formed the basis of Bediako's critique and his corresponding constructive response: "no Christian theology in any age is ever simply a repetition of the inherited Christian tradition . . . all Christian theology is a synthesis, an 'adaptation' of the inherited Christian tradition in the service of new formulations."[29]

Bediako saw Europeans as trying to engraft Africans into their salvation history, and he wanted none of it. For him, one culture could not express the gospel for or to another culture. In Bediako's words, if "we are negative about our own traditions, ashamed of our own cultures, and if we do not really have any confidence, say, in our own language as the language that God also speaks and uses, then the likelihood is that we shall not see what indicators God himself has sown in our traditions and cultures."[30] The deeper spiritual and theological implication is that Africans may not receive the good news of the gospel as intended for them. Instead, Bediako wrote, Africans may "be trying to survive on a borrowed gospel, which, therefore, is not our own deep experience."[31] In the most basic terms, African Christian thought narrates an alternate history that combines the Christian faith with African traditional religious traditions.

A Theology of *Négritude*[32]

Bediako's spiritual journey from atheism to Christianity was paralleled by his intellectual journey from French existentialism to Christian theology. He was driven by questions of identity and belief. Bediako's early academic influences, particularly his study of the French existentialists as an undergraduate, had led him to become a self-avowed atheist in contrast to his upbringing within the Presbyterian Church of Ghana and the traditional religious practices of the Akan people.

Bediako's French master's thesis and doctoral dissertation both demonstrated the outworking of his desire to "understand what had happened

29. Bediako, *Theology and Identity*, 432.

30. Kwame Bediako, "Christian faith and African Culture – An Exposition of the Epistle to the Hebrews," *Journal of African Christian Thought* 13, no. 1 (2010): 57.

31. Bediako, "Christian faith and African Culture," 57.

32. For more on Bediako's theology of négritude, see Tim Hartman, "An Act of Theological Négritude: Kwame Bediako on African Christian Identity" in *Religion, Culture and Spirituality in Africa and the African Diaspora*, ed. William Ackah, Jualynne E. Dodson, and R. Drew Smith (New York: Routledge, 2018).

to"[33] him in his conversion to Christianity. The master's thesis evinces hints of his personal anguish and yearning for a settled existence. The doctoral thesis, completed nineteen months later, was Bediako's awkward first attempt to integrate the experience of Africans with the Christian teachings of the Bible. His research focused on the sources and influences in the work of Tchicaya U Tam'si, a Congolese poet living in Paris.[34]

Bediako had been unable to articulate his understanding of Tchicaya's influences and emphases prior to his conversion,[35] but then wrote his master's thesis in two months. The stated goal of the thesis, "*Négritude et Surréalisme: Essai sur l'oeuvre poétique de Tchicaya U Tam'si*" (*Négritude and Surrealism: An Essay about the Poetic Work of Tchicaya U Tam'si*),[36] was to identify the "spiritual itinerary" of Tchicaya's "poetic consciousness."[37] Bediako was attracted to Tchicaya's constant wrestling with his identity as an African living in Europe. Questions of angst and existential uncertainty in Tchicaya's poetry mirrored Bediako's own self-understanding. He compared the existential "anguish" experienced by the poet Tchicaya to the "first feeling of Christian conversion . . . a broken heart . . . expressed in tears."[38] For Bediako, this common anguish resulted in a shared "humility" for both the Christian and the poet. Bediako dedicated his master's to Jesus Christ: "To Him who saved me."[39]

The anguish Bediako shared with Tchicaya interested him in the sources of Tchicaya's thinking and writing – and no one more so than Aimé Césaire. Césaire, from Martinique in the West Indies, along with Léopold Senghor, later president of Senegal, and Léon-Gontran Damas of French Guiana, coined the term *négritude* while editing their newspaper, *L'Etudiant noir* (The Black Student) in Paris in the mid-1930s. The origin of négritude is in the French

---

33. Bediako and Bediako, "Ebenezer," 4.

34. The pseudonym of Gérald Félix Tchicaya. His pen name means "small paper that speaks for a country" in the language of Kikongo from his native Congo.

35. Personal interview with Gillian Mary Bediako, Akropong, Ghana, 1 June 2012.

36. Kwame Bediako, *Négritude et Surréalisme: Essai sur l'oeuvre poétique de Tchicaya U Tam'si*, T.E.R., Bordeaux III, October 1970. Unpublished M.A. Thesis.

37. Bediako, *Négritude et Surréalisme*, 158.

38. Bediako, 160.

39. Bediako, *Négritude et Surréalisme* opening page:

In tribute
To Him who saved me
That this work of one school year
May be elevated to his glory

word for negro, *negre*.[40] The term is a made-up word used to describe the alienated position of blacks in history. The bond between blacks is the shared experience of suffering. Négritude came to mean a cultural, philosophical, and political movement of suffering peoples recovering their precolonial past histories and current identities.

The theme of identity is central; the precolonial past is used to ground identity for the sake of the future. For Césaire, born on a plantation in the Caribbean, négritude meant a recovery of his African heritage. He sought identity by searching for connection with his lost ancestors and African heritage. For Senghor, as an African, négritude meant to be over and against European colonial influences and developments. He sought identity apart from European colonizers. Négritude became part of the African independence movement.[41]

The assertion of négritude in Tchicaya's poetry is "the cry of the lonely African"[42] living in Paris as his homeland suffered through decolonization. Tchicaya's focus on subjectivity, as one living in two worlds – of the Congo and of France – resonated with Bediako's own experiences as a Ghanaian educated in French existentialism and the European intellectual tradition including Greek, Latin, and the classics of Western civilization. Bediako incorporated Tchicaya's dual themes of protest and the search of identity into his work. As Tchicaya was a second-generation writer within the négritude movement, so also Bediako was a second-generation African theologian. For both authors, whereas the first generation faced toward the white world, the second-generation faced toward Africa, engaging African agonies and African hopes.[43]

Bediako later articulated his theology of négritude – based on Africa's precolonial past and Christianity's patristic (pre-Christendom) past – to ground African Christian identity for the sake of the future. Building on the insights of Kenyan John S. Mbiti, whose work was oriented toward Europe, Bediako then turned his face not just to Europe, but also to himself and to

---

40. The first use of the term "négritude" in print appeared in 1939 in the French version of Césaire's *Notebook of a Return to the Native Land*. See translator's footnote in *Notebook of a Return to the Native Land*, 60. Césaire also spoke of négritude as humanization and believed that many peoples were capable of a négritude of their own. See the film *Aimé Césaire, une voix pour l'histoire* directed by Euzhan Palcy (Martinique: JMJ Productions, [1994] 2006).

41. See Gary Wilder, *Freedom Time: Negritude, Decolonization, and the Future of the World* (Durham: Duke University Press, 2015).

42. Thomas R. Knipp, "Négritude and Negation: The Poetry of Tchicaya U Tam'si," *Books Abroad* 48, no. 3 (Summer 1974): 514.

43. See Gerald Moore, "The Politics of Négritude," in *Protest and Conflict in African Literature*, ed. Cosmo Pieterse and Donald Munro (London: Heinemann, 1969), 38–39.

Africa, criticizing Nigerian theologian Byang Kato for a lack of African-ness and complicity with Western thought patterns.[44] Bediako prepared the way for contemporary third generation theologians who have turned their faces almost exclusively to African concerns with little regard for the West. Bediako's themes of *recovering* an African identity and a reconceived Christian theology surfaced in his early work – to never go away.

An appeal to an authentic genealogy in identity construction pervaded Tchicaya's work and characterized Bediako's search for a true African Christian identity and an alternative history for African Christianity.[45] Much of Tchicaya's corpus wrestled with the relationship of African culture to European missionary Catholicism as well as his own ambivalent and ambiguous relationship to God. When Tchicaya wrote "Christ I hate your Christians," "Le Contempteur" (The Hater/Detractor), in *Epitomé*, he was not rejecting Christ as such but rather Christianity as an institution and European Christians and their African surrogates as oppressors. He demanded that ethical and spiritual standards remain extremely high, even as his own must remain high.[46] Bediako also later employed a similar distinction of Christ from Christianity.

When Bediako juxtaposed elements of the Christian faith and African traditional religions, the true sparks of his vision were ignited. Similar to Tchicaya who was unable to find a clear genealogy for himself and his ideas, particularly his religious ideas, Bediako also invented his own religious genealogy. Whereas Tchicaya juxtaposed elements of African religion to coexist with those of Catholic religion, inventing his own "Tamsien religion,"[47] Bediako could not wholly invent a new religion and remain Christian. Instead, Bediako built a new identity for African Christians. To do so, he utilized the roots of African Christian identity that he found in fellow African theologians such as John Mbiti and Nigerian Bolaji Idowu as well as in second century Christian apologists such as Justin Martyr and Clement of Alexandria.

The path toward integration was not easy for Bediako. Soon after his conversion and the completion of his master's thesis, Bediako struggled with being motivated to continue working on his doctorate, desiring instead to

---

44. See Bediako, *Theology and Identity*, 386–425.

45. Tchicaya addresses this theme most directly in his poem *Epitomé*. See Tchicaya U Tam'si, *Tchicaya U Tam'si: Selected Poems*, trans. Gerald Moore (London: Heinemann, 1970), 33, 34, 40.

46. John Taylor, "Rereading Tchicaya U Tam'si," *The Antioch Review* 66, no. 4, Celebrity Deaths (Fall, 2008): 789.

47. Susan Erica Rein, "Religiosity in the Poetry of Tchicaya U Tam'si," *Journal of Religion in Africa* 10, no. 3 (1979): 249.

abandon it and pursue the formal study of theology. The impact of Bediako's conversion and his participation in an evangelical campus ministry consumed much of his time and intellectual attention. He read the Bible through from cover to cover multiple times in the months following August 1970.[48] He was very active in a local Evangelical Free Church congregation in Bordeaux led by American missionary Bill Adams. He started dating a Christian Englishwoman (whom he would marry three years later) and invited her to join him in running a Good News Club for the Arab children in his neighborhood.[49] Bediako's widow, Gillian Mary Bediako, described the situation following his conversion: "His first impulse was to abandon his studies, and to equip himself at a Bible School in order to serve Jesus Christ. Christians in Bordeaux had a hard time persuading him to complete the course he had been sent to undertake. Eventually he listened."[50]

Bediako's doctorate, *L'Universe Interieur de Tchicaya U Tam'si* (*The Interior Universe of Tchicaya U Tam'si*), delved into Tchicaya's existential realities.[51] His method combined close readings of Tchicaya's poetry with his interpretive analysis based on biblical texts. In contrast with his master's that contained no biblical quotations and cited no Christian authors, entire sections of Bediako's doctorate interpreted and explored Tchicaya's poetry with the use of individual Bible verses, seventy-eight biblical references to seventy-three distinct verses in 213 pages of text. The former influences of surrealism and négritude were still present but were no longer given pride of place in Bediako's analysis.[52] New sources for Bediako included North American evangelicals Francis Schaeffer and J. I. Packer as well as *His Magazine* published by InterVarsity Christian Fellowship, USA. In the bibliography of this dissertation, Bediako lists additional evangelical authors who shaped his analysis, though they are not explicitly quoted: Billy Graham, J. Gresham Machen, D. L. Moody, A. W. Tozer, and B. B. Warfield. Bediako also lists a number of evangelical reviews and magazines in a separate section of his bibliography. He seemed to sense and acknowledge that his use of evangelical reviews and magazines was unexpected

---

48. Visser and Bediako, "Introduction," *Jesus and the Gospel in Africa*, xii.

49. "Call to Glory," 3.

50. "Call to Glory," 19.

51. Kwame Bediako, *L'Univers Interieur de Tchicaya U Tam'si*. Thèse de 3e cycle, L'université de Bordeaux III, July 1973, unpublished doctoral thesis.

52. While there is a significant section on using the influential nineteenth-century French poet Arthur Rimbaud and another on French writer, philosopher, and literary theorist Maurice Blanchot, other authors such as Diop, Sartre, Senghor, Césaire, Levi-Strauss, and Fanon are only mentioned in a footnote or two.

or perhaps even out of place. He defends their inclusion in a footnote within the bibliography where he claims that these magazines intervened in a crucial way for his analysis and were "decisive for our 'evangelical vision.'"[53] Instead of analyzing the text of Tchicaya's poetry (as in his master's), Bediako used Tchicaya's poetry to analyze the internal universe of the poet himself. His doctorate demonstrated Bediako's radical change in thinking following his conversion. He now sought to use Jesus Christ as a lens to understand the world.

Bediako shared his intellectual and spiritual journey in his opening remarks before the jury at his doctoral defense. He spoke of how his interest in Tchicaya U Tam'si began several years earlier and that he "was overwhelmed by a strong sense of affinity with the poet. In some ways, in reading his poems, I believe that I found a way to verbalize my own reactions to life that I did not fully understand: that is, before a life that I believed I understood."[54] Bediako's feelings of connection with Tchicaya's angst and internal unrest led him to admit that he was more taken "with the interior feelings of the man whose work is the object of my study" than with the literary aspect.[55] Bediako's theological interest in the person of Tchicaya overshadowed his literary interest in Tchicaya's poetry.

Bediako saw a parallel between his own spiritual journey and Tchicaya's truncated journey. Whereas Bediako had found inner peace in Jesus Christ, Tchicaya had not come to any such conclusions by the time he died of a heart attack at the age of 56.[56] Bediako alluded to his conversion to Christianity as necessary to understanding Tchicaya and his poetry: "for us, the need is to know Jesus Christ as he is, personal savior and redeemer, the only way to reconciliation."[57] Bediako understood the anguish expressed in Tchicaya's poetry to be a result of his not knowing Jesus Christ as his personal savior. Bediako used these moments before the jury to explain why his thesis seemed to veer off topic at times and also "to communicate what was so freely given to me, because this free gift from God is for everyone."[58] The sharing of his testimony at his doctoral defense demonstrates how Bediako's earliest attempts to express an authentic identity as an African Christian remained within Western, colonial categories. The evangelicalism that Bediako fell into heavily

---

53. Bediako, *L'Univers*, 219n1.

54. Kwame Bediako, "Madame la Présidente," 3. "Madame la Présidente" is an untitled, unpublished 8 page document (undated) in the collection of Gillian Mary Bediako that he read to the jury at his doctoral defense.

55. Bediako, "Madame la Présidente," 5.

56. See Taylor, "Rereading Tchicaya U Tam'si," 790.

57. Bediako, "Madame la Présidente," 7.

58. Bediako, 7.

informed the sources for his doctorate and his style of communication. He could not yet articulate the truly authentic African Christian identity that he was seeking.

Centrality of Theological Questions

Bediako's search for a true, authentic African Christian identity was wrapped up with his own quest for self-understanding. For him, the solution to both was to pursue formal theological education. Bediako described this moment as follows: "This consciousness of having become an African Christian made a profound impression upon me. It gave me a desire to study theology as a discipline, in the hope that it would help me understand what had happened to me."[59] Upon completing his doctorate in July 1973, Bediako immediately moved to London to pursue a bachelor's in theology at London Bible College (LBC, now London School of Theology). His years at LBC further deepened his "conviction that theological questions must stand at the centre of my intellectual concerns and shape my vocational commitments."[60] The seeds of Bediako's critique of Western theology were nurtured as he sought an alternative basis for Christian identity that did not rely on Western culture.

Bediako described the impact of his theological studies as bringing him "to the settled conviction that religious faith, focused on Christ as 'the key to all [God's] wisdom and knowledge' (Colossians 2:3), had a place in the pursuit of the intellectual life. It confirmed to me that in making the transition from Modern Languages (French) to Theology, I was not mistaken, but rather, was finding a new academic vocation."[61] Bediako's theological vocation received high praise, including his election in January 1996 as a fellow of the Ghana Academy of Arts and Sciences.[62] In his obituaries, Bediako was referred to as "the outstanding African theologian of his generation" for his intellect and

---

59. Bediako and Bediako, "Ebenezer," 4.

60. Kwame Bediako, "Memorandum to Christian Service College Council on the work of the College," 29 May 1978, unpublished, 21. Bediako demonstrated a preference at LBC for historical theology – particularly the development of doctrine – over systematic theology. His historical interests were evident in his most formative professors: Tony Lane (patristics) and Leslie Allen (Old Testament). Personal interview with Gillian Mary Bediako, Akropong, Ghana, 1 June 2012.

61. Bediako and Bediako, "Ebenezer," 4–5.

62. "In recommending Rev. Professor Bediako for election to Fellowship of the [Ghana Academy of Arts and Sciences, elected in January 1996], Rev. Professor C. G Baëta, a senior colleague in theology, testified as follows:

vision and for pioneering new directions in African Christian thought,[63] "an outstanding African pastor, teacher and theologian. . . . a scholar with an exceptional pedigree and a forceful writer. . . . an academic genius. . . . [with] great oratorical skills,"[64] "among the pioneers of African Theology,"[65] and "the foremost thinker . . . around the issues of theology, culture, and identity in Africa . . . the most erudite of the contemporary African theologians."[66] Bediako's vocational change paid dividends, including a legacy of influence in Ghana, sub-Saharan Africa, and beyond.

As important as Bediako's classroom education was, he also began to develop relationships "with other 'radical' Christians of evangelical persuasion from the 'Two-Thirds World'"[67] when he participated as a student delegate in the Lausanne Congress for World Evangelization in Lausanne, Switzerland in 1974.[68] At the Congress, Bediako encountered delegates from the Presbyterian Church of Ghana (PCG) who updated him on the happenings in the PCG and "undertook to introduce [him] to the leaders of the church" in Ghana.[69] This meeting with fellow Ghanaians would lead to Bediako's ordination as a pastor in the PCG in 1978. Further, upon returning to London, the Bediakos "opened a file in which [they] began to make occasional entries on 'The idea of a Centre

---

He has applied his considerable expertise as a thinker and a scholar in French literature to his latter found vocation as Pastor and Theologian in his very thorough analysis of the central problem of the African Christian, namely his or her cultural identification with biblical theology. His in depth studies showed that there was no basis for cultural or philosophical incompatibility between the traditional values of the African and his Christian beliefs and precepts.

"Call to Glory," 9.

63. Andrew F. Walls, "Kwame Bediako and Christian Scholarship in Africa," *International Bulletin of Missionary Research* 32, no. 4 (2008): 192.

64. J. Kwabena Asamoah-Gyadu, "Bediako of Africa: A Late 20th Century Outstanding Theologian and Teacher," *Mission Studies* 26 (2009): 7, 9, 11, 10.

65. Chammah J. Kaunda, Kennedy O. Owino, and Isabel A. Phiri, "Applicability of Translatability Theory to European Missionary Masculinity Performance in Africa: Contestations and Reflections," *Alternation* Special Edition no. 14 (2015): 212.

66. Anthony O. Balcomb, "Narrative, Epistemological Crisis and Reconstruction – My Story with Special Reference to the Work of Kwame Bediako," *Scriptura* 97 (2008): 53.

67. Bediako and Bediako, "Ebenezer," 5.

68. Long-lasting friendships began there around common concerns with David Gitari (Kenya), René Padilla (Ecuador/Argentina), Samuel Escobar (Peru), Morris Stuart and Patrick Sookhdeo (both from Guyana and working in the UK), and Vinay Samuel (India) that led to the formation in the early 1980s of the International Fellowship of Evangelical Mission Theologians (INFEMIT). In 1984, the African Theological Fellowship (ATF) was formed as the African network partner within the INFEMIT. See Bediako and Bediako, "Ebenezer," 5.

69. Bediako and Bediako, "Ebenezer," 5.

for Mission research in Ghana.'"[70] The ideas recorded in this file resulted in the founding in 1987 of what is now known as the Akrofi-Christaller Institute (ACI) of Theology, Mission and Culture, a scholarly institution established by the Presbyterian Church of Ghana to serve the wider Christian community in Ghana and Africa.[71]

Bediako's interests and curiosities were not satisfied by a bachelor's in divinity. He had met Professor Andrew Walls of the University of Aberdeen in the spring of 1975 at LBC. Walls' lecture on the shift in the center of gravity of Christianity, with particular attention to Africa's place in Christian history, stirred Bediako's imagination for further study.[72] Upon completing their theology degrees, the couple moved to Kumasi, Ghana, where Bediako taught at the Christian Service College for two years. They joined Ramseyer Presbyterian Church of the PCG, and Bediako began the ordination process. All the while, Bediako was preparing to further pursue his work on identity. For him, "The crucial question is how African theology understands and interprets Jesus Christ in the African situation."[73] At Bediako's ordination as a new minister in June 1978, the moderator, G. K. Sintim-Misa, gave Bediako the charge to "go, study, and return to serve the church."[74] Four months later, the Bediakos each started their doctoral studies at the University of Aberdeen under Walls' supervision.

Bediako's decision to earn a PhD in patristic theology was an attempt to seek the independence of African Christian theology from Western thought. Africans needed theology from other Africans, not simply from Westerners. In his "Brief Statement on a Projected PhD Thesis," Bediako quoted K. A. Busia, a Ghanaian sociologist, to demonstrate that the Christian church in Ghana was popular as a social institution but that the Christian *faith* had little impact in the lives of Ghanaians. Bediako then wrote, "The charge of 'irrelevance' of the Christian Church in Africa is a real problem, and one which is yet to be

---

70. Bediako and Bediako, "Ebenezer," 5.

71. For more information of the Akrofi-Christaller Institute, see www.aci.edu.gh. ACI is accredited by the Ghana Tertiary Education Commission, as a postgraduate research institution, with a presidential charter to award its own degrees.

72. Walls spoke at the college day conference on world mission in response to an invitation from the Bediakos and another student. Bediako, "Andrew F. Walls as Mentor," 7.

73. Kwame Bediako, "Brief Statement on a Projected PhD Thesis," 22 March 1978, unpublished, 7.

74. Bediako and Bediako, "Ebenezer," 7.

adequately encountered."[75] Bediako based his claim on the observation that "the Christianity of the Akan area proves to be the denominational Christianity of the West."[76] In response, he proposed "an African reading" of the Scriptures.[77] His call for authentic, indigenous African theology resulted from both his belief that all theology is and should be contextual as well as the failings of Western Christianity in Africa.[78]

Shaping an African Christian Identity

The question of African Christianity in the postcolonial period was one of identity. Bediako read his conversion to Christianity as a rejection of attempts to define his identity through European existentialist atheism and an embrace of his African identity. Bediako included himself "among those affected by the Enlightenment . . . my culture-heroes were such intellectuals as Jean-Paul Sartre, Simone de Beauvoir, Albert Camus and André Malraux, among others. However, when Jesus Christ became real to me . . . I discovered that I was recovering my African identity and spirituality."[79] Bediako pursued this line of thinking in his theological dissertation, published as *Theology and Identity: The Impact of Culture on Christian Thought in the Second Century and Modern Africa*, that launched his theological career.[80] The two dominant themes of the work, identity and integration (for Bediako, a better term than indigenization) appeared in the original title and never disappeared from his concerns. "The argument of the thesis," according to Bediako, "attempts to

---

75. Bediako, "Brief Statement," 2. Perhaps most interesting in this document is the lack of any mention of any second century apologists. The presence of the patristics in Bediako's dissertation was only to come later, at the suggestion of his supervisor, Andrew Walls.

76. Bediako, 2.

77. Bediako, 4.

78. Bediako later described their time in the United Kingdom as "having benefited from what was probably the best that the West could offer by way of theological education." Bediako and Bediako, "Ebenezer," 16. The Bediakos spent six years in Aberdeen. In 1983, Kwame finished his PhD, and their first of two sons, Timothy Yaw Bediako, was born, with his brother, Daniel Kwabena Bediako, to follow three years later. Bediako taught in a temporary junior faculty position for a year in Aberdeen before they returned to Ghana to begin the process of initiating a centre of mission research.

79. Kwame Bediako, "Worship as Vital Participation – Some Personal Reflections on Ministry in the African Church," *Journal of African Christian Thought* 8, no. 2 (2005): 4.

80. Originally titled, *Identity and Integration: An Enquiry into the Nature and Problems of Theological Indigenization in Selected Early Hellenistic and Modern African Christian Writers*, the dissertation was 536 pages, not including the bibliography, and was defended in July 1983. After light revisions, *Theology and Identity* was published in 1992.

validate the claim that theology is called to deal always with culturally-rooted questions."[81] Kenyan Jesse Mugambi described *Theology and Identity* as "the first book of its kind, illustrating that conceptually the central concerns of the Church have not changed greatly for two millennia."[82] Mugambi acknowledged a change in emphasis historically while applauding Bediako's insight that "the core concerns remain basically the same."[83] His central aim was described by perhaps his harshest critic, South African theologian Tinyiko Maluleke, who observed, "According to Bediako, therefore, the task of African theology is both to *pursue* and *demonstrate* 'the true character of African Christian identity' in a comprehensively religious and intellectual manner."[84]

Bediako's focus on African Christian identity resulted from how Europeans conducted their missionary efforts. The "ethnocentrism of a large part of the missionary enterprise not only prevented sufficient understanding of African religious tradition,"[85] but Europeans' unreflective ethnocentrism forcibly separated Africans from their own history and traditions, resulting in a broader problem. The *theological* myopia of the missionaries conveyed "a theological misapprehension of the nature of the Christian Gospel itself."[86] Bediako offered a theological defense for the possibility of a truly *African* Christian identity based in precolonial African history.

Bediako asserted the need for Africans to think for themselves and not to allow the dominant Western thought patterns to continue unabated. In his very first publication, he questioned the universal validity of Western theology while wondering aloud, "If much of the theological effort in the non-western world merely reproduces replays of the original western versions, we must ask ourselves whether the Christianity that was planted was such as would allow emerging Christian thinkers to answer their own questions."[87] Further, he was convinced of a God who is deeply interested in non-Western minds, hearts,

---

81. Bediako, *Theology and Identity*, xv.

82. J. N. K. Mugambi, "Ecumenism in African Christianity," in *The Routledge Companion to Christianity in Africa*, ed. Elias Kifon Bongmba (New York: Routledge, 2016), 248.

83. Mugambi, "Ecumenism," 248.

84. Tinyiko Sam Maluleke, "In Search of 'The True Character of African Christian Identity': A Review of the Theology of Kwame Bediako," *Missionalia* 25, no. 2 (August 1997): 215, emphasis original.

85. Bediako, *Theology and Identity*, xvii.

86. Bediako, xvii.

87. Kwame Bediako, "Response to Taber: Is There More Than One Way to Do Theology?" *Gospel in Context* 1, no. 1 (1978): 13–14.

and circumstances.[88] Against a critic of contextualizing Christian theology, Bediako responded with characteristic boldness that "the answer to 'false contextualization' is not no contextualization, but faithful contextualization."[89]

Christianity had become too closely associated with Western European thought and culture. In Bediako's view, "Christianity itself has emerged historically as part of the cultural impact of the West on the rest of the world."[90] For Bediako, this historical insight was actually a problem. As an African, non-Western, theologian, his alternate goal was to dissociate the gospel from the trappings of Western culture.[91] Bediako knew that "the Gospel can only be perceived by us in some cultural form or other – a pure Gospel devoid of cultural embodiment is simply imaginary."[92] Bediako's singular insight that "a pure Gospel . . . is simply imaginary" exposes the fallacy of Western thought as universal.

For Bediako, there was no such thing as a "pure Gospel" because humans need a means to apprehend the gospel. Bediako's understanding was that human cultures wrap the gospel like a birthday present so that humanity can comprehend what the good news is. In a similar way, God assumed human flesh in the person of Jesus of Nazareth in order to embody the presence of God on earth. However, Bediako noted, it can be difficult for humans to differentiate between the wrapping paper (culture) and the gift itself (the gospel). He wrote, "The trouble is that we all wear cultural blinkers, and whilst we may affirm an absolute Gospel and accept the relativity of our diverse cultures, each of us fails to perceive some important facets of the one Gospel."[93]

Identity has theological and cultural aspects. Identity can also be shaped by circumstances such as privilege or oppression, wealth or poverty. Nigerian Paulinus Ikechukwu Odozor notes that Bediako's concern for Christian identity is "an assertion that fails to uncover the complex challenges with which African Christians are faced."[94] Maluleke notes two distinct aspects of this complex

---

88. Bediako, "Response to Taber," 14.

89. Kwame Bediako, "[Response to] David Hesselgrave: Dialogue on Contextualization Continuum," *Gospel in Context* 2, no. 3 (1979): 13.

90. Kwame Bediako, "The Willowbank Consultation, January 1978 – A Personal Reflection," *Themelios* 5, no. 2 (January 1980): 28.

91. Bediako, "Willowbank," 28.

92. Bediako, 28.

93. Bediako, 28.

94. Paulinus Ikechukwu Odozor, *Morality Truly Christian, Truly African: Foundational, Methodological, and Theological Considerations* (South Bend, IN: University of Notre Dame Press, 2014), 22.

challenge. First, "the African Christian's identity crisis, like that of African Christian theology, is not merely one of consciousness. . . . there is a 'material basis' for the African Christian's identity problem connectable to colonialism, post-independence oppression and material dispossession."[95] Second, the challenge of this identity crisis can be directly traced to the lack in Bediako's definition of the African Christian's identity of "the scandal of the fact that millions of African Christians (and other African religious people) have been and continue to be enslaved, dispossessed and oppressed by fellow Christians (and fellow religious people) in the name of the very Christianity which they share."[96] Maluleke was convinced that "Bediako's insensitivity to the 'material basis' of the African Christian's identity problem has the potential to reduce his quest for 'the true meaning of African Christian identity' into a superficial, albeit well-meaning, exercise."[97] While Maluleke never drops his concern about Bediako's theology, Bediako and his followers believe that Bediako's theological thought leads to significant, not superficial, transformation for African Christians and Africa as a whole.

Requiring African converts to wear certain types of clothing, usually based on Western notions of modesty (and based in much colder climates) is another example of the theological misapprehension of the gospel. Bediako's theological journey can be understood using an illustration based on clothing norms: Africans learned about wearing neckties from European missionaries and colonial officials at the same time that they learned about Jesus. Bediako and others grew tired of wearing uncomfortable neckties. They then questioned what of their understanding of Jesus was indigenous, authentic, and real. Any of what Africans had been taught about Jesus that was simply fabricated from European culture needed to be thrown away, along with the neckties.

Conclusion

Bediako's thought displays a remarkable amount of consistency throughout his nearly forty years of writing. Bediako's lifelong theological focus on identity remained as the locations and implicit audiences of his writings change. Even two of his harshest critics, Maluleke and Valentin Dedji of Benin, have words of praise for him. Maluleke describes Bediako as an "encouraging voice from

---

95. Maluleke, "In Search of," 217–18.

96. Maluleke, 217.

97. Maluleke, 218.

[an]other part of Africa."[98] Dedji notes that Bediako's "theological agenda and achievement are indeed impressive, consistent, and groundbreaking in many respects."[99] The criticisms by Maluleke and Dedji demonstrate the point that it "is now inconceivable to engage in any consistent theological debate in contemporary Africa without referring to [Bediako's] work."[100] Bediako has been described as "essentially a world Christian"[101] whose intellect, energy, and passion have left a legacy of individuals whom he mentored and of ideas that he published.

In his self-appointed role as an apologist for African Christianity, Bediako offered a very positive and extremely optimistic assessment of the prospects of African Christianity.[102] Bediako's ebullient optimism has been harshly criticized by Maluleke and Roman Catholic theologian Emmanuel Katongole of Uganda. In Maluleke's view, "Bediako's overly optimistic, if not triumphalistic, view of Christianity on the African continent is fraught with many problems."[103] Katongole builds on Maluleke's criticism by questioning its lack of specificity. Katongole wrote that he shares with Bediako the "hope that the future of Christianity is in Africa, but the critical question that concerns me is the type of future, and the type of Christianity that will be associated with Africa."[104] Precisely what "sort of Christianity . . . lies behind this 'phenomenal Christian presence.'"[105] Katongole sought to temper Bediako's unbridled optimism, both regarding the exponential growth of the Christian faith in Africa as well as the very content of that faith in the present and future. Maluleke concurs with the assessment of Bediako's theology as overly optimistic because Bediako failed

---

98. Tinyiko Sam Maluleke, "Black and African Theology after Apartheid and after the Cold War: An Emerging Paradigm," *Exchange* 29, no. 3 (July 2000): 194.

99. Valentin Dedji, *Reconstruction and Renewal in African Christian Theology* (Nairobi: Acton, 2003), 209.

100. Dedji, *Reconstruction and Renewal*, 209.

101. Cephas Omenyo, "Ghana, Liberia and Sierra Leone," in *Christianity in Sub-Saharan Africa*, ed. Kenneth Ross, J. Kwabena Asamoah-Gyadu, and Todd Johnson (Edinburgh: Edinburgh University Press, 2017), 209; and Walls, "Kwame Bediako," 192.

102. Emmanuel Katongole, *A Future for Africa: Critical Essays in Christian Social Imagination* (Scranton, PA: University of Scranton Press, 2005), 155.

103. Maluleke, "In Search of," 215. In an earlier article, Maluleke refers to Bediako's overwhelming optimism about the prospects of Christianity in Africa. See Tinyiko Sam Maluleke, "Black and African Theologies in the New World Order: A Time to Drink from Our Own Wells," *Journal of Theology for Southern Africa* (1996): 10.

104. Katongole, *Future for Africa*, 156.

105. Katongole, 4. Referring to Bediako, *Christianity in Africa*, 3.

to address the "'material basis' for the African Christian's identity problem connectable to post-independence oppression and material dispossession."[106]

Bediako understood this combination organically as an integrated whole, since for him, Christianity is indigenous to Africa. On the contrary, Tarus and Lowery understand African Christian identity as a hybrid between two distinct identities that do not gel seamlessly or automatically.[107] Maluleke agrees noting that identity is *not* a colonial category: "surely African theology in general and African theological concern with questions of identity in particular can neither be solely nor adequately explained with reference to the perceptions, commissions, and omissions of Europeans."[108]

Upon his conversion to Christianity from avowed atheism as a twenty-five year-old African graduate student living in Bordeaux, Bediako employed the tools of the négritude movement that he had learned from the writings of the originators of négritude and the second-generation négritude poet Tchicaya U Tam'si to establish his own personal identity as an African Christian as well as an identity for African Christianity as a non-Western religion. On an individual level, Bediako sought to integrate his African heritage and context with the faith he learned from Westerners in Bordeaux and seventeen hundred years of Western theological scholarship. More basically, Bediako built an identity for African Christianity as a product of precolonial African spirituality and pre-Christendom Christianity.

Bediako sought to articulate and explain the African roots of his personal identity and that of African Christianity as a whole. He considered himself as an intentionally indigenous thinker who understood his entire intellectual project to be indigenous – originating in the place where he was found, that is, in Africa. Yet Bediako's interests were not parochial, but rather universal. By exploring the insights gained through the encounter of the gospel of Jesus Christ with African cultures, peoples all around the world might learn more about the gospel and how to read the Bible differently. Bediako believed that the insights of African Christianity are revelatory for the understanding of the Christian faith worldwide. His belief came from the conviction that "the very process of the cross-cultural transmission of the Gospel can also be

---

106. Maluleke, "In Search of," 218.

107. See Tarus and Lowery, "African Theologies of Identity and Community."

108. Maluleke continued: "To the extent that I may be right in my assessment, the sixth chapter [of *Theology and Identity*] is the lowest point in his book – something of a lost opportunity." Maluleke, "In Search of," 212.

revelatory."[109] The experiments in Christian thought within the "laboratory" of Africa reveal who God is, not only to Africans but to all peoples.[110] The act of divine revelation in Africa and among Africans impacts all Christians and understandings of the essence of Christianity itself. The theme of identity saturated Bediako's work from his earliest publications to his last public lecture. The numerical growth of Christianity in Africa allowed for and necessitated the articulation of a distinct African Christian identity.

Further Reading of Kwame Bediako

"Christian Faith and African Culture – An Exposition of the Epistle to the Hebrews." *Journal of African Christian Thought* 13, no. 1 (June 2010): 45–57.
"Jesus in African Culture: A Ghanaian Perspective." In *Jesus and the Gospel in Africa*, 20–33. Maryknoll, NY: Orbis Books, 2004.
Theology and Identity: The Impact of Culture on Christian Thought in the Second Century and Modern Africa. Oxford: Regnum, 1992. Especially the Introduction and Conclusion.
"The Willowbank Consultation, January 1978 – A Personal Reflection." *Themelios* 5, no. 2 (January 1980): 25–32.

---

109. Bediako, *Christianity in Africa*, 214.

110. Bediako, 252, see also 265; Bediako, "In the Bible," 34; and Bediako, "Types of African Theology," in *Christianity in Africa in the 1990s*, ed. C. Fyfe and A. Walls (Edinburgh: University of Edinburgh, Centre for African Studies, 1987), 456.

2

Translatability

"Relevance without Syncretism"

An authentic African Christian identity is possible because of the infinite translatability of the gospel of Jesus Christ.[1] For Bediako, "Translatability is another way of saying universality. Hence the translatability of the Christian religion signifies its fundamental relevance and accessibility to persons in any culture within which the Christian faith is transmitted and assimilated."[2] Translatability was the starting point for Bediako's own theological reflection.[3]

Infinite Translatability of the Gospel in Human Cultures

Bediako based his understanding of universal translation on this statement: "Our Christian claim is that in Jesus Christ 'Divinity became translated into

---

1. For an extended treatment of translatability, see Kwame Bediako, "Translatability and the Cultural Incarnations of the Faith," in Bediako, *Christianity in Africa*, chapter 7, 109–25.

2. Bediako, *Christianity in Africa*, 109.

3. As early as 1987, Bediako wrote, "with what Professor Andrew Walls has taught us to call the Christian faith's 'infinite cultural translatability.'" See Kwame Bediako, "Christ in Africa: Some Reflections on the Contribution of Christianity to the African Becoming," in *African Futures: 25th Anniversary Conference Proceedings Held in the Centre of African Studies, University of Edinburgh, 9–11 December 1987*, ed. Christopher Fyfe and Chris Allen (Edinburgh: Centre of African Studies, 1987), 453. By 1990, Andrew Walls wrote, "Incarnation is translation. When God in Christ became man, Divinity translated into humanity, as though humanity were a receptor language. Here was a clear statement of what would otherwise be veiled in obscurity or uncertainty, the statement, 'This is what God is like,'" Andrew F. Walls, *The Missionary Movement in Christian History: Studies in the Transmission of Faith* (Maryknoll, NY: Orbis, 1996), 27.

humanity."[4] This initial act of translation, God taking human form in the person of Jesus Christ, mandates both the translatability of the Christian Scriptures as well as the translatability of the gospel.[5] Bediako's basis for this claim was John 1:14: "The Word became flesh and lived among us."[6] Because of the incarnation, Bediako understood translation to be integral to the Christian faith. Translations produce new meaning and generate new insights. The process of translating the Scriptures can (and does) lead to new insights in a particular culture. While these insights are contextual, they are not *confined* to that culture. Others can learn from these "universal" insights,[7] because, "Translatability is another way of saying universality."[8]

Bediako's understanding of translation was directly related to his claim that Christianity is indigenous to Africa and was indebted to Lamin Sanneh.[9] When Bediako pursued his PhD in Aberdeen, Sanneh was a young professor, and the two were part of a tight-knit community of Africans in Aberdeen. In fact, it was said that in the early 1980s, if one wanted to learn about Christianity

---

4. Kwame Bediako, "Christianity, Islam, and the Kingdom of God: Rethinking Their Relationship from an African Perspective," *Journal of African Christian Thought* 7, no. 2 (2004): 6. Indeed as Anthony Balcomb helpfully expressed, "Bediako's theology rests on the single-minded conviction that the Christian gospel has a translatable essence." Anthony O. Balcomb, "Narrative, Epistemological Crisis and Reconstruction – My Story with Special Reference to the Work of Kwame Bediako," *Scriptura* 97 (2008): 53.

5. Bediako's theological claim was that "underlying the translatability of the Christian Scriptures lies the prior act of divine translation, the Incarnation." Kwame Bediako, "Challenges of Ghana's Fourth Republic: A Christian Perspective," The William Ofori-Atta Memorial Lectures, 7–9 October 1992, unpublished, Lecture 2, page 7.

6. See Bediako, *Christianity in Africa*, 110, and Bediako, "The Relevance of a Christian Approach to Culture in Africa," in *Christian Education in the African Context: Proceedings of the First Africa Regional Conference of the International Association for the Promotion of Christian Higher Education (IAPCHE), 4–9 March 1991, Harare, Zimbabwe* (Grand Rapids: IAPCHE, 1991), 31.

7. For more on Bediako's understanding of translation, see Benno van den Toren, "Kwame Bediako's Christology in Its African Evangelical Context," *Exchange* 26, no. 3 (1997): 218–32, esp. 229.

8. Bediako, *Christianity in Africa*, 109. See also Bediako, "Relevance of a Christian Approach," 31, and Kwame Bediako, "Biblical Exegesis in the African Context: The Factor and Impact of Translated Scriptures," *Journal of African Christian Thought* 6, no. 1 (2003): 17.

9. In his writings, Bediako cited Sanneh over seventy-five times. Most often, Bediako cited Lamin Sanneh, "The Horizontal and the Vertical in Mission: An African Perspective," *International Bulletin of Missionary Research* 7, no. 4 (1983): 166; Lamin Sanneh, *Piety and Power: Muslims and Christians in West Africa* (Maryknoll, NY: Orbis, 1996), x; Lamin Sanneh, *West African Christianity: The Religious Impact* (Maryknoll, NY: Orbis, 1983), 250; and Lamin Sanneh, *Translating the Message: The Missionary Impact on Culture* (Maryknoll, NY: Orbis Press, 1989), 1.

in Africa, one of the best places to go was Aberdeen because of the numerous African graduate students and scholars there.

Christianity and Islam are understood to spread differently. Islam spreads faith by *diffusion* – expanding from its geographical starting point to other societies with certain inalienable cultural assumptions, including the indispensable use of the Arabic language in Scripture, law, and religion.[10] In the diffusion approach, there is no distinction between the message of the missionary and the culture of the missionary. The cultural assumptions of the missionaries are inalienable and as such unassailable and non-negotiable. In contrast, Christianity has spread through an approach of mission by *translation*, where the recipient culture is "the true and final locus of the proclamation, so that the religion arrives without the presumption of cultural rejection."[11] In this understanding of translation, the recipient culture is adapted to, not merely imposed upon. Instead of believing that their message is culturally bound, Christian missionaries seek to change, to *translate* their message into cultural forms that can be understood by the recipient culture.

The primary contention is that Christianity, from its origins, has been a religion of translation beginning with Aramaic and Hebrew into Greek.[12] Thus Christianity at its core is based on the impulse, the necessity even, to translate its message to any human culture. For Sanneh and then for Bediako, two complementary forces in Christianity's historical development can be identified in early Christian history. On one hand, the nascent Christians sought to relativize their Jewish roots, resulting in the promotion of significant aspects of those roots. On the other hand, Christians sought to destigmatize Gentile culture and adopt that culture as a natural extension of the life of the new religion.[13]

This intrinsic interplay between relativizing and destigmatizing has shaped the course of the church's history and the path of theological development. Every time Christians encountered a new culture, these two forces were unleashed. When European Christian missionaries first came to Africa, starting in the late fifteenth century, they brought with them a theological model of translation that incorporated some elements of the Jewish, pre-Christian religion and a desire to destigmatize African cultures and create African Christians. As these missionaries claimed that the names Africans used for

10. Sanneh, *Translating the Message*, 29.
11. Sanneh, 29.
12. Sanneh, 1.
13. Sanneh, 1.

God actually called on God in Jesus Christ, they attempted to destigmatize traditional African religions. From this perspective, Bediako's elaboration of translation can be understood as a metaphor for inculturation.[14] Bediako understood that the task of African theology does not consist in indigenizing Christianity or theology, but rather, as Diane Stinton described it, "in allowing the Christian Gospel to encounter the African experience, as well as be shaped by it."[15] Bediako further pointed out that African Christians could proceed with this task without apology to Western traditions of Christianity, since these do not enshrine universal norms.

Names for God

The names used to refer to God was a main topic of discussion for Bediako in relation to the indigenous nature of Christianity in Africa. The basic contrast that he drew was between what happened when Christianity was introduced in Europe and what happened when Christianity was introduced in Africa. As Bediako narrated the history, when Christianity was first proclaimed in northern and western Europe, the names of traditional deities were "swept away . . . with the neutral name of 'God.'"[16] This neutral name was used by Hellenistic Christians to identify "the God of the Bible with the 'God' of Plato and the concept of the highest good in the Greek philosophical tradition – a 'God' without a name, generally described in negative categories and usually spoken of in abstract terms."[17] This characterization and naming of the Divine dominated European Christian thought. In Africa, the situation was different.

Instead of a plurality of powerful gods, pre-Christian Africans espoused "a well-rooted belief in one great God, Creator and Moral ruler of the universe and one not too distinguishable from the God of the Old and the New Testament traditions."[18] The God of the Bible was then identified with this One who held "a traditionally venerated name in indigenous languages and it is the divine name

---

14. Gerald O. West, "Mapping African Biblical Interpretation: A Tentative Sketch," in *The Bible in Africa: Transactions, Trajectories, and Trends*, ed. Gerald O. West and Musa W. Dube (Leiden: Brill, 2000), 46.

15. Diane B. Stinton, "Jesus Christ, Living Water in Africa Today," in *The Oxford Handbook of Christology*, ed. Francesca Aran Murphy (New York: Oxford University Press, 2015), 441.

16. Kwame Bediako, "The Holy Spirit, the Christian Gospel and Religious Change: The African evidence for a Christian theology of religious pluralism," in *Essays in Religious Studies for Andrew Walls*, ed. James Thrower (Aberdeen: Department of Religious Studies, University of Aberdeen, 1986), 47.

17. Bediako, "Holy Spirit," 47.

18. Bediako, 47.

in the vernacular which has on the whole passed into Christian devotion."[19]
Bediako further noted the immense significance of beginning African
Christian thought from a place of continuity with traditional African religions
rather than beginning from the radical discontinuity with so-called pagan
spiritualities in Western Europe. Bediako describes this alternate "starting point
for theological thought" as producing an effect that is "incalculable."[20] Indeed,
a whole cluster of ideas emerged: from translation, indigeneity, continuity,
mother-tongue vernaculars, Christianity as a non-Western religion, and the
remaking of Christian theology. Continuity between the pre-Christian African
past and present-day African Christian thought offers a different foundation
than Western Christian thought.

Bediako's understanding was that even though "Europe shares with
Africa an identical pre-Christian heritage in the primal religious traditions
of the world,"[21] the Christianization of Europe happened through conquest
that "proceeded on a basis of substitution to such an extent that the primal
traditions were virtually completely wiped out."[22] Scant traces of European
primal religions remain in Western culture today. The wholesale substitution
of the Christian religion in place of European primal religion "together with
the fact that there was no sustained interest in the use of indigenous European
languages and their pre-Christian world-views for Christian purposes,"[23] has so
radically altered the Western religious memory that it will never be recovered.
Yet as Bediako points out, "the old beliefs had not entirely lost their hold
upon people's minds" as "Christians continued to name the days of the week
after pre-Christian deities, and pre-Christian elements and notions made
their way into the celebration of Christian festivals."[24] Little remains of the
European primal imagination, except Sun-day, Mo(o)nday, etc. The conquest
and Christianization of Europe eradicated Europeans' primal imagination.

Many European missionaries simply proceeded to "do" missions as missions
had been "done" to their ancestors – by wiping out the local traditions and
wholly substituting a Western understanding of the Christian God. European
colonization in Africa was not (primarily) by means of military conquest but
instead a process of attempted "civilization" with an economic upside. However,

---

19. Bediako, 47.
20. Bediako, 47.
21. Bediako, *Christianity in Africa*, 260.
22. Bediako, "Understanding African Theology," 59.
23. Bediako, 59.
24. Bediako, 59.

the European colonizers did not eliminate all traces of African primal religions. Bediako saw this restraint as a tremendous opportunity for African Christian thought. He wrote, "It may be that in Africa the opportunity lost in Europe for a serious and creative theological encounter between the Christian and primal traditions, can be regained."[25] Bediako saw this opportunity as a gain for African theology, a reward of sorts for the tough work of standing in the interface between the Christian faith and the "spiritualities of their African primal heritage."[26] He describes the process this way: Having "to internalize that dialogue within themselves, African theologians have restored the character of theology as Christian intellectual activity on the frontier with the non-Christian world as essentially *communicative, evangelistic* and *missionary*."[27] From its origins, African Christian thought has had Christianity modelled as an encounter between gospel and culture.

Many missionaries to Africa, in contrast to the conquerors of Europe, sought out the name for God within an African culture and identified that name with God in Jesus Christ. While this may certainly be viewed as a totalizing move by an occupying power, it has allowed for continuity between African primal religions and Christianity which has encouraged the primal religions to continue. The result of this method was that, "The God of the Bible turned out to be the God whose name has been hallowed in vernacular usage for generations."[28] Bediako illustrates the specific implications: "in Africa the God whose name had been hallowed in indigenous languages in the pre-Christian tradition was found to be the God of the Bible, in a way neither Zeus, nor Jupiter, nor Odin could be. Onyankopon, Olorun, Ngai, Nkulunkulu are the names of the God and Father of Jesus Christ; Zeus, Jupiter, and Odin are not."[29] This move by the European missionaries to use the African names for God – which has been accepted and used for generations by African Christians – points to continuity between African traditional religions (ATRs)[30]

---

25. Bediako, 59.

26. Bediako, 59.

27. Bediako, 59; emphasis original.

28. Bediako, *Christianity in Africa*, 99.

29. Kwame Bediako, "The Significance of Modern African Christianity – A Manifesto," *Studies in World Christianity The Edinburgh Review of Theology and Religion* 1, no. 1 (1995): 54. See also Bediako, *Jesus and the Gospel in Africa*, 8–15; and Patrick J. Ryan, "'Arise O God!': The Problem of 'Gods' in West Africa," *Journal of Religion in Africa* 11, no. 3 (1980): 161–71.

30. I use the descriptor African traditional religions (ATRs), not African indigenous religions, out of deference to Bediako and other African Christian theologians such as Bénézet Bujo and John Mbiti who seek to articulate indigenous African understandings of the Christian faith based in their belief that God in Jesus Christ has always been present and active on the

and Christianity, at least from the side of the Christians, but raises the question of the monotheistic view of God in Christianity and the multiple divinities of many African religions.

Bediako proposed the Trinity as a method to deal with multiple African divinities so that the one-in-the-many conception of African divinity could continue.[31] He used Bolaji Idowu's assertion that all African primal religions are monotheistic where the multiplicity of "spirits" or "divinities" can be seen as manifestations of "a single God."[32] Bediako later backed off the claim that ATRs are inherently monotheistic in his book *Christianity in Africa* and affirmed continuity while reminding himself and his readers of the empirical experiences of practioners of ATRs that cannot simply be overrun by Christian assumptions. He notes the "positive gain in the near-unanimous affirmation through African scholarship that much in the primal religious experience and heritage is genuinely contiguous with Christian understanding and religious experience."[33] Yet he cautions that this "religious and spiritual continuity has been used to buttress a presumed African monotheism. A misreading of the spiritual realities of the African primal world has often resulted from this process, for example the failure to engage adequately with the dimension of multiplicity."[34]

Translation and Its Critics

One difficulty with Bediako's understanding of translation is that the concept of translatability seems to take on a life of its own in becoming an independent actor. For Emmanuel Katongole, "There is something misleading about

---

African continent and with African peoples. From their point of view, both African traditional religious beliefs and rituals as well as African Christianity are indigenous religions of Africa. For representative examples, see Bediako, *Christianity in Africa*; Bénézet Bujo, *African Theology in Its Social Context*, trans. John O'Donohue (Maryknoll, NY: Orbis, 1992); and John S. Mbiti, *New Testament Eschatology in an African Background: A Study of the Encounter between New Testament Theology and African Traditional Concepts* (Oxford: Oxford University Press, 1971).

31. Kwame Bediako, "Christian tradition and the African God revisited: A process in the exploration of a theological idiom," in *Witnessing to the Living God in Contemporary Africa*, ed. David Gitari and Patrick Benson (Nairobi: Uzima, 1986), 77–97; and *Theology and Identity*, 288–89.

32. For more on Idowu's position, see Bolaji Idowu, *African Traditional Religion: A Definition* (Maryknoll, NY: Orbis, 1973), 205. For more on Bediako's discussion of Idowu, see *Theology and Identity*, 286–88 and on monotheism in African traditional religions, see *Theology and Identity*, 291–93.

33. Bediako, *Christianity in Africa*, 99.

34. Bediako, 99.

[Bediako's] attempt to prove the non-foreignness of Christianity by setting up an infinitely translatable Gospel – not Christianity – as the crucial factor in missionary work."[35] Bediako believed that it is only by understanding and appreciating the inherent translatability of the Christian faith "that we can appreciate the true character of continuing Christian witness and enhance the genuine development of new indigenous traditions of Christian thought."[36]

Bediako's writings emphasize what he calls "the depth of the impact that the Bible has made upon Africa."[37] Gerald West countered the impression Bediako gave that "the encounter between the Bible and Africa is in one direction: from the Bible to Africa."[38] West was concerned that Bediako's approach treated the Bible as the subject – with a static and self-evident message – with Africa as the passive object. West proposed reversing Bediako's statement to read: "*Further developments in African Christianity will test the depth of the impact that Africa has made upon the Bible.*"[39] In this way, African agency in translation is emphasized. Bediako focused on the Bible's answers rather than Africans' questions; the Bible has answers to Africans' questions, not only Europeans' questions.[40] West, on the other hand, preferred to emphasize Africans' questions not the Bible's answers, implying that Africans' questions (rather than Europeans' questions) might produce different answers – from the same Bible.[41] Maluleke offered a similar critique about the lack of African agency in Bediako's translation metaphor: "Apart from attributing almost everything creative done by Africans to the genius and logic of the gospel, rather than Africans, the proposal seems more concerned with the activities of missionaries and colonialists than those of Africans."[42]

The failure of many European missionaries was to assume that the translation process was complete – once and for all – when the gospel was

---

35. Katongole, *Future for Africa*, 162.

36. Bediako, *Christianity in Africa*, 110.

37. Kwame Bediako, "Epilogue: The Impact of the Bible in Africa," in Ype Schaaf, *On Their Way Rejoicing: The History and Role of the Bible in Africa* (Carlisle: Paternoster, 1995), 254.

38. Gerald O. West, "Mapping African Biblical Interpretation: A Tentative Sketch," in *The Bible in Africa: Transactions, Trajectories, and Trends*, ed. Gerald O. West and Musa W. Dube (Leiden: Brill, 2000), 29.

39. West, "Mapping African Biblical Interpretation," 29, emphasis original.

40. Bediako, *Christianity in Africa*, 63.

41. Gerald O. West, *The Stolen Bible: From Tool of Imperialism to African Icon* (Leiden: Brill, 2016), 243n55.

42. Tinyiko Sam Maluleke, "The Rediscovery of the Agency of Africans: An emerging paradigm of post-cold war and post-apartheid black and African theology," in *African Theology Today*, ed. by Emmanuel Katongole (Scranton, PA: University of Scranton Press, 2002), 166.

translated into Western culture. In a sense, the tactics of these missionaries resembled more of an approach of diffusion where Africans needed to conform to European customs, theological concepts, and languages. Instead of bringing the gospel to Africa, as they naively assumed, the missionaries brought a bastardized version of Christianity – a hybrid of the gospel of the Christian faith and Western culture – which they passed on as the pure gospel alone. Bediako was charitably understanding toward the missionaries and particularly grateful to them for bringing the Bible to Africa and translating it into so many African mother tongues.

However, Bediako's charity has been harshly criticized by other African theologians. Chammah Kaunda, Kennedy Owino, and Isabel Phiri, believe that Bediako seemed "to view translation like a robotic and mechanical process where the passive missionaries witnessed Christian faith extracting itself in its purity from their cultures and translating itself into Africa cultures."[43] They echo Katongole's fear that if Bediako's understanding of translatability was an independent actor, the Bible would translate itself. This trio does not view translation as a neutral act or the missionaries as impartial actors. Instead, they write, "When we understand that translatability is a political ideology, then we begin to understand that the missionaries utilised translation to achieve total control of the African mind and render them subservient to colonial domination and exploitation."[44] While Bediako certainly acknowledged the power of translation, particularly of the Bible, he viewed translation as an inherent good – a sharing of ideas, wisdom, and the word of God. He viewed the missionaries as servants of God rather than as colonial minions, self-serving individualists, or malevolent actors. Contrary to Bediako, Kaunda, Owino, and Phiri understand translatability as political theology.

Taking this criticism a step further, Martin Ngodji of Namibia urges readers of Bediako (and Sanneh) to acknowledge the role of the translator in the process of translation. Texts do not translate themselves, and the Bible is no exception. The implicit biases of a translator seep into every translation. For example, Ngodji notes the impact of European gender bias on vernacular African translations of the Bible. He writes, "In many African languages gender-sensitivity does not exist, and neither does gender-bias. In the African

---

43. Chammah J. Kaunda, Kennedy O. Owino, and Isabel A. Phiri, "Applicability of Translatability Theory to European Missionary Masculinity Performance in Africa: Contestations and Reflections," *Alternation* Special Edition 14 (2015): 216.

44. Kaunda, Owino, and Phiri, "Applicability of Translatability Theory," 216–17.

language a person is just a person and God is God."[45] The question then arises why so many translations of the Bible in African languages use male pronouns for humans and for God.[46]

Bediako's understanding of translation and of the gospel have been challenged as too positive and naive. Katongole criticized "the language and logic of 'translatability' which Bediako appeals to [that] rests on an outdated premise of a foundational epistemology, which only serves the promotion of a putative universality. Translation is never innocent or ideologically neutral."[47] While there is no pure gospel for Bediako, he does appear to hold onto a belief in the purity of the translation process. Bediako failed to acknowledge (or address) that, in the words of Musa Dube of Botswana, translation is one of the most effective tools for "colonizing minds and spaces."[48] Bediako's theology of translation, according to Katongole, is an "attempt to unhinge Christianity from its past (even a colonial past) [that] simply drives an unfortunate wedge between that gospel and history."[49] The gospel will continue to be transmitted in the future, regardless of the actions or inactions of Christians and the church.[50]

Alongside his belief in the power of the gospel and its transmission through translatability, Bediako did foresee a significant role for Africans. In one of his final lectures, Bediako urged his Ghanaian audience not to dwell on the gifts or burdens of the missionaries, but rather to engage the work of the gospel in the present. He exhorted his listeners as follows: "In this era of the African significance in Christian history in the world, it is not what missionaries did or did not do, but what African Christians do with the gospel, that matters. There is here no inevitability of African success. We have work to do!"[51]

---

45. Martin Ngodji, "The Applicability of the Translatability and Interpretation Theory of Sanneh and Bediako: The Case of the Evangelical Lutheran Church in Namibia, in Northern Namibia" (PhD dissertation, University of Kwazulu-Natal, Pietermartzburg, South Africa, 2010), 54.

46. Maluleke makes a similar point: "While the gospel may indeed be eminently translatable, human intervention can affect the pace and quality of such translation – even arresting it into all sorts of orthodoxies." Tinyiko Sam Maluleke, "Half a Century of African Christian Theologies: Elements of the emerging agenda for the twenty-first century," *Journal of Theology for Southern Africa* 99 (November 1997): 20.

47. Katongole, *Future for Africa*, 162.

48. Musa W. Dube, "Consuming a Colonial Cultural Bomb: Translating *Badimo* into 'Demons' in the Setswana Bible (Matthew 8:28–34; 15:22; 10:8)," *Journal for the Study of the New Testament* 73 (1999): 33, 44.

49. Katongole, *Future for Africa*, 162.

50. Katongole, 163.

51. Bediako, "Missionaries Did Not Bring Christ to Africa," 29–30.

Surprisingly, given how much attention Bediako paid to the *Western* and *European* versions of Christianity that the missionaries brought to Africa, he did not offer the same critiques or cautions of European translations of the Bible into African mother tongues. Bediako saw the encounter of Western Christianity with African culture not as invalidating Christianity, but as unmasking Western Christianity for what it is. Bediako wrote,

> Not only in demographic terms, but in some other respects too, Christianity has become a non-Western religion. . . . It is not that Western Christianity has become irrelevant, but rather that Christianity may now be seen for what it truly is, a universal religion, infinitely culturally translatable – capable of being at home everywhere without loss to its essential nature.[52]

Through the christologically understood translation principle, Bediako asserted that "Christianity . . . [is] capable of being at home everywhere without loss to its essential nature."[53] Tanzanian theologian Laurenti Magesa refers to this assertion of Bediako's as, "The translatability of the Gospel message means its transculturality."[54] Translation overcomes any and all cultural barriers.

Therefore in Africa, *even* in Africa, the gospel of Jesus Christ can take an authentic form. In doing so, not only will the Christian faith not lose its essential nature, but the faith will be revealed for what it truly is: a gospel present in, but not captured by, human cultures. The infinite translatability of the gospel debunks any notions of Christianity as a "white man's religion" for Bediako. "African Christianity is no less Christian for being mediated through African languages, whilst Western Christianity does not enshrine universal standards,"[55] he wrote. For him, the possibility of Scripture translation demonstrates that "an African 'incarnation' of the Faith is valid too."[56] Because of the incarnation of God in the human being Jesus Christ, an African incarnation of the Christian faith is not only possible, but is valid.

---

52. Bediako, "Impact of the Bible in Africa," 244.

53. Bediako, 244.

54. Laurenti Magesa, *Anatomy of Inculturation: Transforming the Church in Africa* (Maryknoll, NY: Orbis, 2004), 148.

55. Bediako, *Christianity in Africa*, 121.

56. Bediako, 121.

Gospel and Culture

All translation occurs in the encounter between gospel and culture. Bediako offered a positive assessment of his African cultural heritage. For him, culture is full of possibilities in the divine-human encounter. Culture is not inhibiting but freeing for African Christians. Bediako wrote,

> Rather than constituting a prison that inhibits our human development, and therefore a prison from which we are to break free in order to experience salvation in a so-called "Christian culture" brought in from outside, our African cultural heritage is in fact the very place where Christ desires to find us in order to transform us into his image.[57]

This process of encounter and translation emphasized for Bediako the "demanding task . . . [of] *Africanisation* of its Christian experience" which follows – historically – "the 'Christianisation' of African tradition."[58] This positive valuation of African culture emphasizes continuity between traditional African religions and African Christianity.

For Bediako, the gospel of Jesus Christ does not change, but its cultural form (i.e. Christianity) must change as the gospel is translated from one host culture to the next. His understanding was that as the gospel was translated from European cultures to African cultures that the cultural form of the gospel would change from European Christianities to African Christianities, but that the gospel of Jesus Christ never changes. Bediako wrote, "The gospel . . . does not need to be changed or modified in order to speak to the conditions of modern life."[59] The result of Bediako's claims is that Christianity, in fact "all Christian theology is a synthesis, an 'adaptation' of the inherited Christian tradition in the service of new formulations . . . no Christian theology in any age is ever simply a repetition of the inherited Christian tradition."[60] As a synthesis, the timeworn category of syncretism is revealed as hollow. For Bediako, the gospel must be contextualized, but not to the point where the distinctiveness of the gospel is lost to the host culture, or context. There is no such thing as a pure gospel. Or at least if there is, no human being can encounter a pure gospel without any cultural "blinkers."[61] So on the one hand,

---

57. Bediako, "Their Past Is also Our Present," 8.

58. Bediako, *Christianity in Africa*, 4, emphasis original.

59. Kwame Bediako, "'In the Bible . . . Africa Walks on Familiar Ground': Why the World Needs Africa," *AICMAR* 6 (2007): 37.

60. Bediako, *Theology and Identity*, 434.

61. Bediako, "Willowbank Consultation," 28.

purity is not the goal, or even a possibility, for the church's understanding of the gospel. On the other hand, the gospel must not be so fused to its host culture that the "blinkers" obscure the distinctiveness and divine foreignness of the gospel. Though he never expressed it directly, Bediako seems convinced that Western Christianity is not faithful to the gospel but is actually a syncretistic form of Western culture. As a graduate student, he wrote, "it may well require a more active partnership with Third World churches to effect the rescue of Western churches from their captivity to culture."[62] This quotation lays bare Bediako's central claim about Western Christianity: its captivity to culture. For him, the church in the West traded the gospel for a poor substitute, Western culture. Thus, instead of the church being founded on the unchanging gospel of Jesus Christ, Western churches have placed their confidence in the shifting sands of culture.

Bediako identified the stakes of the discussion for the interaction between gospel and culture when outsiders enter a culture seeking to "bring" the gospel with them: "In short, the challenge is that of relevance without syncretism."[63] Bediako sought an integrated understanding of the Christian faith in African culture, and he did so by asserting the presence of the gospel in Africa prior to the arrival of European missionaries. He stated this succinctly, borrowing from Kenyan theologian John S. Mbiti, in the title of a 2006 lecture: "Missionaries did not bring Christ to Africa; Christ brought them."[64] Bediako's christological view of history extended to prior to the New Testament era. He wrote, "Indeed, the gospel was before the New Testament. In that sense, the gospel existed before our traditions, before our cultures."[65] While Bediako's understanding of the gospel is universal (as discussed above), he understood theology to be provisional because "all theology, wherever it is produced, is contextual and therefore provisional rather than universal, and that theology itself is always a struggle with culturally-related questions."[66] The work of translation is participating in the tension of these struggles with culturally related questions. Contextual theologies emerge from these interactions of the gospel and human cultures.

62. Bediako, 32.

63. Bediako, *Christianity in Africa*, 85.

64. Bediako, "Missionaries Did Not Bring Christ to Africa," 17–31.

65. Kwame Bediako, "Scripture as the Hermeneutics of Culture and Tradition," *Journal of African Christian Thought* 4, no. 1 (2001): 2.

66. Bediako, *Christianity in Africa*, 129.

Understandings of the gospel are always culturally bound and subject to error and misinterpretation. No theology can be universal; a "theology can be authentic only in context."[67] Any attempt at a universal theology creates a false gospel. The consequences of a misplaced cultural confidence in a false gospel were devasting for Bediako. He wrote, "The price that is paid by converts to such a truncated Gospel is incalculable."[68] Bediako's deep concern – that the scriptural witness of the gospel can be corrupted by blind adaptation of cultural assumptions – motivated his work. He was constantly pushing back against the Western, colonial (mis-) formulations of the gospel of Jesus Christ and sought to rehabilitate and re-examine African culture in light of his understanding of that same gospel.

A challenge in Bediako's thought is whether his understanding of the translatability of the gospel inadvertently becomes a universal theology. He was deeply wary of the universalizing tendencies of Western theological thought and consequently distrusted universalities and many Western theologians. Bediako's emphasis on the receiving, or host, culture encouraged the flourishing of non-Western contextual theologies. Yet Bediako's understanding of the universal translatability of the gospel of Jesus Christ at times seemed to overwhelm the contextual particularities in a given gospel and culture interaction. He sought to navigate a very narrow path between the universal gospel as understood as the same for all peoples and the possibility that disparate contexts could understand the good news differently. He gave no guidance as to how any differences in understanding might be adjudicated. On one side lies a static gospel, on the other side, contextual theology. For Gerald West, "What 'the gospel' is is always contested, precisely because post-colonial 'others' can and do speak (back)."[69] Bediako, however, did not allow the gospel to be contested. He sought an unideological Christianity without a pure Christianity. Whether such a distinction is possible is debatable.

Bediako offered a formal definition of "culture" in the 1988 *New Dictionary of Theology*.[70] He begins his entry with a disclaimer: "Culture is a term that is not easily definable."[71] Then he continues, pushing his main point: "However,

---

67. Kwame Bediako, "Biblical Christologies in the Context of African Traditional Religion," in *Sharing Jesus in the Two-Thirds World*, ed. Vinay Samuel and Chris Sugden (Grand Rapids: Eerdmans, 1984), 98.

68. Bediako, "Willowbank Consultation," 29.

69. West, *Stolen Bible*, 241.

70. Kwame Bediako, "Culture," in *New Dictionary of Theology*, ed. Sinclair Ferguson and David Wright (Downers Grove, IL: InterVarsity, 1988), 183–85.

71. Bediako, "Culture," 183.

if we take culture to mean the ways of thinking (culture begins internally) and behavior shared by a substantial social grouping of persons, which give them identity in relation to other social groupings, then it is evident that all persons participate in one culture or another. There is no individual who has no culture."[72] Bediako routinely insisted that no person or group of people could exist outside of culture. Thus not only people, but also their thoughts, convictions, and theologies are rooted within culture. Culture for him is "all-embracing" and "inescapable."[73] Culture is not fixed but instead "like human life itself, culture is dynamic, adaptable and open to transformation both within itself, and in response to new and external factors."[74] Culture for Bediako is the collection of human thinking and behavior that is shared by a group of people that gives the group their identity. Individual cultures are fluid and ever changing in response to internal and external developments.

In contrast to his understanding of culture as dynamic, Bediako's understanding of the gospel was fixed on the person of Jesus Christ. He defined "the Gospel" as follows:

> The Gospel, in the true sense of the word, is who Christ is, and what he means, in his person, his life on earth, his work, his death, his resurrection and its aftermath, and how all that concerning him relates to all human beings, in all our cultural traditions, histories, and environments. The Gospel, therefore, is not like a mathematical formula.[75]

Though fixed on the person of Christ, Bediako's understanding of the gospel is not reducible to a mathematical formula because the meaning is not self-evident. In part this conviction amounts to the rationale for why the "Gospel and culture cannot be separated."[76] Since the claim in John 1:14, "'The Word became flesh' [was] not some abstract, general humanity,"[77] but instead the real flesh of a Jewish man living in first-century Palestine, the gospel, God's Son coming to earth as a human being, is concretized in a specific way. This connection of gospel with culture is rooted in the incarnation. For Bediako,

---

72. Bediako, "Culture," 183; see also Kwame Bediako, "Gospel and Culture: Some Insights for Our Time from the Experience of the Earliest Christians," *Journal of African Christian Thought* 2, no. 2 (1988): 8.

73. Bediako, "Gospel and Culture," 8.

74. Bediako, 8.

75. Bediako, 8.

76. Bediako, 9.

77. Bediako, 9.

"the Gospel can no longer be viewed as independent of culture" because Jesus of Nazareth was a human being who existed within culture.[78]

As with any situation when the gospel and culture become intertwined, questions and accusations of syncretism lurk at every bend. Bediako tackled this challenge head-on. He desired relevance without syncretism. He knew that Christian theology can be captured by culture – in fact, this is precisely the claim he made about most Western theologies and some African theologies, such as Afrikania.[79] He was wary of any theology claiming to be above, outside of, or apart from *culture*. That is, Bediako was clear that there is no such thing as a pure gospel. The gospel is always intermingled with human cultures. If it were not, humans would be unable to hear or understand a gospel delivered without form or vessel. God assumed humanity in the person of Jesus Christ so that humans might have a clear example of who God is and how we as humans are to live.

For Bediako, there is a mutually enlightening relationship between gospel and culture. In the interaction between the two, the gospel teaches about culture, and culture teaches about the gospel. He believed that "through the Gospel, and through the interface with culture, we also gain fresh understanding of culture itself . . . the engagement between Gospel and culture is what God has been about all along."[80] Bediako did not fear the interaction of gospel and culture. He believed that such interaction is an inevitable part of human existence and as such should be welcomed and probed for meaning without trying to escape or avoid it. Even more than understanding the inevitable, however, Bediako saw potential learning through the interaction.

Culture was not a neutral quantity for Bediako. He believed that, "There is within every tradition of culture, history, identity and continuity, elements which lead to Jesus and affirm him as Lord; but equally, there are within every tradition, elements that lead away from Jesus and deny him."[81] Culture then is very powerful in shaping the identities of individuals and in pointing them toward or away from Jesus Christ.

Historically, Bediako saw a tremendous amount of Western attention devoted to possible syncretism in churches and theologies of the developing

---

78. Bediako, 8–9.

79. Kwame Bediako, "African Identity: The Afrikania Challenge," in *Christianity in Africa: The Renewal of a Non-Western Religion* (Edinburgh: Edinburgh University Press, 1995), 17–38.

80. Bediako, "Gospel and Culture: Guest Editorial," *Journal of African Christian Thought* 2, no. 2 (1988): 1.

81. Bediako, "Gospel and Culture," 12.

world, as well as "an insufficient alertness to similar phenomena threatening the churches of the West."[82] Bediako's view of Western theology was that it is syncretistic with Western culture and distorts the gospel. Therefore, translating this distorted, Western gospel was not enough for churches in the global South. They must go further. He wrote, "the question will be falsely put if it is assumed that Third World churches will need merely to 'translate,' albeit in their own thought-forms and idioms, the theological reflection of Western Christianity."[83] There is much more work to be done than the mere translation of words or ideas from Western cultures to African ones. In fact, according to Bediako, "it is quite conceivable that the fundamental theological concerns of the Christian Church in our time will be given new direction and form by the responses emerging from the reflection of the Third World churches."[84] The insights gleaned will not be trivial. Instead for Bediako, Christians in Africa and other parts of the developing world may well "discover fresh insights . . . [that] Western Christianity has culturally been unable to see."[85] The interaction of gospel and culture in the developing world demonstrates significant potential for the remaking of Christian theology.

The distinctions between the gospel and culture and between gospel and theology are underscored by Bediako's distinction between Christ and Christianity. In Bediako's final analysis, "it is not any system of Christianity but *Christ* himself who saves, who redeems, and who gives light to everyone who comes into the world."[86] For Bediako, "Christianity" is used as a term indicating the too cozy relationship of gospel and culture where the cultural claims and assumptions dominate the gospel. Christ himself as the truest expression of the gospel is the uncorrupted presence of God within human culture.

Yet "Christianity, in becoming a non-Western religion, has become in actual experience the most universal of all religions."[87] Here Bediako played with the definition of universal. Since Christianity is widespread, Christianity is practiced around the world by a wide variety of peoples. These demographic realities make Christianity to be sociologically universal, which is a different claim than Bediako's understanding of the gospel as theologically universal. Since for Bediako the gospel is universal, then the conditions of possibility

---

82. Bediako, "Willowbank Consultation," 26.

83. Bediako, 31.

84. Bediako, 31.

85. Bediako, 31.

86. Bediako, "Christianity, Islam, and the Kingdom of God," 6, emphasis original.

87. Bediako, *Christianity in Africa*, 186.

exist for the universal practice of the Christian faith across cultures throughout the world. God speaks directly to Africans, not through European mediators; the gospel is translated into human language using African vernaculars and concepts.

Further Reading of Kwame Bediako

"Biblical Exegesis in the African Context: The Factor and Impact of Translated Scriptures." *Journal of African Christian Thought* 6, no. 1 (2003): 15–23.

"The Impact of the Bible in Africa." Epilogue in Ype Schaaf, *On Their Way Rejoicing: The History and Role of the Bible in Africa*, 243–54. Carlisle: Paternoster, 1995.

"'Missionaries Did not Bring Christ to Africa – Christ Brought Them': Why Africa Needs Jesus Christ." *AICMAR* 6 (2007): 17–31.

"Translatability and the Cultural Incarnations of the Faith," chapter 7, 91–108. In *Christianity in Africa: The Renewal of a Non-Western Religion*. Edinburgh: Edinburgh University Press, 1995.

3

History

"Christianity as a Non-Western Religion"

Bediako primarily performed the task of narrating the African experience of the gospel by connecting twentieth-century African Christianity with its Christian past. He clearly articulated his goal in the Introduction to *Theology and Identity*:

> Whilst the book seeks to make a contribution to the understanding of modern African Christianity, it seeks to do so by situating twentieth-century African theology within the organic tradition of Christian theology as a whole. Accordingly, the book attempts to remove African theology from the historical limbo in which it has often been held, caught between African "non-Christian" beliefs and values on the one hand, and Western "Christian" ideas on the other.[1]

Bediako understood African Christianity as "within the organic tradition of Christian theology." So it is not a foreign element that needs to be grafted in, but instead African Christianity is a natural part of Christian theology that goes back to its beginnings. Yet African Christian thought has been accused of not being African enough because it is Christian, and of not being Christian enough, because it is African. As a result, Bediako sought to connect twentieth-century African Christianity to its precolonial Christian past, thereby removing African Christianity from its "historical limbo." For Bediako, a line can be

---

1. Bediako, *Theology and Identity*, xii.

drawn from the earliest Christian theologians directly to modern African theologians – without having to go through European mediators.

Situating African Christianity Historically

As Christian theologians started to emerge from within African Christianity in the mid-twentieth century, most had to relocate to the United Kingdom or France for doctoral training. However, as Bediako observed, when these theologians returned to Africa, they were "forced by the very demands of Africa's religious pluralism, to move into areas of theological activity for which no Western syllabus prepared them."[2] The understanding of the Christian faith that developed in Europe was in an environment of unrivaled cultural influence. Religious minorities and dissenters had been driven out. Christianity in Western Europe was in decline, while African Christianity was growing exponentially. African theologians, in their quest to understand their identity as African Christians, found themselves seeking out their own religious heritage, rather than their teachers' European Christianity.

Bediako noted that this quest to identify a religious heritage for African Christians was "indeed, a proper task of theology. . . . [Although] this new theological approach had no counterpart in the more recent Western theological thought forged within the context of Christendom."[3] As long as the Christian faith was connected to political power, religious identity was inherited from one's surrounding culture without intentional effort. In Europe from the medieval era forward, where one was born generally determined one's religion: i.e. Germans were Lutherans; Scots were Presbyterians; and Italians were Roman Catholics. Geography of birth and ethnicity determined identity with the type of Christianity reinforcing ethnic identity. Yet in the postcolonial African context, identity became a primary, even *the* primary, theological category, not a secondary accessory. Bediako notes that "the development of theological concern and the formulation of theological questions were linked as the inevitable by-product of a process of Christian self-definition."[4] The search for an authentic African Christian identity was a truly theological endeavor as Christians sought traces of religious memory in the past to better understand themselves in the present. Bediako's background in the study of the négritude

---

2. Bediako, *Christianity in Africa*, 258. See also Bediako, "Understanding African Theology," 52.

3. Bediako, "Understanding African Theology," 53.

4. Bediako, *Christianity in Africa*, 256.

movement prepared him to do the work of theological retrieval for the sake of African Christian identity.

Bediako stressed that African Christians have an important, significant past and that they needed to know it. Bediako believed that God in Jesus Christ has been active in Africa for as long as humans have dwelled on the continent, and even before. He also believed that the gospel of Jesus Christ is at home in every culture. These dual beliefs formed the basis for his claim that the Christian faith is indigenous to Africa. He wrote, "For theological consciousness presupposes religious tradition, and tradition requires memory, and memory is integral to identity: without memory we have no past, and if we have no past, we lose our identity."[5] For Bediako, a people without a history have no present identity. As Aimé Césaire and other authors of négritude reconnected the black peoples brought to Martinique and the Antilles to their African past in an analogous manner, Bediako sought to connect African Christians to their dual heritage – as Africans and as Christians.

Bediako's work sought to bring African Christian thought out from the looming shadow of Western Christian thought. Even after Europeans stopped overtly trying to impose Western Christianity on Africa through the colonial project, *truly* African theology has not been widely welcomed within Western theological circles. Through much of his work, Bediako sought to overcome this impasse. He articulated the overall goal of African theology: to show that "there were genuinely and specifically *African* contributions – derived from the twin heritage of African Christianity, namely, the African primal tradition and the African experience of the Christian Gospel – to be made to the theology of the universal Church."[6] Bediako rooted African Christian identity in the twin heritage of African Christianity which is comprised of the African experience of the Christian gospel and the African primal tradition.[7]

Bediako sought to establish the idea that the Christian faith is indigenous to Africa, and in the words of Tinyiko Maluleke, "to exorcise the phantom foreignness of Christianity."[8] Bediako believed that the preoccupation of African theologians in prior decades with the foreignness of Christianity and with the African past is no longer necessary. Particularly in *Theology and Identity*, he addresses these historical issues of identity, then seeks to move forward building on that foundation. Bediako's exploration of the roots of African

---

5. Bediako, "Understanding African Theology," 51.

6. Bediako, 56, emphasis original.

7. Bediako, 56.

8. Maluleke, "Half a Century of African Christian Theologies," 20.

Christianity had a wide lens because there are "*African* contributions . . . to be made to the theology of the universal Church."

Connecting African Christianity with Its Christian Past

The result of connecting the present African Christianity to its Christian past allows African Christians to articulate their own understanding of the gospel within their own contexts, a religiously pluralistic modern world, in a way that, in Bediako's analysis, Western theologies based in a worldview shaped by Christendom and the Enlightenment have seemed chronically unable to do. In *Theology and Identity*, Bediako focuses "on the problems of forging Christian identity in the context of the religious pluralisms of the second century of the Christian era and modern Africa."[9] The thrust of the project is "to suggest that it is possible to ask fresh questions of the Christian tradition of the past, questions which can in turn illuminate the task of constructing local theologies and the doing of theology in our religiously pluralistic modern world."[10] With this goal in mind, Bediako employs *sankofa* to articulate his theology of négritude.

Sankofa is a word in the Twi language of Ghana that literally means "go back and get it" and is also translated "go back to the past and bring forward that which is useful." The idea is represented by an Akan adinkra symbol of a rooster with its feet facing forward toward the future and its head reaching backward toward the past with an egg in its beak. Bediako went back to the precolonial, Christian past of Africa to gain insights on how to understand and articulate the Christian faith in modern, religiously pluralistic societies. In doing so, he made a powerful political statement about the independence and self-sufficiency of theologies birthed by Africans and on the African continent. African theologies are indigenous, legitimate, and self-sufficient.

In *Theology and Identity*, Bediako analyzes four Christian authors from the second century: Tatian the Syrian; Tertullian of Carthage; Justin Martyr of Rome; and Clement of Alexandria. These four authors were all first-generation converts to Christianity who reflected on how to interpret their pagan past in Greco-Roman religions in light of their newfound faith in Jesus Christ.[11] These second-century apologists saw "no more pressing problem to be faced by Gentile Christians in the Graeco-Roman world than the question of their

---

9. Bediako, *Theology and Identity*, xii.

10. Bediako, xii.

11. Bediako, 32.

heritage and historical roots."[12] The similar concerns of these apologists and four modern African theologians – Bolaji Idowu of Nigeria, John Mbiti of Kenya, Mulago gwa Cikala Musharhamina of Congo, and Byang Kato of Nigeria – formed the basis for *Theology and Identity*. In his analysis, Bediako's preference for the thought of Justin Martyr and Clement shine through.

In Justin Martyr, Bediako saw an apologist who while "interpreting the past . . . is also explicating the present."[13] Justin Martyr claimed that there were Christians before Christ and "that he and the Christians of his own day had a common cause with those of the past."[14] Thus in Justin Martyr, Bediako found an early example of continuity between a pre-Christian past and a Christian present. For Justin Martyr, as later for Bediako, "the truth of the Christian Gospel is the truth of the person rather than of the religious tradition to which one belongs."[15] The person of Jesus Christ, "the Word Himself,"[16] is the source of Christian knowledge and the conduit for participation in God.

Bediako used Clement of Alexandria to build on the continuity articulated by Justin Martyr. In doing so, Bediako saw a "universalizing of 'salvation-history' . . . [that] involves the Christianising not only of Hellenistic tradition, but the Jewish also; 'holy pagans' and Jewish saints become 'Christians before Christ,' on the same terms; and the Old Testament, by virtue of Christ foreshadowed therein, becomes a Christian book."[17] Bediako latched on to the universalizing approach of Clement perhaps to the detriment of the particularities in other religious traditions, including African traditional religions. Bediako described how, for Clement, "the Christian account of reality . . . supersedes the entire history of intellectual and philosophical speculation in Hellenistic tradition . . . by absorbing it."[18] The superiority of the Christians' understanding of cosmology, ethics, and the like allowed them to absorb the Hellenistic tradition within it. For Bediako, this process of absorption is acceptable in regard to the Hellenistic tradition but not in regard to African traditions. Perhaps one could use Bediako to reread the Hellenistic tradition as pre-Christian, but distinctive. In this way, while the Christianity of Bediako, and Clement, would still be universalizing, it would

---

12. Bediako, 35.
13. Bediako, 149.
14. Bediako, 150.
15. Bediako, 156.
16. Bediako, 152.
17. Bediako, 160.
18. Bediako, 203–4

not be totalizing. Bediako hinted in this direction in his concluding comments on Clement: "Advancing beyond Justin, Clement even postulated a tradition in Hellenistic culture which bore witness to an apprehension of the divine truth in the Hellenistic past."[19]

Bediako sought a similar presence of divine truth within the African past. The advantage of Clement's views, according to Bediako, was that he connected Christians to an ancient people through the Old Testament "with laws and traditions which entitled them to a place in the common history of mankind, a right that was being denied them by Graeco-Roman traditionalists."[20] All told, Clement's task was "integrating Christian faith with culture,"[21] and Bediako understood himself to be doing the same as a modern-day apologist for Christianity in Africa with implications for Christianity in the wider world.[22]

While the thrust of Bediako's work built on the view of history and the universalizing role of the Christian faith espoused by Justin Martyr and Clement of Alexandria, the deeper connection still is with the person of Jesus Christ revealed in the Scriptures of the Old and New Testaments. Bediako's underlying theological conviction was that Africans are humans, created by God, and equal to Europeans. "The fact of the matter is," says Bediako, "if Jesus Christ is not in the cultural heritage of African peoples, then Africans as human beings would not have been created in and through Jesus Christ, the Word of God, Agent of creation, and the Second Adam and New Man."[23] Since Africans as human beings are created by God in the image of God, then Jesus Christ is the cultural heritage of Africans just as much as Europeans.

Sidestepping the Enlightenment

Bediako's historical project was to connect modern African Christianity with pre-Christendom Christianity. Once the Christian faith was yoked with political power in the fourth century, Christian theology went astray. Throughout his early work, Bediako demonstrates a distrust of Western thought, yet only later is his deep antipathy toward the Enlightenment revealed. Bediako desired to skip the Enlightenment and its dichotomies all together. At the least, he wanted

---

19. Bediako, 207.

20. Bediako, 203–4.

21. Bediako, 207.

22. In his final public appearance, a tribute to Andrew Walls, Bediako compared himself to Clement of Alexandria and Walls to Clement's teacher, Pantaenus. Bediako, "Andrew F. Walls as Mentor," 8.

23. Bediako, "Missionaries Did Not Bring Christ to Africa," 21.

to avoid Christendom entirely. His analysis skips from the second century to the twentieth century without engaging any Christian writings or traditions from the intervening years. He read all Western theologians from Aquinas to Calvin to Schleiermacher to Barth with intense skepticism. However Bediako was only willing to engage, carefully, Western theological sources dated after the conclusion of the failed European colonial project. Practically, this stance left him extremely skeptical of all Western theologies. Perhaps a theologian from the West who wrote after 1970 might garner Bediako's attention, but such work would be closely scrutinized for signs of Western, Christendom bias.

The possibility of an African Christianity without Enlightenment thought was very appealing to Bediako. He wrote: "the secret of the success of African Christianity may well lie in the fact that it is not bound by Enlightenment doubts, strictures, and limitations."[24] He identified three major problems with the Enlightenment. His first critique was that Enlightenment ideals "have gradually drained the vital power out of Christian theology by shunting its affirmations into the siding of mere opinion."[25] Bediako believed that religious convictions are primary to human identity construction, not secondary. He articulates his objection as follows: "The Enlightenment denied to religious affirmations the status of public truth, . . . Essentially, the Enlightenment exalted the autonomous individual self and so undermined the claims of divine revelation and corporate religious consciousness."[26] For Bediako, the Enlightenment exalted the autonomous self over and against divine revelation and communal spiritualities. In these ways, for him, Enlightenment ideals were both un-Christian and un-African.

On the individual level, "The real harm that the Enlightenment has done, has been to separate knowledge from character, intellectual development from spiritual growth."[27] These separations of beliefs from actions, of theology from ethics, produced scholars, intellectuals, and theologians who are "morally weak" because they have not experienced the discipline of connecting ideas and behaviors. Bediako's analysis is that the "theory of knowledge on which they have been brought up is not holistic and so does not produce integral

---

24. Kwame Bediako, "A New Era in Christian History – African Christianity as Representative Christianity: Some Implications for Theological Education and Scholarship," *Journal of African Christian Thought* 9, no. 1 (2006): 7.

25. Bediako, *Christianity in Africa*, 104.

26. Bediako, "Worship as Vital Participation," 3.

27. Kwame Bediako, "The African Renaissance and Theological Reconstruction: The Challenge of the Twenty-First Century," *Journal of African Christian Thought* 4, no. 2 (2001): 32.

development."[28] Thus Enlightenment ideals not only relegate God and religion to the margins, but also seek to prevent personal integration and holism.

Further, the Enlightenment generated "destructive dichotomies in epistemology."[29] While not inventing dichotomies such as saved/damned, master/slave, rich/poor, colonizer/subject, white/black, etc., these Enlightenment ideals reinforced these fluid or amorphous distinctions into fixed categories. For example, the category of "race" was invented to justify the slave trade for the economic benefit of Europeans. Bediako suggested that the way forward is "to reformulate the Christian faith drawing on aspects of the primal imagination . . . [so] that we can achieve a unified and organic view of the knowledge of truth."[30] Here Bediako's method is on full display. For Africans, avoid the European Enlightenment because it has nothing helpful to offer; Africans do not need European history, since they have their own traditional, primal histories. For European Christians, African primal understandings have something helpful to offer, a type of antidote to the Enlightenment.

"Primal" as a Positive Term

Bediako used "primal" as a positive term.[31] For him, "Primal means, therefore, universal, basic elements of human understanding of the transcendent and of the world, essential and valid religious insights that may be built upon or may be suppressed but that cannot be superseded."[32] For Bediako, "primal" is not a euphemism for primitive, but a positive term in its own right. The uniqueness of African Christian thought lies in its appropriation of this primal imagination; Bediako turned to the primal to articulate an authentic African Christian identity. He constantly sought to bring together the ancient Christian tradition, including the gospel, with the present context (i.e. culture).

The work of translation into and out of African languages and thought forms highlights the intersection of gospel and culture. Bediako followed in the line of Ghanaian philosopher J. B. Danquah who understood how to link the

---

28. Bediako, "African Renaissance," 32.

29. Bediako, *Christianity in Africa*, 104.

30. Bediako, 104.

31. For more on the relationship between the Christian faith and primal religion, see Gillian M. Bediako, *Primal Religion and the Bible: William Robertson Smith and His Heritage* (Sheffield: Sheffield Academic Press, 1997).

32. Kwame Bediako, "Recognizing the Primal Religions," Stone Lecture No. 2, Princeton Theological Seminary, 21 October 2003.

past with the present so as to lead on to the future.[33] Bediako aimed to diminish the influence of the Enlightenment and increase the influence of traditional African religious culture, particularly of primal religions. He wrote, "If primal religion is the Christian substructure, then we are researching the foundation of Christian faith."[34] Bediako's major claim is that the entire Christian faith is built upon primal spiritualities and religiosity. The problem is that "the Enlightenment project obscured this understanding."[35] All Christian thought is constructed upon "the primal substructure, which is not to be dismissed as 'pagan.'" His call is for a theological (re-)interpretation of primal religion as the Christian substructure.[36]

The foundation of African Christianity must be African primal religions, not Enlightenment philosophy. For Bediako, following Clement, as the Christian faith *absorbs* the pre-Christian religion, then this prior religion impacts the Christianity that emerges afterwards. The early church was deeply influenced by Greco-Roman religion, and Western Christianity is deeply influenced by the Enlightenment. Bediako's argument is that African Christianity *must be* influenced by African culture and primal religion. Of course, there remains a more fundamental substructure to Christianity: Israelite cultic religion and Second Temple Judaism.

As Bediako saw it, the implications of the Enlightenment, or at least of the Enlightenment's relationship to Christian theology, are dire: a failed Western theology. "The Western Christian theology that emerged from that bruising struggle," in Bediako's assessment, "[is] a Christian theology shaved down to fit the Enlightenment world-view."[37] Additionally, he claims that "modern, western theology is enlightenment theology. Theology pared down. Theology cut and shaved to fit a small-scale universe. A theology that has made its peace with the enlightenment."[38] For Bediako, the insights of the Enlightenment are to be resisted, not embraced. Bediako sought to take African theology *around* the

---

33. Kwame Bediako, *Religion, Culture and Language: An Appreciation of the Intellectual Legacy of Dr. J. B. Danquah*, J. B. Danquah Memorial Lectures, Series 37, 2–4 February 2004 (Accra: Ghana Academy of Arts and Sciences, 2006), 36.

34. Kwame Bediako, "Thoughts on the Nature of the Project," *Journal of African Christian Thought* 11, no. 2 (2008): 4.

35. Bediako, "Thoughts on the Nature," 4.

36. Bediako, 4.

37. Kwame Bediako, "Conclusion: The Emergence of World Christianity and the Remaking of Theology," in *Understanding World Christianity: The Vision and Work of Andrew F. Walls*, ed. William R. Burrows, Mark R. Gornik, and Janice A. McLean (Maryknoll, NY: Orbis, 2011), 253.

38. Kwame Bediako, "What Kind of People Should We Be?," Stone Lecture No. 5, Princeton Theological Seminary, 23 October 2003, audio recording.

Enlightenment in a way that is seemingly not possible for Western theologians who need to wrestle with the legacy of the Enlightenment in Western theology by moving *through* it in some way.

Bediako also believed that African Christianity has something unique to offer to the universal conversation. He wrote, "in order to understand Christianity as a religious faith, one needs to understand African Christianity.... African indigenous knowledge systems may have something to contribute here in their holistic, integrating and reconciling nature, and their profound tolerance of diversity. African indigenous knowledge systems could become a positive resource in a new polarized world."[39] In this new era in Christian history, as Bediako described the early twenty-first century, Africans can help Christianity to connect with the primal substructure of the Christian faith and to positively engage the religiously pluralistic contexts of the twenty-first century world.

The African Past of African Christianity

Instead of seeking the roots of an African Christian identity in Enlightenment values, Bediako appealed to African philosophers – particularly J. B. Danquah[40] and Kwame Gyekye[41] – to "demonstrate the African participation in a common humanity under God as Head."[42] In contrast to the Enlightenment tendency to emphasize difference and distinction between autonomous human beings, Bediako emphasized a common humanity under God. Bediako believed that Africans are fully human beings created by God in the image of God and as such possess a common humanity with all other peoples. This common Creator means for Bediako (following Danquah) that "Christianity is the fulfillment of the religious conception of our own people."[43] Again, the African people are organic to Christian history. The Christian faith is indigenous to the African people. Yet though equal, Africans are distinct, especially from Europeans

---

39. Bediako, "New Era in Christian History," 4.

40. Bediako wrote: "*The Akan Doctrine of God* ... is primarily 'an exercise in the philosophy of religion,' in which Dr. Danquah attempts to use the philosophical scheme of the German philosopher, Fredrich Hegel, in a systematic presentation of Akan religious ideas. The aim is partly, or perhaps even largely, polemical, to show that Akan, and for that matter, African, religious, ideas and practices are not 'primitive, lacking in intellectual vigour,' as had been presumed and concluded by early European interpreters, most of whom had little close contact or inside knowledge of African traditions." *Religion, Culture and Language*, 40.

41. See Kwame Gyekye, *Essay on African Philosophical Thought* (Cambridge: Cambridge University Press, 1987).

42. Bediako, *Religion, Culture and Language*, 18.

43. Bediako, 16.

after the Enlightenment. Bediako quotes Gyekye who observes that, "The Akan universe is a spiritual universe, one in which supernatural beings play significant roles in the thought and action of the people. What is primarily real is spiritual."[44] In opposition to Enlightenment assertions, many Africans believe that what is *primarily* real is not what is seen, but what is unseen. The spiritual, the spirit world, is the primary reality of human existence; the tangible, visible world is secondary and subservient.

Bediako understood the Christian gospel as sharing and preserving this view within African life, not condemning it as many Europeans had. "Far from obliterating the African primal view of things," he wrote, "in its essentially unified and 'spiritual' nature and replacing it with a two-tier modern Western view comprising sacred and secular dimensions, the Christian faith has in fact reinforced the African view."[45] Thus when Bediako engaged tradition, he considered the Scriptures of the Old and New Testaments and African philosophy, culture, and traditions.

Connecting African Christianity with Its African Past

The second aspect of the twin heritage of African Christianity is its history within the traditional religions and spiritualities of Africa. As Bediako understood it, "African theology has been about the redemption of African culture."[46] The first step in identifying and articulating the African aspect of this heritage is to dismantle the assumptions of many Western colonial missionaries. The first assumption to undo is that of a religious vacuum, that Africans are a religiously *tabula rasa* (blank slate). Following Mulago, Bediako embraced the role of a Christian theologian shaping African Christian identity by taking "theological responsibility for one's cultural community."[47] Bediako's work has valorized the traditions and rituals of African traditional religions. He has demonstrated that Africans have a spiritual past. Africans have worshipped God – even before they knew the name of God as Jesus Christ. Once an African religious past was established, the question of how to assess that tradition came next. As opposed to treating African traditional religions as "paganism" (similar to Hellenistic religion), Bediako followed Mbiti's claim that African primal religions are in fact *praeparatio evangelica* (preparation for

---

44. Bediako, 8, citing Kwame Gyekye, *Essay on African Philosophical Thought*, 69.

45. Bediako, *Christianity in Africa*, 176.

46. Bediako, 177.

47. Bediako, *Theology and Identity*, 353.

the gospel).[48] Bediako found a pre-Christian African religious history that he claimed prepared Africans for Christianity. In this way, Bediako sought and established a precolonial Christian history for Africa.

Bediako's reading and appropriation of African history has not been universally accepted. African non-Christian intellectuals, most notably Ali Mazrui and Okot p'Bitek, have criticized Bediako's view. Bediako, however, remained undeterred in continuing to claim that "Christianity as a religious faith is not intrinsically foreign to Africa. It has deep roots in the long histories of the peoples of the continent."[49] This long history preceded the arrival of European missionaries. Bediako approvingly quoted Danquah to support his perspective. In Danquah's words, "Christianity is a fulfillment of the religious conceptions of our own people. But long before Christianity came, we can be certain that God had himself been his own witness, he had given evidence of his existence and his goodness, to lead to the development of a high religion in the Ghanaian society."[50] While not questioning God's presence and work in Africa for as long as there have been human beings on the continent (and even before), Katongole criticized Bediako's overreliance on "the 'gospel' as a category in its own right, distinct from 'Christianity,'" rather than "provid[ing] a narrative display of the agency of African Christians in their historical and social context."[51] Bediako's argument against the foreignness of Christianity remained theoretical, not empirical.

Bediako's embrace of *preparatio evangelica* (evangelical preparation) received numerous, vigorous critiques from Maluleke and others. Maluleke believes that treating African traditional religions (ATRs) as preparation for Christianity is "inadequate and incorrect"[52] and "dishonest"[53] because Bediako did not show sufficient "respect for African culture and African traditional religions than to

---

48. Bediako, "Their Past Is also Our Present," 9.

49. Bediako, "Understanding African Theology," 55. See also Ali M. Mazrui, *The African Condition: A Political Diagnosis* (London: Faber and Faber, 1980); Okot p'Bitek, *African Religions in Western Scholarship* (Kampala: East African Literature Bureau, 1970); and Bediako, *Christianity in Africa*, 5.

50. Kwame Bediako, "Religion and National Identity: Assessing the Discussion from Cicero to Danquah," Bediako Law and Religion Inaugural Lecture, 25 June 1997 (Accra: Ghana Academy of Arts and Sciences, 2006), 16. From Kwesi Dickson's introduction to *The Akan Doctrine of God*, xxv, quoting an unpublished paper of Danquah's in J. B. Danquah, *The Akan Doctrine of God: A Fragment of Gold Coast Ethics and Religion* (1944, New York: Routledge, 2006, reprint of 1968 2nd ed.).

51. Katongole, *Future for Africa*, 162.

52. Maluleke, "In Search of," 216.

53. Maluleke, "Black and African Theologies," 8.

see them merely as preparations for the Christian gospel."[54] Bediako's "fail[ure] to regard ATRs in their own terms" incited Maluleke to brand Bediako as an example of p'Bitek's "intellectual smuggler."[55] For Maluleke, African traditional religions are not merely "'traditions' which were waiting to be fulfilled by the Christian gospel."[56] There is a sense in Bediako's treatment of African traditional religions that they are minor or developmental customs that are preparing Africans for a more advanced religious system, that is, for Christianity.

Cameroonian theologian David Tonghou Ngong launched a similar critique claiming that "ATRs should be treated as complete systems that need no further completion."[57] Instead, Ngong claims, similar to p'Bitek's argument, that Bediako's Christian perspective hinders Bediako from developing a theology of African traditional religions. Ngong proposes that "the theology of ATRs should be developed within the framework of ATRs rather than through Christian theological perspectives."[58] In this way, Ngong accuses Bediako of being too Christian in his approach to African traditional religions, an accusation that Bediako might readily accept. He also accuses Bediako of being not Christian enough in his approach because he minimized the differences and discontinuities between the Christian imagination and the primal imagination. For Ngong, "it must be stressed that becoming a Christian entails changing one's imagination in a significant way."[59] With a more nuanced analysis, Gerald West offers a slightly different reading of the primal worldview within Bediako's thought: "while some African theologians have argued that this primal world-view was primarily preparatory, preparing Africans for 'the gospel'/Christianity, others like Bediako have argued that this primal world-view was/is also constitutive of African Christianity."[60] Instead of viewing African culture as a problem for African Christianity, Bediako viewed African culture and spirituality as full of possibilities.

---

54. Maluleke, 16.

55. Tinyiko Sam Maluleke, "African Traditional Religions in Christian Mission and Christian Scholarship – Re-Opening a Debate That Never Started," *Religion and Theology* 5, no. 2 (1998): 131. See also Okot p'Bitek, "Intellectual Smugglers in Africa," *East Africa Journal* 8, no. 12 (1971): 7–9.

56. Maluleke, "In Search of," 216.

57. David Tonghou Ngong, *The Holy Spirit and Salvation in African Christian Theology: Imagining a More Hopeful Future for Africa* (New York: Peter Lang, 2010), 6.

58. Ngong, *Holy Spirit and Salvation*, 6.

59. Ngong, 7.

60. Gerald O. West, "The Role of the Bible in African Christianity," in *Anthology of African Christianity* (Oxford: Regnum, 2016), 82. See the nearly identical quotation in West, *Stolen Bible*, 241.

African Culture and African Christianity

Bediako's positive assessment of African culture and African traditional religions counters the prevailing assumptions of European colonial missions and the 1910 Edinburgh conference in particular which declared Africans as without a religious heritage and described African rituals as pagan.[61] He sharply disagreed with any descriptions of African culture as backward or as "constituting a prison that inhibits our human development . . . a prison from which we are to break free in order to experience salvation."[62] In no way was a so-called "Christian culture" to replace African cultures. Instead Bediako wrote, "our African cultural heritage is in fact the very place where Christ desires to find us in order to transform us into his image."[63] For Bediako, African culture is at best neutral, and more likely a positive asset for encountering the gospel of Jesus Christ. Africans do not need to become less African in order to become Christian. Instead, Bediako valorizes African traditional religions, without endorsing every rite or action, as an intrinsic, foundational aspect of African Christian thought.

While for Bediako the primal religions of Africa belong to the African religious past, this is *not so much a chronological past as an 'ontological' past.*[64] Bediako was clarifying that even when Africans convert to Christianity, they do not, in fact cannot, simply leave the primal religions behind them. Instead, the impact of the primal religions remains with them in their being. Primal religions have shaped who they are and who they will be. According to Bediako, "For the African theologian, however, the traditional religions, even if they constitute his past, are of the nature of an 'ontological' past, which means that together with the profession of the Christian faith, it gives account of the same entity – namely the history of the religious consciousness of the African Christian."[65] The identity of an African Christian is shaped by the past through the influences of pre-Christendom Christian theology and precolonial

---

61. Of particular note is the final chapter of the Commission IV report. For more on this significant moment in missionary history and the delimiting of Christendom, see Brian Stanley, *The World Missionary Conference, Edinburgh 1910* (Grand Rapids: Eerdmans, 2009), especially 235–45. See also Bediako's assessment: "The missionary enterprise of the nineteenth century did not see in African traditional religion and culture a partner for dialogue the way in which it viewed Buddhism and philosophical Hinduism in Asia." *Christianity in Africa*, 69.

62. Bediako, "Their Past Is also Our Present," 8.

63. Bediako, 8.

64. Bediako, "Understanding African Theology," 4, emphasis added.

65. Bediako, *Christianity in Africa*, 258.

African primal religions. This twin heritage of African Christianity describes the presence of an indigenous Christianity within modern African culture.

Even with Bediako's careful exposition of his understanding of the twin heritage of Christian thought in Africa, Tinyiko Maluleke was not satisfied. He articulates two overarching concerns about Bediako's assertion of Christianity as a non-Western religion, an indigenous African religion. Maluleke asserts that, "Simply to declare Christianity a non-Western religion is therefore grossly inadequate." His concern is that such a declaration ignores what he calls "the 'vulnerability' of the Christian gospel at the hands of human cultures."[66] Bediako was unwilling to consider any potential vulnerabilities of the gospel. Maluleke also sees a basic disconnect between the assertion of the non-foreignness of Christianity and peoples' experience. Maluleke states, "The fact that many African churches, for example, are still Western in polity, theology, doctrine and worship cannot be swept aside by mere enthusiasm for an African brand of Christianity."[67] Bediako, of course, agreed that many of the expressions of Christianity in Africa are too Western, but he also believed wholeheartedly that Christianity is a non-Western religion and turned toward indigeneity as a way of better understanding and conveying his view.

For Bediako, the presence of Christianity in Africa is the result of a movement from within African culture, not a foreign imposition from without. He wrote, "African theological literature in the twentieth century has therefore been an effort toward indigenization, a rooting of Christianity in African life by claiming for it a past in the spiritual harvests of the African pre-Christian religious heritage."[68] African theology and African Christianity have a twin heritage: the gospel of Jesus Christ in Africa and African cultures and religions. Bediako's understanding of the process is insightful. For Christianity in Africa, "it was indigenization by Christianization of the religious past, rather than by any serious adaptation or contextualization and inculturation – to use two current words – of Christianity as such."[69] For Bediako, the terms adaptation, contextualization, and inculturation all emphasize the gospel as something foreign to Africa that needs to be massaged in order to fit within African categories. Instead for him, the gospel is indigenous to Africa, not foreign, as indigeneity and translation are interconnected. Drawing from the twin heritage of African Christianity, the precolonial African past, and the pre-Christendom

---

66. Maluleke, "In Search of," 217.
67. Maluleke, "Black and African Theologies," 8.
68. Bediako, *Christianity in Africa*, 76.
69. Bediako, 76.

Christian past, Bediako grounded the translation of Christian Scriptures and concepts into African languages and cultural terms. The translation process is ongoing and mutually enlightening, teaching both about culture and the God who reveals.

Bediako connected translation to indigeneity: "If it is translatability which produces indigeneity, then *a truly indigenous church should also be a translating church*, reaching continually to the heart of the culture of its context and incarnating the translating Word."[70] For him, the connection is through the incarnation: "For the Word who took flesh and dwelt among us, not only exegetes (and so translates) God (John 1:18), but also exegetes the human predicament (John 4:29), bringing the two together in a mutually intelligible communication."[71] This communication is based in translatability which is the starting point for seeking indigeneity. Bediako is clear that "indigeneity does not lie at the *end* of a quest. Rather it is presumed within the very translatability of the Christian religion."[72] Thus Bediako's understanding of indigeneity is a direct implication of his belief in translatability. Indigeneity becomes as much "a matter of recognition within the Gospel as it is an achievement of actual Christian witness."[73] The gospel of Jesus Christ is then recognized within a host culture, in this case, African culture. What this means for Bediako is that it "is only by a serious misconception then that we can call [Christianity] a Western religion."[74] Christianity is indigenous to Africa. African Christians have their own distinct history rooted in patristic Christian theology and traditional African cultures and religions.

Further Reading of Kwame Bediako

"A New Era in Christian History – African Christianity as Representative Christianity: Some Implications for Theological Education and Scholarship." *Journal of African Christian Thought* 9, no. 1 (2006): 3–12.

"Understanding African Theology in the Twentieth Century," 49–62, and "Towards a New Understanding of Christian History in the Post-missionary Era," 108–20. In *Jesus and the Gospel in Africa*.

---

70. Bediako, 122, emphasis added.
71. Bediako, 122.
72. Bediako, 123, emphasis added.
73. Bediako, 123.
74. Bediako, 123.

4

Mother-Tongue Scriptures and Indigenous Translations

"The Word of God Is Always Vernacular"

For Bediako, Scripture is at the center of the interaction between gospel and culture. He offered the image of a prism to describe his understanding of the role of Scripture in the engagement of gospel and culture:

> Scripture is like a prism that refracts light, separating it out into its different, constituent colours. It is as the colourless light passes through the prism that the rainbow is revealed. In the gospel and culture engagement, our concern is to seek ways in which the gospel may be relevant to our cultures. In order to discover this, culture must practically pass through Scripture for its light and shade to be discerned.[1]

Part of the significance of this image for Bediako was that it asserts the centrality of Scripture as "more than the importance of texts of the Bible, and more than the importance of certain verses and chapters that one may quote as proof text to support a particular position . . . Scripture is more comprehensive and more overarching than just the sum of passages of Scripture."[2] Bediako's theological starting point is the gospel of Jesus Christ. The gospel is prior to culture. The gospel, not our human cultures, defines humanity.[3] Scripture then

---

1. Bediako, "Scripture as the Hermeneutics," 2.
2. Bediako, 2.
3. Bediako, 2.

interprets us – both as human beings created by God and as human beings in our specific cultural identities.[4] As culture is read in light of Scripture, the cultural wheat and chaff are sorted out. While Bediako believed that traditional African cultures and religions prepared Africans to embrace the Christian faith, some aspects of the tradition are to be rejected; polygamy was one frequent target of Bediako's criticisms.[5]

Scripture is not identical with the gospel, but served for Bediako more like a record of the gospel. He defined Scripture as "the authoritative, normative deposit given to us of the divine-human encounter, that lies at the heart of our faith."[6] Scripture then becomes "the authoritative 'road map' for our religious itinerary . . . the effective 'compass' on our journey of faith as the people of God."[7] Scripture interprets a Christian's spiritual journey. Scripture is the story in which Christians participate. Scripture speaks to humanity because Scripture speaks about humanity.[8] These various roles allow Bediako to claim that "Scripture is life . . . that gives us the record of the word of God made life in the incarnate Son."[9] Scripture is not only about belief but about life itself through the power of the Spirit to enliven bodies and inspire creativity. Scripture is the story of life itself.

The story of Scripture is both text and context.[10] In addition to the words on the page, Bediako believed that it is "possible to think of the Scriptures also as context, a context that the reader (or hearer) may enter and so actually participate in their world of meaning and experience."[11] The Scriptures invite the reader in to participate in the events and meanings described. Bediako was positing something other than learning the skills of exegesis and hermeneutics. Rather, he viewed Scripture as "also a context in which modern Christians can share as illuminating of their own human experience."[12] As the story of the Scriptures sheds light on the lives of contemporary Christians, Bediako believed that "the Scriptures become *our* story, illuminating our past, reflecting the triumphs of our dependence on God, as well as our failures in disobedience

---

4. Bediako, 2.

5. For example, see Bediako, *Christianity in Africa*, 66–67, 183–85.

6. Bediako, "Scripture as the Hermeneutics," 2.

7. Bediako, 2.

8. Bediako, 5.

9. Bediako, 6.

10. Bediako, "Biblical Exegesis in the African Context," 18.

11. Bediako, 18.

12. Bediako, 18.

and idolatry. We come to *participate* in the meaning of the scriptural events, as anyone who shares in African Christian worship services knows."[13] The invitation to enter into the Scripture and to participate in the scriptural world of meaning was based upon Bediako's conviction that God is still speaking. After speaking in Hebrew, Aramaic, and Greek, God keeps speaking in vernacular languages. God did not finish speaking when the biblical canon was finalized. God speaks in and through translation.[14]

Time and time again, Bediako returned to the power and impact of Scripture translation on African Christianity. He saw it as "the credit of the modern missionary movement from the West that, in contrast to the mission to Europe in earlier times, the history of modern mission could be written as the history of Scripture translation."[15] The narrative of Scripture translation and the spread of vernacular translations of the Bible from the coasts of Africa inland begins to paint a picture of how the Christian faith grew in Africa. In Bediako's analysis, "There is probably no more important single explanation for the massive presence of Christianity on the African continent than the availability of the Scriptures in many African languages."[16] Enabling everyday Africans to hear the Scriptures in their own mother tongues allowed the texts of the Bible to spread freely while inviting hearers into the scriptural world by making the context accessible through African vernaculars. Vernacular translations allowed for the indigenization of the Christian faith. Succinctly, Bediako wrote, "African Christianity today is inconceivable apart from the existence of the Bible in African indigenous languages."[17] In spite of objections from some Europeans, one of the significant results of the proliferation of translations into African vernaculars is that they do not "entrench ethnic exclusiveness."[18] Many Africans know multiple languages (unlike many North Americans); translating the Bible into African vernaculars has both strengthened the understanding of the Christian faith and strengthened the African languages.

Theologically, the significance of having Scripture in vernacular African languages is that it demonstrates the point that God speaks directly to all

---

13. Bediako, *Christianity in Africa*, 227, emphasis original.

14. Bediako, "Biblical Exegesis in the African Context," 23.

15. Kwame Bediako, "Cry Jesus! Christian Theology and Presence in Modern Africa," in *Jesus and the Gospel in Africa* (Maryknoll, NY: Orbis Books, 2004), 8–15.

16. Bediako, *Christianity in Africa*, 62.

17. Kwame Bediako, "A Half Century of African Christian Thought: Pointers to Theology and Theological Education in the Next Half Century," *Journal of African Christian Thought* 3, no. 1 (2000): 8.

18. Bediako, "A Half Century," 9.

peoples. Thus, "if the Word of God is always vernacular," wrote Bediako, "then Biblical exegesis includes paying attention to how and in what terms the Word is heard and received in the process of its transmission in the vernacular."[19] Not only do vernacular translations demonstrate that God speaks directly to all peoples, but they further reinforce that "the gospel has no permanent resident culture."[20] No individual culture or people can claim God in Jesus Christ for themselves. God is before culture and transcends all human cultures. Translating the Scriptures into African vernaculars provided two-way interpretation: vernacular translation allows people of that culture to understand Scripture in light of their traditional culture, *and* the vernacular Scriptures allow for a means of gaining a further insight into their traditional culture.[21]

Mother-Tongue Scriptures and Vernacular Concepts

Bediako identified the single greatest contribution of European missionaries as the translation of the Bible into African languages.[22] He referred to the existence of the Bible in African indigenous languages as "probably the single most important element of the missionary legacy."[23] The impact of these translation efforts bore the greatest dividends for African Christianity in the years following decolonization and the departure of most European missionaries. Instead of the Christian church languishing in the absence of missionaries, Africans shared the Christian faith with other Africans using the Scriptures in their mother tongues translated through the efforts of European missionaries. The dramatic and rapid growth surprised many Western observers who conceived of Christianity as a Western religion. Bediako attributed the growth of the Christian faith in Africa to the presence of the Bible in African languages. He wrote,

> There is a common perception in many Western circles – Christian and non-Christian – that Christianity in Africa is connected necessarily with Western forms of the faith. It is less well known that African Christianity, as we have it today, is inconceivable apart from the Bible in African mother tongues. Just as the strength

---

19. Bediako, *Christianity in Africa*, 71.
20. Bediako, "Scripture as the Hermeneutics," 6.
21. Bediako, *Christianity in Africa*, 71.
22. Bediako, 62.
23. Bediako, "A Half Century," 8.

of the Christian faith in Africa derives from its independence of Enlightenment views on life, so in an age of globalization, strange as it may sound, the prospects of Christianity are not tied to the dominance of English as a so-called global medium.[24]

The growth and spread of Christianity are not dependent upon Western missionaries, Western categories of thought, nor Western languages. Instead, African Christianity emerged from the Scriptures of the Old and New Testaments in African mother tongues. Though the concept of "mother-tongue Scriptures" is absent from Bediako's early work, it takes on increasing importance in *Christianity in Africa* and afterwards.[25]

Weakened Western Hegemony; Strengthened African Christianity

The lingering results of translating the Scriptures into African vernaculars parallels the impact of the Protestant Reformation in sixteenth-century Europe.[26] Through translation, the Protestant missionaries prevented colonial languages from being treated as sacred in the way that Arabic is in Islam or even as Latin was in the Roman Church in the Middle Ages. At the same time, the translation of the Scriptures destabilized Western hegemony in Africa and opened up the possibility of God speaking directly to Africans. Bediako wrote, "Whenever Western missionaries or a missionary society made the Scriptures available to an African people in that people's own language, they weakened

---

24. Bediako, "Worship as Vital Participation," 6.

25. The phrase "mother-tongue Scriptures" does not appear in *Theology and Identity*. Bediako's first mention of "the Bible in mother tongues" (though it is not developed) appeared in Kwame Bediako, "Into all the world," in *Jesus 2000*, ed. Richard Bauckham et al. (Oxford: Lion, 1989), 223.

26. Bediako described the work of the Basel Mission in the Gold Coast (later Ghana):

It is hard to ignore the influence of the Protestant Reformation tradition out of which a missionary society like the Basel Mission emerged. Believing so intensely that the Bible was the sole source of divine truth, the Mission would naturally insist that converts should be able to read and understand the Bible for themselves. The logical outcome of the conviction was a recognition of the importance of the vernacular language in much the same way that a vernacular Bible had affected their lives in Europe. Basel Mission instructions to its missionaries included the specific one that the "vernacular of the people should never be suppressed by the English language" and, for the missionaries themselves, the learning of the vernacular was compulsory. In the Gold Coast this meant, of course, the two "mission" languages, so to speak, of Twi and Ga.

Bediako, *Christianity in Africa*, 51.

any Western bias in their presentation of the Gospel."[27] The theological and spiritual impact of vernacular translations cannot be overemphasized: "African Christians, with access to the Bible in their mother-tongues, could truly claim they were hearing God speak to them in their own language. It amounts to the awareness that *God speaks our language too*."[28]

Africans with Bibles in their mother tongue could truly claim to hear God speaking to them.[29] They were given access to the original sources of Christian teaching and could respond to it in their own terms.[30] In and through the process of translation, Bediako was careful to note that "the vernacular remains in every respect the Word of God."[31] Bediako's confidence in God's sovereignty throughout the process of translation was unshakable. He was convinced that the

> significance of Pentecost, therefore, has to do with more than answering to the chaos of Bethel and restoring harmony between God and humanity, and between human beings. Its deeper significance is that God speaks to men and women – always in the vernacular. Divine communication is never in a sacred, esoteric, hermetic language; rather it is such that "all of us hear . . . in our own language . . . the wonders of God"(Acts 2:11).[32]

Yet though God can communicate God's word in any and every language, human beings cannot understand every language. For Bediako, "In Christian theology, God is held to speak through the translatable Bible, in human languages."[33]

Bediako's claim that the Bible equals the word of God drew the ire of Maluleke who criticized Bediako for not fundamentally "question[ing] the validity of the equation: Bible = Word of God."[34] According to Maluleke, this equation formed the basis for Bediako's arguments about translation and vernacularization. In Maluleke's eyes, "What is being translated, according

---

27. Bediako, "Understanding African Theology," 57–58.

28. Bediako, 57–58, emphasis original.

29. Bediako, "Jesus in African Culture," in *Jesus and the Gospel in Africa*, 32.

30. Bediako, "Challenges of Ghana's Fourth Republic," 7.

31. Bediako, "Jesus in African Culture," 32.

32. Bediako, *Christianity in Africa*, 60.

33. Kwame Bediako, "Danquah's Use of Mother Tongue in Intellectual Discourse and Its Relevance in Our Time," in *Religion, Culture and Language: An Appreciation of the Intellectual Legacy of Dr. J. B. Danquah*, Ghana Academy of Arts and Sciences (Accra: Black Mask, 2006), 43.

34. Maluleke, "Black and African Theologies," 11.

to [Bediako], is the very Word of God itself."[35] Maluleke considers Bediako's equation to be idolatrous – accusing Bediako of "bibliology"[36] – and very dangerous. Maluleke concludes, "The equation of colonialism with Christianity if and where it has occurred, has done far less harm to Black and African theologies than the equation of the Bible with the Word of God."[37]

On this question of the character of the Bible's presence in Africa, Maluleke and Bediako occupy opposite poles. Maluleke understands the Bible as damaging, a tool of colonialism, while Bediako "emphasized its potential to recover and revitalise what has been damaged by colonialism and even to correct destructive aspects of traditional culture."[38] Gerald West rightly states, "The Bible is an ambiguous presence in Africa. The legacy of its partnership with colonialism lives on."[39] West, Maluleke, and Bediako all agree that the Bible, and its interpretations, have great power in Africa.

Mother-Tongue Thought and Religious Ideas

Bediako was convinced that a person's mother tongue is particularly formative in shaping thought and religious ideas. Translation into African vernaculars not only strengthened African Christian autonomy over and against Western hegemony, the use of the mother tongue radically altered what was possible for thinking about God and the world. Bediako described his understanding of the relationship between language, the mother tongue, and theological formation in *Christianity in Africa*:

> The ability to hear in one's own language and to express in one's own language one's response to the message which one receives, must lie at the heart of all authentic religious encounter with the divine realm. Language itself becomes, then, not merely a social or psychological phenomenon, but a theological one as well. Though every human language has its limitations in this connection, yet it is through language, and for each person, through their

---

35. Maluleke, 10.

36. Maluleke, 12.

37. Maluleke, 12.

38. Gerald West, "African Biblical Hermeneutics and Bible Translation," in *Interacting with Scriptures in Africa*, ed. Jean-Claude Loba-Mkole and Ernst R. Wendland (Nairobi: Acton, 2005), 5.

39. West, "African Biblical Hermeneutics," 5.

mother tongue, that the Spirit of God speaks to convey divine communication at its deepest to the human community.[40]

Bediako believed that the mother tongue penetrates most deeply into a person's being and forms part of individual identity. Bediako demonstrated the place and impact of the mother tongue using the example of cursing: "In Africa, no one curses their neighbor in English, French or Portuguese. We curse in mother tongues. It is with the deep penetration of the heart with the mind of Christ in our mother tongues, that one is exorcised from a cursing mind and given a redemptive mind."[41] The mother tongue has a power all its own that connects to a person's deepest emotions. Bediako believed that "nothing communicates more effectively to heart and mind than the mother-tongue. In this sense, language, as an aspect of cultural identity, takes on theological importance as the vehicle of divine truth."[42] One's mother tongue speaks most deeply and clearly to one's person. For Bediako, "Taking the vernacular seriously then, becomes not merely a cultural but also a theological necessity."[43] While the first translators likely were seeking to give Africans access to theological ideas, the result of vernacular translations has been a reformulation of the ideas themselves. Richard Fox Young comments on Bediako's understanding of the need and role of vernacularization: "For faith to seek understanding and find it, a borrowed language would not do. Only a mother-tongue theology would have the potential to liberate African theology from its long-standing Latin Captivity (as it were) – from, that is, normative models of exogenous origin."[44] Mother-tongue translations gave birth to distinctly *African* theologies.

Bediako appealed to Danquah who wrote first in his mother tongue, Twi, and then translated to English. Wrote Bediako: "Here we have an extraordinary situation: One of our most brilliant ancestors seems, in his maturing scholarship, to have worked from his mother-tongue insights into his English expression!"[45] To demonstrate his conviction about the power of the mother tongue and its theological importance, Bediako required students at the Akrofi-Christaller Institute to write an abstract for their theses, both master's and doctoral, in

---

40. Bediako, *Christianity in Africa*, 60.

41. Bediako, "Missionaries Did Not Bring Christ to Africa," 28.

42. Bediako, "Challenges of Ghana's Fourth Republic," 7.

43. Bediako, *Christianity in Africa*, 73.

44. Richard Fox Young, "Clearing a Path through *Jesus of the Deep Forest*: Intercultural Perspectives on Christian Praise and Public Witness in Afua Kuma's Akan Oral Epic," *Theology Today* 70, no. 1 (2013): 39. Young is commenting on Bediako, *Christianity in Africa*, 69–70.

45. Bediako, "Danquah's Use of Mother Tongue," 39.

their mother tongue. While the thesis itself would likely be written in English, or maybe in French, the abstract had to be written in the vernacular so as to force the student to translate his or her theological and academic ideas into vernacular words and concepts.

Forced Dialogue between Gospel and Culture

Not only did the translation of the Christian Scriptures into African languages destabilize Western hegemony and enable Africans to hear the word of God in their own languages, but the act of translation necessitated a dialogue between gospel and culture. Without an understanding and appreciation of a vernacular language, a faithful translation of the Bible would not be possible. Instead "the possession of the Christian Scriptures in African languages ... ensured that an effectual rooting of the Christian faith took place in African consciousness ... not in the terms of a foreign language or of an alien culture, but in the categories of local languages, idioms and world-views."[46] Bediako understood the Scriptures themselves, once translated into a local vernacular, to then serve as an interpreter of that culture. He wrote,

> When the Scriptures come into a language, they become an element of the culture, and can, therefore, serve as the hermeneutic, the interpreter, of that culture. While in one sense, the Bible may be said to come from "outside," in another sense, it comes from within. We may not, therefore, separate Gospel and culture when we consider the role of mother-tongue Scriptures.[47]

The refusal to separate gospel and culture emerges from Bediako's belief that the gospel is indigenous to African cultures.

The stakes for theological reflection without mother-tongue Scriptures could not be higher according to Bediako. For him, "What is at stake is nothing less than the quality of the Christian interaction with African culture,"[48] since "the Gospel spoken in Twi, Ga, and Kasem, sounds different from the Gospel spoken in English."[49] In order to truly communicate the gospel to an individual or a people, their mother tongue must be used. The translation of the words

---

46. Bediako, "Understanding African Theology," 54.

47. Bediako, "Gospel and Culture: Guest Editorial," *Journal of African Christian Thought* 2, no. 2 (1999): 1.

48. Bediako, "Guest Editorial," *Journal of African Christian Thought* 5, no. 1 (2002): 3.

49. Bediako, "Gospel and Culture: Guest Editorial," 1.

of Scripture allow for the translation of Christian ideas and concepts into the vernacular.

Biblical narratives are not simply legends or fanciful tales. The worldview and the Scripture's "ever-renewed stress that the lives and careers of the 'ancestors' – Adam, Eve, Noah, Enoch, Abraham, Isaac, Jacob, Moses, David – have a relevance for every succeeding generation, assuring us that they have something to do with us too."[50] The stories in the Bible tell Africans of their spiritual ancestors, their predecessors in faith.

Indigenization as Translation

Bediako's understanding of indigeneity was a direct implication of his belief in translatability. Bediako addressed the relationship between translation, indigeneity, and particularly his understanding that

> translatability is the only true basis and starting point for seeking indigeneity. . . . Universality, translatability, incarnation and indigeneity belong in a continuum and are integral to the warp and woof of the Christian religion.[51]

In Western theology, Christian witness has often meant bringing in a new idea or new information to non-Christian peoples. Bediako offered an alternate definition, using recognition rather than imposition or other type of import. His approach was similar to the apostle Paul's words on Mars Hill in Athens as recorded in Acts 17. Paul encountered an altar with the inscription: "To an unknown god." And he announced to all who would listen: "What therefore you worship as unknown, this I proclaim to you" (Acts 17:23). Bediako urged Africans to recognize the ways that God has always and already been active in Africa. In terms of time, the work of divine translation preceded the incarnation of Jesus Christ and the coming of missionaries to Africa. God, the Father of Jesus Christ, translates divine presence and activity into every culture. The gospel of Jesus Christ is indigenous to Africa because God has *translated* God's own self within African cultures.

Bediako considered indigeneity as intrinsic to the Christian faith. Christianity is always translated into local customs and languages. For Bediako, "The single most important element for building such an indigenous Christian

---

50. Bediako, *Christianity in Africa*, 227.
51. Bediako, 123.

tradition is therefore the Scriptures in the vernacular language of a people."[52] Thus for Bediako, the role of the missionaries was essential for two reasons. They brought the name of Jesus Christ so that Christ could be recognized within African cultures, and they translated the Bible into vernacular African languages so that Africans might read God's word for themselves, without European intermediaries. To be clear, the missionaries did not bring the presence or activity of God.

In their quest to understand the African side of the twin heritage of African Christianity, African theologians are forced to wrestle with the question of whether Christianity is foreign to Africa or indigenous to it. From Bediako's vantage point, "African theological writing came to focus on giving a more positive interpretation of the African religious past than the missionary assessment had done, and so demonstrated the continuity of the religious past with the Christian present."[53] For Bediako, indigeneity was intimately connected to continuity.

Two of the authors that Bediako analyzes in *Theology and Identity*, Idowu and Mbiti, offer opposite positions on the question of indigeneity. In Bediako's words, "Idowu remained haunted by the 'foreignness' of Christianity, and having started from that foreignness, was never able to arrive at indigeneity."[54] For Idowu, the Christian gospel was always external to African culture and thus had to be indigenized from the outside. Idowu did not believe that Christianity could be made to take African cultural forms, since it is always a foreign element. Bediako followed Idowu's sympathetic understanding of African cultural contexts for theology and his understanding of the continuity of Christianity and African traditional religions. Bediako also was inclined to follow Idowu's claim that all African primal religions are monotheistic, even though their claim could not be proven based on the empirical evidence.

Bediako sided with Mbiti's belief that the Christian gospel is indigenous to Africa. Mbiti believed that the gospel should be appropriated in African terms. Since Mbiti viewed African traditional religions as *praeparatio evangelica* for Christianity, Christianity is understood as a non-Western religion. (Significantly, Mbiti also considered Islam to be a traditional African religion.) Thus, "Mbiti rejected the very idea of the quest for indigenization of Christianity or of theology in Africa."[55] Since Christianity was always and already indigenous

---

52. Bediako, 62.

53. Bediako, 76.

54. Bediako, 116.

55. Bediako, 117.

to Africa, Christianity could not be indigenized. Mbiti rejected the concepts of the indigenization of Christianity and the indigenization of theology. The gospel of Jesus Christ already was indigenous to Africa; no additional processes were needed. Bediako interpreted Mbiti's claim, writing "for theology is always indigenous, resulting from the effort to articulate the meaning of the Gospel in a particular cultural milieu in response to the realities of that milieu."[56]

While many theologians might claim that theology is always contextual, containing the insights and biases of a given culture, Bediako made a different, prior claim: theology is always indigenous. While God remains apart from and outside of creation, divine revelation is understood to be embedded within human cultures. God is present with and among creation including humankind. God then uses human cultures to reveal Godself, at least partially, to the people of any given culture. Bediako saw continuity in God's activity in traditional African cultures, in the Scriptures of the Old and New Testaments, and in contemporary African Christianity. Bediako took Hebrews 13:8 literally: "Jesus Christ is the same yesterday and today and forever." The same Jesus Christ has been active in Africa yesterday, today, and forever. All told, Bediako followed Mbiti's thinking in this debate. In light of an indigenous Christianity with corresponding indigenous African Christian theologies, Bediako then sought to identify expressions of this indigenous faith within African culture.

Perhaps the clearest example of Bediako's perspective can be found in his hope for his own Ghanaian Presbyterians. Every Christmas Day, the Presbyterians in Akropong sing a hymn celebrating Jesus's birthday:

> They sing this hymn without any awareness that Christmas itself was originally a Christian substitute for a pre-Christian New Year religious festival in pagan Northern Europe. My earnest prayer and hope is that they will one day sing it at the traditional New Year festival of Odwira to welcome and worship the one who achieved once and for all purification for their sins, their greater Ancestor, Nana Iesu Kristo.[57]

Bediako's intent was to expose the pre-Christian foundations of many Western Christian traditions and to yearn for African pre-Christian customs to come alongside or replace them. Bediako understood the crucifixion of Jesus Christ to be the fulfillment of the traditional *Odwira* festival of purification and renewal: "The *Odwira* to end all *odwiras* has taken place through the death

---

56. Bediako, *Theology and Identity*, 306.
57. Bediako, *Christianity in Africa*, 86.

of Jesus Christ."[58] The use of African mother tongues opened up Christian theological understandings not available solely through Western languages.

Further Reading of Kwame Bediako

"The Afrikania Challenge," chapter 2, 17–38, and "Translatability and the Cultural Incarnations of the Faith," chapter 7, 109–25. In *Christianity in Africa: The Renewal of a Non-Western Religion*. Edinburgh: Edinburgh University Press, 1995.

"Biblical Exegesis in the African Context: The Factor and Impact of Translated Scriptures." *Journal of African Christian Thought* 6, no. 1 (2003): 15–23.

"'In the Bible . . . Africa Walks on Familiar Ground': Why the World Needs Africa." *AICMAR* 6 (2007): 32–50.

"Jesus in African Culture: A Ghanaian Perspective," 20–33. In *Jesus and the Gospel in Africa*. Maryknoll, NY: Orbis Books, 2004.

"Scripture as the Hermeneutics of Culture and Tradition." *Journal of African Christian Thought* 4, no. 1 (2001): 2–11.

---

58. Bediako, "Jesus in African Culture" in *Jesus and the Gospel in Africa* (Maryknoll, NY: Orbis Books, 2004), 33.

5

Contextual Theology

"A Struggle with Culturally Related Questions"

Bediako framed his entire theological project as "a struggle with culturally related questions."[1] For Bediako, *all* theology is contextual whether that theology emerges from Europe, Africa, Asia, or Latin America, the city, rural areas, or wherever. Theology can never emerge from a vacuum. There is always a context that produces theological reflection. The contextuality of theology means that all theology is provisional – articulated for a particular time and place – rather than universal – for all times and places. Theology then is not fixed, but dynamic, "always a struggle,"[2] in Bediako's words.

Bediako's understanding of the nature of theology was shaped by his view of history. The work of theological reflection is not a new development in Africa following the arrival of Europeans. The European missionaries did not bring Christ to Africa; Christ brought them: "Christ, already present in the situation, called in His messengers so that by proclamation and incarnation, He might be made manifest."[3] Part of Bediako's reasoning was that if Christ had been brought into Africa, then Christ would be "a disposable divinity, actually able to be taken, carried and brought . . . and presumably also, disposed of if not needed."[4]

Bediako's starting point for his theological reflection and, in his view, for all African theologies is the preexistent presence of Jesus Christ in Africa. Bediako

1. Bediako, *Christianity in Africa*, 129.
2. Bediako, 129.
3. Bediako, 226.
4. Bediako, 226.

even claimed that "Jesus Christ too was in that African cultural heritage." Bediako applied the prologue of the gospel of John – John 1:3–4: "All things came into being through him, and without him not one thing came into being. What has come into being in him was life, and the life was the light of all people." – to include "all humanity, and therefore African peoples, in their cultural heritage."[5] In this way, Bediako grounded African Christianity in the spiritual presence of Jesus Christ in Africa even before any Africans had heard of the name of Jesus Christ.

The early task of theology in Africa was to seek to indigenize the message of the gospel of Jesus Christ as brought by European missionaries. Translating the Bible into vernacular languages and beginning to articulate Christian concepts in African terminology gave African Christian thought tentative beginnings. Bediako noted that "African Traditional Religion has been a serious preparation for the Gospel in Africa and forms the major religious substratum for the idiom and existential experience of Christianity in African life."[6] African traditional religions prepared Africans to embrace the Christian faith, according to Bediako. Contrary to European presuppositions, Christianity is not synonymous with Western culture, and Africans have become Christians – in vast numbers – without becoming Western.

The wrestling with culturally related questions in African Christianity is a distinctive feature of African Christian thought. For Bediako, this distinction shapes Africa's contribution to contemporary theological reflection. The dramatic growth of Christianity in Africa demonstrated "the viability of Christian religious discourse, as not outworn and to be discarded, or about which to be embarrassed, but rather as fully coherent with human experience, and fully meaningful within the history of the world's redemption."[7] Bediako saw the contextual experiments of African Christian thought as having exportable lessons for other parts of the world, especially the increasingly secularized societies of Europe and North America.

While in much of his thought Bediako did seek to assert African Christian thought over and against Western culture and theology, he was also keenly interested in his theological reflection in the health and future of African theology. Bediako was especially concerned with the authenticity of African theology. He wrote, "If it is adequately to reflect the experience of faith in Christ in African life, African theology will have to make greater use of the Scriptures

---

5. Bediako, "Missionaries Did Not Bring Christ to Africa," 21.

6. Bediako, *Christianity in Africa*, 83.

7. Bediako, 265.

in the vernacular, thus hearing and perceiving the Word of God in much the same way as the majority of Africa's Christians do."[8] He was concerned that African theologians not try to impress Westerners with their theological abilities and thereby lose connection with African Christians. One key way to maintain this connection is through the use of the Scriptures in vernacular languages. For Bediako, "Taking the vernacular seriously then, becomes not merely a cultural but also a theological necessity. For it is only through the vernacular that a genuine and lasting theological dialogue with culture can take place."[9] This dialogue, this struggle with culturally related questions, is a necessity of theological reflection. For Bediako, there was no such thing as pure theology, as there is no such thing as a pure gospel; theology is always contextual and provisional.

Bediako's emphasis on contextual theology worried some evangelicals who feared that Bediako "dangerously leaves aside" God's constancy "in his study of the contextuality of theology."[10] For Benno van den Toren, "Bediako's theology lacks stability and is in the end a risky enterprise."[11] Van den Toren believes that Bediako's understanding of translation is too contextual, or at least too contextually bound.[12] All of these are more worrisome to van den Toren because Bediako made them "without explicitly denying" that his emphasis on context might challenge Western assumptions about immutability and theological method.[13] The concern is that Bediako's contextual theology is heterodox.

For Africans, Bediako hoped that, "African theology [would] therefore fulfil a crucial pastoral function: nurturing and equipping a people of God, who have heard in their own languages the wonders of God."[14] Through the focus on the particular in African theology – the Scriptures in vernacular languages, the vital preparation of African traditional religions, and the ongoing presence and work of Jesus Christ – it is possible to both help Africans and to offer a model of gospel-culture engagement to the wider world. Succinctly Bediako wrote that, "Christianity may now be seen for what it truly is, a universal religion."[15]

---

8. Bediako, 73.

9. Bediako, 73.

10. Benno van den Toren, "Kwame Bediako's Christology in Its African Evangelical Context," *Exchange* 26, no. 3 (1997): 230.

11. van den Toren, "Kwame Bediako's Christology," 230.

12. Specifically, van den Toren criticizes Bediako's article "How Is Jesus Christ Lord," in *Jesus and the Gospel*, 40.

13. van den Toren, "Kwame Bediako's Christology," 230.

14. Bediako, *Christianity in Africa*, 73.

15. Bediako, "Cry Jesus!" 3.

The grand reversal that Bediako identified is that Western theology has been understood to be universal, and its theological understandings as acontextual and universally applicable. Instead for Bediako, "Christianity, in becoming a non-Western religion, has become in actual experience the most universal of all religions."[16] The universality possible through African Christianity results from the intentional contextuality of African Christian thought. By deeply delving into questions of gospel and culture and engaging traditional African religions as the foundation for African Christian thought, African Christianity provides a model for contextual theological reflection in other parts of the world.

Further according to Bediako, Africans have gained theological insights from which others can learn. His focus always remained on the role of African Christians and African theologians. He wrote, "Not what Western missionaries did (or did not do), but what Africans did, and have done with the Gospel, is what has proved the more enduring element in the making of Christian Africa in the twentieth century."[17] The making of Christian Africa has in turn remade the Christian faith as a *non-Western* religion.

Christology

Accordingly, Bediako's Christology defies Western categorization. Victor Ezigbo describes Bediako's approach as a "culture-oriented Christology . . . to re-express Jesus Christ in terms of some indigenous cultures and religious thought forms."[18] Bediako valued Jesus Christ higher than all other theological ideas; he was a self-described African evangelical theologian. However, he was not particularly interested in the councils such as Nicaea in 325 or Chalcedon in 451, in doctrinal formulas such as two natures in one person, nor in even descriptors like a high or low Christology. He assumed the orthodoxy of the patristic church and did not question it.

Bediako was more interested in the connection between Jesus Christ and translatability as well as quite interested in asserting and exploring what it means for Jesus to be the greatest ancestor, the Supreme Ancestor. When Bediako articulated his ancestor Christology, he did not play by Western rules or within Western categories. Bediako believed that, "the renewal of society

---

16. Bediako, *Christianity in Africa*, 186.

17. Bediako, 206–7.

18. Victor I. Ezigbo, *Re-Imagining African Christologies: Conversing with the Interpretations and Appropriations of Jesus in Contemporary African Christianity* (Eugene, OR: Pickwick, 2010), 64.

is not achieved by jettisoning the spiritual roots of ancient wisdom but by the redemption of the totality of culture and history and their application in new settings."[19] He paraphrased and adapted the fourth-century christological maxim: "what is not assumed is not redeemed," and applied it to Africa's pre-Christian past, saying: "if our past is not redeemed, neither is our present redeemed, nor can our future be redemptive."[20]

For Bediako, the initial focus within African Christian thought on identity, with the quest to situate African Christianity historically and to pursue the indigenous nature of the Christian faith in Africa through the use of mother-tongue Scriptures and vernacular concepts, inevitably led to the development of a theology of ancestors. By asserting the "continuity of God in African-experience . . . a theology of ancestors becomes, therefore, the corollary and unavoidable by-product."[21] African theologians needed to interpret "the past in a way which shows that the present experience and knowledge of the grace of God in the Gospel of Jesus Christ have been truly anticipated and prefigured in the quests and the responses to the Transcendent in former times."[22]

Bediako's hope was that the vernacular terminology related to Jesus would penetrate the spirituality of African Christianity. In this way, the vernacular, the mother tongue, and a theology of ancestors comes together: "In my experience in Ghana," Bediako wrote, "hardly anyone will pray in English to 'Ancestor Jesus' or 'Chief Jesus,' but many will pray in Akan to 'Nana Yesu.' 'Nana' means 'ancestor' and is the title for ancestors (and chiefs)."[23] The use of *Nana Yesu* allows the person and message of Jesus Christ to be internalized and contextualized within Akan culture.

Following Danquah's 1944 book *The Akan Doctrine of God*, according to Bediako, "no African Christian theology that took seriously its African context, could ignore ancestors."[24] For him, Danquah "had virtually set the agenda for all subsequent intellectual discourse on the matter."[25] In his work, Bediako understood his need to get his own mind around the possibility of an African Christian identity historically before engaging a theology of ancestors. Bediako

---

19. Bediako, "Danquah's Conception of Culture and Its Place in the Renewal and Enhancement of Society," in *Religion, Culture, Language*, 36.

20. Bediako, "Danquah's Conception of Culture," 36.

21. Bediako, *Christianity in Africa*, 225.

22. Bediako, 224–25.

23. Bediako, "One Song in Many Tongues," in *Jesus and the Gospel in Africa*, 78.

24. Bediako, "Religion and National Identity," 6.

25. Bediako, 6.

believed that "the continued significance of ancestors within the life of African Christianity comes to pass through the prism of Christology."[26] Though the Old Testament in particular "validates . . . a theology of ancestors,"[27] Jesus Christ has revealed who the ancestors truly are. And though Bediako did not share the beliefs of practioners of African traditional religions regarding ancestors, he did believe that ancestors are essential for all Christians. He wrote, "all Christians in every place and time, not only need to have a past, but indeed do have a past, a pre-Christian past that connects with the present. All Christians have need of ancestors, pre-Christian ancestors!"[28] In short, the ancestors are the most direct link to the African heritage of African Christianity.

Sin

Bediako differed from many Western evangelicals in his understanding of sin. In Bediako's published writings, there is a general lack of discussion of sin. In his most sustained treatment of sin, Bediako wrote, "In our [African] tradition, the essence of sin is in its being as an antisocial act. This makes sin basically injury to the interests of another person and damage to the collective life of the group. . . . [Yet] Sin is more than antisocial act; the sinner sins ultimately against a personal God with a will and purpose in human history."[29] Bediako sought to hold together an African understanding of sin and wrongdoing as a communal act which damages the whole clan and a more Western, evangelical understanding of sin as an individual act against God. When Bediako trained local pastors, he presented a more Augustinian understanding of sin and its effects on individuals.

Bediako's understanding of sin is consistent with other African Christians who view salvation as a "holistic experience . . . [of] total well-being,"[30] that "embrac[es] both the physical and the spiritual,"[31] and addresses "physical and immediate dangers that threaten individual or community survival, good health and general prosperity or safety. . . . Salvation is not just an abstraction,

---

26. Bediako, *Christianity in Africa*, 228.

27. Bediako, 226.

28. Bediako, "'Their Past Is also Our Present," 2.

29. See Bediako, "Jesus in African Culture," 26.

30. Cyril Okorocha, "The Meaning of Salvation: An African Perspective," in *Emerging Voices in Global Christian Theology*, ed. William Dyrness (Grand Rapids: Zondervan, 1994), 76.

31. John Mbiti, *Bible and Theology in African Christianity* (Nairobi: Oxford University Press, 1986), 158–59.

it is concrete."[32] Consistent with an African cosmology, Bediako in his understanding of the Christian faith sought access to God without needing to overcome separation from God. For Bediako, "the real problem of our sinfulness is the soiled conscience."[33] The wages of sin, in this understanding, are primarily guilt and shame. Such human emotions and the corresponding social dis-ease are not addressed by "purificatory rites and sacrificial offerings to achieve social harmony . . . [they are] ineffectual."[34]

Yet for Bediako, the universal revelation called for an individual, personal response. Without this individual response, salvation is not possible. Neither as individual rebellion against a sovereign Lord, nor as systemic injustice in a fallen world, does sin feature prominently in Bediako's understanding of humanity, atonement, or Christianity.

Ancestors in General

Beyond these personal and individual questions, the broader cultural questions must be addressed. An understanding of ancestors, at the heart of African traditional religions,[35] "represent a more enduring problem theologically than divinities."[36] Bediako describes the relationship between the dead and the living in traditional Akan understanding as follows: "the dead and the prominent dead especially – go to join the ancestors bearing messages from the living."[37] Those members of the clan who have died and who are honored for their life by being designated as ancestors continue to live on from the other side of the grave.[38] These "ancestors, from the realm of their continuing existence, [are held to] play a decisive role in the affairs of the society."[39] Bediako approvingly

---

32. John Mbiti, "Some Reflections on African Experience of Salvation Today," in *Living Faith and Ultimate Goals*, ed. S. J. Samartha (Geneva: World Council of Churches, 1974), 112–13. See also Kofi Opoku, "Toward a Holistic View of Salvation," in *Healing for God's World: Remedies from Three Continents* (New York: Friendship Press, 1991), 41–60.

33. See Bediako, "Jesus in African Culture," 26.

34. See Bediako, 26.

35. Anthony Ephirim-Donkor, *African Religion Defined: A Systematic Study of Ancestor Worship among the Akan* (New York: University Press of America, 2010), v.

36. Bediako, *Christianity in Africa*, 98.

37. Bediako, "Challenges of Ghana's Fourth Republic," 13.

38. According to Bediako, "not all the dead are ancestors. . . . For ancestors become so not solely by association in blood lineage, but also by quality of life, by the social significance and impact of their work; in other words, the dead become ancestors by achievement in life and not solely for having lived in the community." Bediako, *Christianity in Africa*, 80.

39. Kwame Bediako, "Death and the Gospel in the Ghanaian Context," *Exchange* 20, no. 2 (1991): 147.

quoted fellow Ghanaian theologian Christian Baëta who said that Africans "*live* with their dead."[40]

Bediako describes the role and significance of ancestors as based on the traditional belief that "the well-being of the society depends upon the maintenance of good relations with the ancestors on whom the living depend for help and protection." In this way, the ruler fulfills "an important function as intermediary between the living and ancestors." The ruler's role is to ensure harmony between the living and the ancestors who "continue to show interest and to participate in the affairs of the society through the channels of spiritual intervention by the appropriate rituals."[41] Frequently when someone is ill or if the crops are not producing, the first explanation is that the ancestors are unhappy; the first recourse, then, is to find a way to appease them. The deep interconnection of the living and the dead within the belief of the Akan people, and many other African peoples, reveals a great deal about their understanding of human community and their culture. Bediako explains, "The Ghanaian attitude to death and funeral observances therefore also reveals much about Ghanaian ideas of personal and group security and well-being."[42] Thus the understanding of the place and role of the ancestors within Ghanaian society cuts to the heart of cultural assumptions and the articulation of an African Christian identity. The connection between generations is understood to pass from an ancestor to his or her descendants.[43] What this all means for Bediako's theology is that "an Ancestor-Christology in African theology . . . is meant to show that Christ, by virtue of his Incarnation, death, resurrection and ascension into the realm of spirit-power, can rightly be designated, in African terms, as Ancestor, indeed Supreme Ancestor."[44]

---

40. C. G. Baëta, "The Challenge of African Culture to the Church and the Message of the Church to African Culture," in *Christianity and African Culture* (Accra: Christian Council of the Gold Coast, 1955), 59, emphasis original. Quoted in Bediako, *Christianity in Africa*, 60.

41. Bediako, "Challenges of Ghana's Fourth Republic," 4–5.

42. Bediako, "Death and the Gospel in the Ghanaian Context," 148.

43. Danquah described this connection as a "spark": "For the Akan the central fact of life is not death but life, the means whereby the blood of an ancestor, the spark of the race, is generated for a descendent, bearer and vehicle of the spark." J. B. Danquah, *The Akan Doctrine of God*, 168. Quoted in Bediako, "Religion and National Identity," 14.

44. Bediako, *Christianity in Africa*, 217.

Connecting Jesus with the Ancestors
Jesus as an ancestor

Starting from the conviction that Jesus Christ is the "*Universal* Saviour,"[45] Bediako wrote that there has been a "continuity of God from the pre-Christian African past into the Christian present . . . [such that African traditional religions were] . . . a vital preparation for the Gospel."[46] Bediako's belief in Christ's universality leads him to assert that, "Christianity is, among all religions, the most culturally translatable, hence the most truly universal, being able to be at home in every cultural context without injury to its essential character."[47]

Bediako's belief in continuity comes from an underlying biblical assumption: "Jesus Christ is not a stranger to our heritage, starting with the universality of Jesus Christ rather than from his particularity as a Jew, and affirming that the Incarnation was the incarnation of the Saviour of all people, of all nations and of all times."[48] Based on an interview, Bediako's emphasis on Christ's divinity is described as follows:

> Bediako thinks that it is the divinity of Jesus that is the point of contact with the universality of Jesus. Therefore, to start with his divinity is to make him universal. If I start with him as human, Bediako said, I have to see him as a Jew and will have problems accepting him as an Akan ancestor. Jesus needs to be human first in order to live, and die in order to become an ancestor, but as a universal ancestor he must communicate from the other side.[49]

While Bediako's views on the Jewishness of Jesus seem to come dangerously close to supercessionism, Diane Stinton reassures Bediako's readers: "Without downplaying the particularity of Jesus' Jewishness, Bediako emphasizes his incarnation for all of humanity of all times."[50] In a similar manner, though Bediako did not deny Jesus's embodied flesh, he was not particularly interested in Jesus's humanity. For Bediako, concentrating on the particular humanity of

---

45. Bediako, "Jesus in African Culture," 20, emphasis original.

46. Bediako, 21.

47. Bediako, 32.

48. Bediako, 24.

49. Roar Fotland, "Ancestor Christology in Context: Theological Perspectives of Kwame Bediako" (PhD dissertation, University of Bergen, 2005), 292–93.

50. Diane B. Stinton, *Jesus of Africa: Voices of Contemporary African Christology* (Maryknoll, NY: Orbis, 2004), 11.

Jesus of Nazareth conflicted with his emphasis on Jesus's universality through his divinity.

The question for Bediako was not merely theoretical but practical and one he claimed that early Jewish Christians wrestled with in the Epistle to the Hebrews. Bediako believed

> that the new African theology will have to attempt what the writer of the *Epistle to the Hebrews* did: that is, to make room, within an inherited body of tradition, for new ideas, for new realities which, though – seemingly entering from the outside, come in to fulfil aspirations within the tradition, and then to alter quite significantly the basis of self-understanding within that tradition.[51]

Bediako's ancestor Christology is one of those ideas. His quest was to discover what Jesus Christ might look like if Christ is the answer to questions that Africans, not Europeans, are asking.[52]

Priestly mediation

For Bediako the fundamental question, not only for early Jewish Christians but also for contemporary Africans, is this: how do you relate to someone of a different tribe? Jewish priests only came from the tribe of Levi. Jesus of Nazareth was born of the tribe of Judah. Jesus of Nazareth was not a priest and could not become a priest. Jesus became a priest not through Aaron, but through Melchizedek. The Epistle to the Hebrews makes a "Christological argument . . . that we have a priest, and more than a priest,"[53] a High Priest. The theological insight that Bediako draws from the Epistle to the Hebrews is that "Melchizedek is the pattern, not Aaron."[54] Bediako continues explaining the significant meaning of his insight: "'Jesus is the High Priest that meets our needs,' meeting and fulfilling all the aspirations and yearnings expressed and anticipated in all the rituals of atonement and redemption presided over by Aaron and his successors."[55]

"Therefore," Bediako wrote, "the priesthood, mediation and hence the salvation that Jesus Christ brings to all people everywhere belong to an entirely

---

51. Bediako, *Christianity in Africa*, 84.
52. Bediako, "Jesus in African Culture," 20.
53. Bediako, *Christianity in Africa*, 84.
54. Bediako, 84.
55. Bediako, 84.

different category from what people may claim for their clan, family, tribal and national priests and mediators."[56] Through Jesus's divinity, he is the Supreme Ancestor of all peoples:

> Our Saviour is our Elder Brother who has shared in our *African* experience in every respect, except our sin and alienation from God, an alienation with which our myths of origins make us only too familiar. Being our true Elder Brother now in the presence of his Father and our Father, he displaces the mediatorial function of our natural "spirit-fathers."[57]

Jesus Christ became the high priest and the sacrifice by functioning as the true ancestor.

This priestly mediation of Jesus Christ extends to Bediako's understanding of sacrifice. For Bediako, Jesus

> attains his singular position not by legal succession, but by divine designation, not by physical descent, but by spiritual achievement – by a quality of life that triumphed over evil, by an inimitable passion and death, and the power of an indestructible life in resurrection – in short, in the realm of power, in the realm of spirit. On that basis He becomes significant for all, and available to all.[58]

Bediako connects his account of atonement – how humanity is united to God – to Jesus as ancestor: "Jesus becomes *the Ancestor* of all."[59]

Impact of death and resurrection

Unpacking *how* the universality of Jesus Christ can be understood to penetrate African culture in integrative ways remains. For Bediako, the answer lies in the death and resurrection of Jesus Christ. In agreement with the apostle Paul, Bediako wrote that "the death of Jesus . . . reveals death itself to be a *theological* problem which calls for a *theological* response."[60] Therefore, any theological consideration of ancestors must begin with a theological consideration of death itself and Christ's death in particular. In general terms, the first aspect

---

56. Bediako, "Jesus in African Culture," 28.

57. Bediako, 26, emphasis original.

58. Bediako, *Christianity in Africa*, 85.

59. Bediako, 85.

60. Bediako, "Death and the Gospel in the Ghanaian Context," 148, emphasis original.

to keep in mind is philosopher Kwame Gyekye's claim: "What is primarily real is spiritual."[61] The central feature of Jesus's death then is less a sacrifice than it is a return to the spirit world through his resurrection and ascension.

Significantly, though Bediako emphasized the sacrifice of Jesus, he preferred a *Christus Victor* model of the atonement over a substitutionary model.[62] Bediako's preferred model of the atonement is consistent with his social, not individual, understanding of sin. Jesus waged a spiritual battle for the universe against demonic spirits and evil forces. Humanity benefits from Christ's cosmic, victorious power. Through this power, "In Christ, then we receive 'an adoptive past' through our 'Abrahamic link.'"[63] Because of Christ's cosmic victory over sin and death, Christians become children of God adopted through the great ancestor, Abraham. The victory of Christ through his death on the cross and resurrection from the dead defines what it means to be human. This is the good news; for Bediako, "Jesus Christ and his gospel are *prior*, and constitute the foundation of our cultures."[64]

Destabilizing traditional politics

Bediako believed that the death and resurrection of Jesus exposed the ancestors for what they really are: "the death of Jesus is also the defeat of Satan and of all the elemental demonic terrors which masquerade behind the presumed activity of ancestors."[65] Since Jesus "is Lord over the living and the dead, and over the 'living-dead,'"[66] ancestors do not have any real power over the living.

---

61. Kwame Gyekye, *Essay on African Philosophical Thought: The Akan Conceptual Scheme* (Cambridge: Cambridge University Press, 1987), 69. Bediako sought to connect the death of Jesus with its impact in the spiritual world. He wrote, "the victory of the Cross was achieved in the realm of spiritual power, that is, in the very realm where ancestors, spirit-powers and magical forces are believed to operate." Since Jesus's death has spiritual ramifications, his death can affect the ancestors and the spiritual realm in which they are understood to preside. Bediako, *Religion, Culture and Language*, 8.

62. Bediako, "Jesus in African Culture," 22.

63. Bediako, 227. See also Bediako, "Scripture as the Hermeneutics," 3.

64. Bediako, "Missionaries Did Not Bring Christ to Africa," 19, emphasis original.

65. Bediako, "Death and the Gospel in the Ghanaian Context," 149.

66. Bediako, "Jesus in African Culture," 27. Bediako continues: "From the standpoint of Akan spiritual beliefs, Jesus has gone to the realm of the ancestor spirits and the 'gods.' We already know that power and resources for living come from there, but the terrors and misfortunes which could threaten and destroy life come from there also. But if Jesus has gone to the realm of the 'spirits and the gods,' so to speak, he has gone there as Lord over them in the same way that he is Lord over us. He is Lord over the living and the dead, and over the 'living-dead,' as ancestors are also called."

Bediako asks, "[A]re not ancestors in effect a projection into the transcendent realm of the social values and spiritual expectations of the living community?" Then he continues, "[the] ancestors have no existence independent of the community that produces them. . . . Strictly speaking, the cult of ancestors, from the intellectual point of view, belongs to the category of myth, ancestors being the product of the myth-making imagination of the community."[67] For Bediako, the death and resurrection of Jesus reveals that the ancestors are a myth.[68] Jesus Christ holds spiritual power over all lesser spiritual forces. The dead one, Jesus Christ, has power while the dead ancestors do not. Bediako wrote, "The potency of the cult of ancestors is not the potency of ancestors themselves; the potency of the cult is the potency of myth."[69] Jesus Christ surpasses and replaces the cult of ancestors. Only Christ can bestow the benefits believed to be given by lineage ancestors.[70] Just as each ancestor remains the spirit of a formerly living human being with his or her own personality and life experiences, Jesus also retains his personal identity while in the spiritual realm.[71]

Bediako's description of the cult of ancestors as a myth has been critiqued by Victor Ezigbo and Benhardt Y. Quarshie. Ezigbo refers to Bediako's argument as suffering from "internal incoherence" because he "designates the ancestral cult as a myth . . . [and] tends to eclipse the historical reality of the cult."[72] Bediako's approach is "misleading. . . . [because] Many Africans continue to believe that they can communicate with their ancestors through divination and other metaphysical means."[73] Quarshie counters Bediako's claim, writing: "The ancestors are too real for the African to be simply attributed to myth."[74] Both theologians agreed that the unintended consequence of Bediako's argument

---

67. Bediako, "Jesus in African Culture," 30.

68. Bediako, 30.

69. Bediako, 30.

70. Bediako, 31.

71. In this way, Bediako insisted on holding together the person and work of Jesus Christ – just as he would for any ancestor. Bediako wrote, "who Jesus is in the African spiritual universe must not be separated from what he does and can do in that world. The way in which Jesus relates to the importance and function of the 'spirit fathers' or ancestors is crucial." Bediako, "Jesus in African Culture," 22.

72. Ezigbo, *Re-Imagining African Christologies*, 77.

73. Ezigbo, 78, 77.

74. Benhardt Y. Quarshie, "'Jesus, Pioneer and Perfecter of Faith' (Heb. 12:2): Kwame Bediako's Hebrews-based Ancestor Christology Revisited," in *Seeing New Facets of the Diamond: Christianity as a Universal Faith, Essays in Honour of Kwame Bediako*, ed. Gillian Mary Bediako, Benhardt Y. Quarshie, J. Kwabena Asamoah-Gyadu (Eugene, OR: Wipf & Stock, 2014), 30.

about the ancestors as a myth undercuts his assertion of Jesus Christ as ancestor. In Quarshie's words, "if the ancestors are regarded as mere myth with interest only in their function, then Christ may also be reduced to myth with only interest in his function."[75] Quarshie, for one, prefers an understanding of the ancestors as "very active participants in the [day-to-day] life of the community and of the individuals who make up the community. . . . The ancestors police the community and they summon, question, guide, direct, instruct, cajole, judge, rebuke, punish and bless."[76] Replacing Bediako's understanding of the ancestors as myth with a more robust understanding of ancestral function, Quarshie then embraces Bediako's ancestor Christology. Quarshie's summary of the gospel of Jesus Christ as understood by Africans is deeply indebted to Bediako:

> God (*Onyankopɔn, Nyɔnmɔ*) had spoken to both the pre-Christian Jewish and African ancestors in many and various ways, but that self-revelation of God had been partial, incomplete and imperfect and had consequently attained imperfect results. Speaking to us in these days by a Son, God offers us his full-self-disclosure, which effectively supersedes the earlier partial revelation in content and in results or impact.[77]

In spite of their disagreement over the role and place of the ancestors in African societies, Bediako would applaud Quarshie's clear and succinct summary.

Bediako is not unique in articulating an ancestor Christology. Though different theologians may use different christological titles, Bediako saw all of them as seeking to connect African culture with the gospel of Jesus Christ: "African Christological titles like 'Eldest Brother' (H. Sawyerr), 'Ancestor,' 'Great Ancestor' (J. S. Pobee, C. Nyamiti, K. Bediako), are neither 'from below,' nor strictly 'from above;' rather they are indicative of the way the primal imagination grasps the reality of Christ in terms in which all life is essentially conceived – as spiritual."[78] All articulations of an ancestor Christology destabilize the traditional political structure. Bediako identified the power dynamics at stake: "in the profound relating of Christ to the living forces

---

75. Quarshie, "Jesus, Pioneer and Perfecter," 30. Ezigbo makes a similar point in a footnote: "If Bediako's contention for the invalidity of the cult of the ancestors is correct, then it follows that there is no convincing correlation between Jesus and the ancestors." Ezigbo, *Re-Imagining African Christologies*, 78.

76. Quarshie, "Jesus, Pioneer and Perfecter," 30.

77. Quarshie, 33.

78. Bediako, *Christianity in Africa*, 176.

of the traditional religion there would also be a power-encounter since the traditional religion, centered at its most vital points on ancestors, was at heart about power."[79] In disrupting the traditional understanding of the ancestral cult, Bediako knew he was desacralizing traditional politics and upsetting long held ways of governing.

Ancestral function

Bediako understood the impact of the dead among the living to be confined to Jesus Christ alone. He was not willing to grant lineage ancestors the power of saints as in the Roman Catholic tradition or influential spirits as in African traditional religions. Due to the close connection in African life between ancestral function and politics, particularly tribal politics, Bediako acknowledges that "the whole realm of politics is sacralised . . . the traditional world-view makes no sharp dichotomy between 'secular' and 'sacred' realms of existence."[80] Authority belongs to and derives from the transcendent, spiritual realm. Bediako wrote, "If authority does not reside with the merely human, then why should it be located in the realm of the essentially *human* spirits of the ancestors?"[81] So in the perspective of Christian ideas, ancestors too are desacralized. For Bediako, "Jesus' way of dealing with political power represents the perfect desacralisation of all worldly power."[82] Authority truly belongs only to God.[83] Every challenge to political authority is an attack on the ancestors.[84]

Bediako saw one "of the values of an Ancestor-Christology is precisely that it helps to clarify the place and significance of 'natural' ancestors. . . . Just as there exists a clear distinction between God and divinities, so also there exists a qualitative distinction between Christ as Ancestor and natural ancestors."[85] Bediako's formulation remains vulnerable to the critiques of African Christianity made by the prominent non-Christian African philosophers Ali Mazrui and Okot p'Bitek.

Taking up these lines of critique, Maluleke named Bediako's approach to the ancestors as overly triumphalist. "We must do better," he wrote. "[T]

---

79. Bediako, 71–72.

80. Bediako, 241.

81. Bediako, 244, emphasis original.

82. Bediako, "Challenges of Ghana's Fourth Republic," 8.

83. Bediako, *Christianity in Africa*, 244.

84. Bediako, "Challenges of Ghana's Fourth Republic," 5.

85. Bediako, *Christianity in Africa*, 217–18.

he possibility is not only for Jesus to become the Supreme Ancestor, but he could simply join the ranks of other ancestors who are at the service of the Supreme Being in Africa."[86] While Maluleke criticizes Bediako for replacing the cult of ancestors with Jesus Christ on behalf of all Africans, the significance of Maluleke's critique here is that he wholly agrees with Bediako that the dead have an impact on the living in African culture.

Neither theologian sides with the initial Western viewpoint that the ancestors are demonic. As such, both can be seen to offer a positive assessment of African primal religions. Maluleke criticizes Bediako's view that African traditional religions are legitimate religious traditions *only* as preparation for Christianity. Such debates about the role of the dead among the living can sound quite strange to Western ears. However given the implications, not only for theology but also in politics, Western listeners can appreciate the stakes within African cultures.

Bediako's reading of Colossians 1:15–17 – "He is the image of the invisible God, the firstborn of all creation; for in him all things in heaven and on earth were created, things visible and invisible, whether thrones or dominions or rulers or powers – all things have been created through him and for him. He himself is before all things, and in him all things hold together" – functions as an effective case study of his method of reading a mother-tongue Scripture passage to explore theological and cultural insights that serve to desacralize the ancestors and offer a revelation of God in Jesus Christ.[87] When Bediako read Colossians 1:15–17 in his own indigenous language, Twi, alongside an English translation, he noticed the Greek word "θρόνοι" (1:16) was unremarkably translated into English as "thrones." However when translated in Twi, the word "*nhengua*" was used. Bediako notes the significant cultural implications of this translation for Twi speakers: in the "Akan cultural heritage of Twi-speaking people of Ghana, '*nhengua*' are not the publicly visible thrones on which royals sit. . . . Rather, '*nhengua*' are the sacred, ritually preserved thrones of departed royals." These *nhengua* are associated with the mysteries of sacred rule and the operations of ancestral authority and power: "Every reigning king sits upon the stool (throne) of a royal ancestor and becomes an embodiment of his royal grandsires." Thus according to Bediako, by translating θρόνοι as *nhengua*, "the Scriptures clearly declare that Jesus Christ reigns supreme over that world also, as living Ancestor there in his own right." Jesus reigns over all who sit upon the ancestral thrones and all who look to these earthly kings (and their ancestral

---

86. Maluleke, "Black and African Theologies," 16.

87. See Bediako, "Missionaries Did Not Bring Christ to Africa," 25–26.

forebearers) for power. These *nhengua* are not separate from the Christian faith, but rather Jesus has something to do in and with the throne room itself. "To hear from the first time in the medium of his own language," wrote Bediako, "that '*nhengua*' were created through Christ and were created for Christ, was a revolution and a new revelation!"[88]

Based on his underlying belief that the gospel of Jesus Christ is infinitely translatable, Bediako used his understanding of pre-Christendom Christianity and precolonial Africa to shape a history for the Christian faith that is indigenous to Africa. This faith then can be integrated in and expressed through mother-tongue Scriptures and vernacular concepts including, significantly, a theology of ancestors. Bediako captures the path of his argument in the following quotation:

> The cross-cultural transmission did not *bring* Christ into the local African situation. . . . The deeper insight is, however, that Christ, already present in the situation, called in His messengers so that by proclamation and incarnation, He might be made manifest. The cross-cultural transmission is thus a confirmation of the divine initiative in the local situation, extending its ramifications beyond the range of former horizons, and demonstrating the ecumenical significance of local history.[89]

Since God is at work in every culture, local theologies must be articulated that are authentic and indigenous to each context.

Further Reading of Kwame Bediako

"Christian Religion and the African World-View: Will Ancestors Survive?," chapter 12, 210–33. In *Christianity in Africa: The Renewal of a Non-Western Religion*. Edinburgh: Edinburgh University Press, 1995.

"Jesus in African Culture: A Ghanaian Perspective," 20–33. In *Jesus and the Gospel in Africa*. Maryknoll, NY: Orbis Books, 2004.

"'Missionaries Did not Bring Christ to Africa – Christ Brought Them': Why Africa Needs Jesus Christ." *AICMAR* 6 (2007): 17–31.

"'Their Past Is also Our Present.' Why All Christians Have Need of Ancestors: Making a Case for Africa." *AICMAR* 6 (2007): 1–16.

---

88. Bediako, 26.

89. Bediako, *Christianity in Africa*, 226, emphasis original.

6

Remaking Christian Theology

"Africa . . . Leads the Way"

Bediako understood Western Christianity to have been fatally wounded by the elimination of religious differences in Christendom. "When the context of religious pluralism is succeeded," he wrote, by "a Christendom from which all possible alternatives are presumed eliminated, not only from the context, but from theological existence too, [then] the theological enterprise ceases to need to make Christian decisions. Because no other kinds of decisions are conceivable, the character of theology itself becomes changed."[1] In Bediako's analysis, Western theology failed by eradicating religious pluralism which eliminated theological alternatives.[2] Bediako repeatedly referred to Christendom as a "disaster,"[3] and was certain that "Africa has not produced, and is not likely to produce, a new Christendom."[4] Instead African Christianity – an understanding of the Christian faith within a religiously pluralistic environment – can offer hope and guidance to those stuck within a Christendom mindset.

According to Bediako, Western theologies – in the period from Emperor Constantine's conversion in 313 until at least the colonial independence movements around 1960 – did not display much ability to engage religious

1. Bediako, *Christianity in Africa*, 257.

2. Bediako, 257.

3. See Kwame Bediako, "Africa and Christianity on the Threshold of the Third Millennium: The Religious Dimension," *African Affairs* 99 (2000): 316.

4. Bediako, *Christianity in Africa*, 249. Of no minor significance here is that Bediako published these words seven years *prior* to Philip Jenkins, *The Next Christendom: The Coming of Global Christianity* (New York: Oxford University Press, 2002).

pluralism. Many Christian theologians developed an inability to dialogue with people outside the Christian faith, aside from proseletizing. For Bediako, a non-Christian could not "encounter Christ except on the terms of a Christian theology whose categories have been established with little reference to the faiths of others."[5] Western Christians cannot continue to operate on a Christendom-era model; there must be a "remaking" of Christian theology to address the contemporary challenges presented by religious pluralism.

Bediako describes the problem and the need for Western Christians to ask new questions:

> theology cannot be done, studied and taught in quite the same way in which it has been in the Western European tradition, where the challenge of pluralism was virtually unknown or else was minimal for a very long time. It also means that the intellectual framework as well as the kind of questions that will be posed, will differ from those that have characterized the Western European tradition in theology.[6]

Since the experience of African Christians has always included religious pluralism, both in the form of primal religions and Islam, Bediako believed that Africans can help Western Christians in remaking their theology. In the process, the complex character of Christianity will be revealed and explored. Bediako believed that "African theologians [had] recaptured the character of Christian thought as Christian intellectual activity on the frontier with the non-Christian world, and as essentially *communicative* and *missionary*."[7] For Bediako, the gift of African Christianity to the Western world is to point toward the true Christian faith, an authentic understanding of Christian identity that is not corrupted by Christendom.

World Christianity, Not Global!

One clear consequence of Bediako's views on Christianity, politics, authority, and power is that the exponential growth of Christianity in Africa and other areas in the developing world will not produce a new (or a next) Christendom – not now, not ever. Bediako's main reasoning is that Christian churches in Africa exist in

---

5. Bediako, *Christianity in Africa*, 257.

6. Bediako, *Theology and Identity*, 434.

7. Kwame Bediako, "African Christian Thought," in *Oxford Companion to Christian Thought*, ed. A. Hastings and A. Mason (Oxford: Oxford University Press, 2000), 10, emphasis original.

contexts of religious pluralism. The goal of the church should not be to eliminate or conquer non-Christians or their beliefs, but rather that the Christian churches should "learn to continue to worship God and His Christ, witness to the Gospel, learn to survive in joy, and strive for peace and justice and democratic freedom for all."[8] The character of the democratic freedom that Bediako called for encompasses "ethnicity, race, social class, culture and customs."[9] Bediako desired that these "elemental forces" that had "shaped individual and social identity and destiny in the old order" would become sites of the full, concrete expression of "Christian conversion and Christian discipleship."[10]

With the geographic shift in the center of gravity of the worldwide Christian population, Bediako strongly argued for a corresponding intellectual shift away from treating Western thought as the center, the reference point, for Christian theological reflection. Importantly, Bediako did not simply want to replace the former center of Christian thought in the West with a new center. The presence of vibrant and growing African Christianity demonstrates that there can be no single definition of Christianity today. Since Christianity does not radiate from a single geographic center, but multiple centers, a single meaning or message of Christianity is not possible.

Bediako's insightful claim on this topic is that in the present situation, "it becomes less helpful to speak of a 'global Christianity' whereby, presuming a contest for 'global' hegemony, the new centres of Christian vitality are represented as 'the next Christendom' – a relocation of power from Western churches, and therefore a global threat to the West."[11] Bediako, while aware of power dynamics, did not primarily think about the Christian faith in terms of power. The growth of Christianity in Africa and the global South did not come at the expense of or take anything away from Christianity in the global North. The growth of Christian faith is not a zero-sum game. For Bediako, there are multiple centers leading to multiple Christianities. Not only is there "no *one* centre from which Christianity radiates," claims Bediako, "it was never intended to be so."[12] The implication is that there are multiple centers for Christianity, not just one and certainly not just one in the West.[13]

---

8. Bediako, *Christianity in Africa*, 249.

9. Bediako, 249.

10. Bediako, 249.

11. Bediako, "Conclusion: The Emergence of World Christianity," 248.

12. Bediako, *Christianity in Africa*, 164, emphasis original.

13. Bediako, "New Paradigms on Ecumenical Co-operation: An African Perspective," *International Review of Mission* (July 1992): 376. See also Bediako, *Christianity in Africa*, 164, 167, 169.

Rather, it is more helpful and more accurate, as Bediako wrote, "to recognise the emergence of a 'world Christianity,' the result of diverse indigenous responses to the Christian faith in various regions of the world, the emergence of a positive polycentrism, in which the many centers have an opportunity to learn from each other."[14] Bediako much preferred the language of *world* Christianity as opposed to *global* Christianity. To him, world Christianity emphasizes indigenous responses to the Christian faith, a more bottom-up understanding, while global Christianity is more hegemonic and too concerned with issues of power within the Christian faith around the world. The learning opportunities between different cultures and contexts are a significant implication of the positive polycentricism of contemporary world Christianity.

Bediako criticized Philip Jenkins for referring to Christianity in the global South as "a very exotic beast indeed, intriguing, exciting, and a little frightening."[15] The underlying impetus for Bediako's harsh critiques of Jenkins' *The Next Christendom* concerned Jenkins' fear that the rise of global Christianity is a threat to the West and the geopolitical order.[16] Bediako read Jenkins as painting "a frightening scenario that he does little to dispel" where the Christian South is ostracized by the increasingly secular North which prides itself on being rational and tolerant.[17] Further, Bediako attacks Jenkins's search for "a new Christendom, a new 'power block.'"[18] In Bediako's view, Jenkins desired to understand the new emergence of Christianity in the southern continents "in terms of world geopolitics."[19] Jenkins' approach fuels polarizations and minimizes the African significance "because it [does] not fit his geopolitical

---

14. Bediako, "Conclusion: The Emergence of World Christianity," 248.

15. Kwame Bediako, "'Whose Religion Is Christianity?': Reflections on Opportunities and Challenges in Christian Theological Scholarship: The African Dimension," in *Mission in the Twenty-first Century: Exploring the Five Marks of Global Mission*, ed. Andrew F. Walls and Cathy Ross (Maryknoll, NY: Orbis, 2008), 211n4; citing Jenkins, *Next Christendom*, 220.

16. For Bediako's earliest critique of Jenkins, see his 2003 Stone Lecture at Princeton Theological Seminary, published as Kwame Bediako, "'Ethiopia Shall Soon Stretch Out Her Hands to God' (Ps. 68:31): African Christians Living the Faith: A Turning Point in Christian History," in *A New Day Dawning: African Christians Living the Gospel: Essays in Honour of Dr. J. J. (Hans) Visser*, ed. Kwame Bediako, Mechteld Jansen, Jan van Butselaar, and Aart Verburg (Zoetermeer: Boekencentrum, 2004), 30–40, esp. 32–38.

17. Bediako, "New Era in Christian History," 7n9. Bediako is referring to Jenkins, *Next Christendom*, 161–62.

18. Bediako, "New Era in Christian History," 3.

19. Bediako, 3.

perspective."[20] Bediako acknowledges that in Jenkins' subsequent work, he dropped the "frightening aspect" of the rise of global Christianity; however the exotic and intriguing descriptors remained.[21] Jenkins' core problem, according to Bediako, is that Jenkins' analysis assumes a dichotomy between the global North and South that is defined by the economic and political realities of late capitalism.[22] Jenkins' analysis relies on a colonial paradigm, an assumption that Bediako wholly rejected.

Postcolonial Theology as too Colonial

Bediako's commitment to the local and the indigenous in theological reflection also caused him to be skeptical of the movement toward postcolonial theology. For Bediako, "In positioning oneself as postcolonial, one is handicapped to understand one's indigenous heritage."[23] Bediako did not want to lose the insights of the primal imagination from the precolonial period through a too hasty jump to the postcolonial. Bediako's understanding of the term "postcolonial" is primarily historical, consistent with the use of the hyphen, rather than theoretical.[24] Though Bediako's project is consistent with the postcolonial thread of pushing back against colonizing powers and influences, he insists that "the nature and the significance of African Christian life reach[es] beyond the Western colonial connection. This means that the postcolonial paradigm can be restrictive and, when used exclusively, can be distorting."[25] To shape an African Christian identity, Bediako looked to the twin heritage of African Christianity in precolonial Africa and pre-Christendom Christianity. He sought "a larger intellectual framework than post-coloniality for describing, analyzing and interpreting African Christian history, life, and thought. . . . the

---

20. Bediako, 4. See also James Ferguson who describes Africa as "an inconvenient case" for globalization theorists, since it does not fit the story line for either proponents or opponents of globalization. Instead, "the recent history of Africa does pose a profound challenge to ideas of global economic and political convergence." James Ferguson, *Global Shadows: Africa in the Neoliberal World Order* (Durham, NC: Duke University Press, 2006), 26, 28.

21. Kwame Bediako, "'Why Has the Summer Ended and We Are Not Saved?': Encountering the Real Challenge of Christian Engagement in Primal Contexts," *Journal of African Christian Thought* 11, no. 2 (2008): 5. See Philip Jenkins, *The New Faces of Christianity: Believing the Bible in the Global South* (New York: Oxford University Press, 2006).

22. See Bediako, "Whose Religion Is Christianity?," 211.

23. Bediako, 212n33.

24. For more on the use of the hyphen in post-colonial, see Bill Ashcroft, Gareth Griffiths, and Helen Tiffin, *The Empire Writes Back: Theory and Practice in Post-Colonial Literatures*, 2nd ed. (Routledge, 2002), especially 193–222.

25. Bediako, "Whose Religion Is Christianity?," 115.

Christian faith in Africa is not ultimately determined by Western paradigms of interpretation."[26] For Bediako's interests in African Christianity, the colonial period brought the Bible – translated into African mother tongues – and the name of God in Jesus Christ. Aside from these not insignificant contributions, the colonial period need not impact African Christianity any more than it already has.

Bediako was more interested in theology that is indigenous, precolonial, and emerging from Christianity as an indigenous African religion, rather than postcolonial and defined as a response to Western culture and theological concepts. From this perspective, Bediako sought to be post-postcolonial by moving toward an indigenous African Christian identity that is not shaped, much less defined, by Western or European colonial history and ideas.[27] He rejected the secularity of modern Western thought and skepticism of the transcendent and religious phenomena. By the end of the twentieth century, Bediako was quite clear that, "Christianity has now entered a post-Western phase."[28] In fact, he understood "the post-colonial crisis in mission" to be a part of "the dying stages of Western ethnocentrism."[29] As long as the church in Europe and North America remains unaware or unwilling to engage the shift of the center of gravity, they perceive a crisis in their historically self-appointed roles as sending churches and the peoples of the global South as receiving churches.

Bediako preferred the language of postmissionary to postcolonial. The growth of the Christian faith has radically altered the demographics of the Christian faith worldwide, and this situation calls for similar changes in mindset. He wanted to stress the African role in the growth of the Christian faith as well as what Africans have to offer to the world. "The experience of African Christianity," Bediako wrote, "[vindicated] the transcendent as a specifically religious phenomenon and experience [that] need not be surrendered in a culturally and religiously plural world."[30] In this sense for Bediako, "the African experience may have anticipated some aspects of post-modernity!"[31] by valuing the spiritual over the material and experience over rationality.

---

26. Bediako, 115.

27. For an opposing interpretation, see Tinyiko Maluleke who believed that Bediako's understanding of African Christianity is "too thickly clouded by the mist of colonialism." Maluleke, "Black and African Theologies," 8.

28. Bediako, "Whose Religion Is Christianity?," 115.

29. Bediako, *Christianity in Africa*, 131.

30. Bediako, "A Half Century of African Christian Thought," 8.

31. Bediako, 8.

In the early twentieth century, according to Bediako, "The missionaries were completely unaware that there could be other 'Christianities' than the form they knew. This problem persists right up to our day."[32] Thus not only were the missionaries mistaken for presuming their understanding of Christianity as the only possibility, Western Christianity has not learned any different in the ensuing hundred years. Christianity is not a Western religion, but rather a non-Western religion: "This is not to say that Christianity has ceased to exist in the West, but simply that the faith and its expression are no longer determined by dominant Western cultural and social norms."[33] Yet, "the sheer number of African Christians makes it difficult to ignore what African theologians say and write."[34] Even still, his real concern lay with the future of the church worldwide as a result of "the increasing intellectual stiffening of African Christian conviction."[35]

Remaking of Theology: "Africa . . . Leads the Way"

The implications of the global shift in Christian faith were clear to Bediako. The peoples of Latin America, sub-Saharan Africa, and Asia are going to show the future of Christian theology. The demographic changes necessitate theological changes: "it may well require a more active partnership with Third World churches to effect the rescue of Western churches from their captivity to culture."[36] While the theology of European Christians may remain important to them, it will only serve as an historical footnote to the theologies written in the developing world.[37] This shift provides an opportunity for the developing world to help the West, not that the former colonial powers deserve to be helped by those who they oppressed.

Bediako saw the shift in the center of gravity as preserving the Christian faith that had come under threat in Europe. He was grateful for this movement from the North to the South since by "becoming a non-Western religion,

---

32. Bediako, "Biblical Christologies," 121.

33. Kwame Bediako, "'In the Bible . . . Africa Walks on Familiar Ground': Why the World Needs Africa," *AICMAR* 6 (2007): 36.

34. Kwame Bediako, "Review of *African Theology en Route*," *Journal of Religion in Africa* 11, no. 2 (1980): 159.

35. Bediako, "Review of *African Theology en Route*," 159.

36. Bediako, "Willowbank Consultation," 32.

37. Andrew F. Walls, "The Gospel as Prisoner and Liberator of Culture," in *The Missionary Movement in Christian History: Studies in the Transmission of Faith* (Maryknoll, NY: Orbis, 1996), 10.

Christianity has also become a true world faith."[38] Noting the significance of the shift for the future of Christianity and of Christian theological reflection, Bediako claims that significantly "the present shift in the centre of gravity may have secured for Christianity a future that would otherwise be precarious in the secularized cultural environment of the modern West."[39] Becoming a non-Western religion has required considerable intellectual adjustment for many and changes how Christianity is understood. Simply, Christianity "has now ceased to be shaped primarily by the events and processes at work in Western culture."[40] The intellectual adjustment then "requires nothing less than the complete rethinking of the Church history syllabus."[41] The focus now should be on the ongoing developments of the church in the global South, not the fossilized remains of European churches and theologies.

Bediako believed that by extricating African Christianity from the influence of Western Christianity, "African Christian theological scholarship will be making African Christianity less provincial but instead more truly universal!"[42] As Christians reconnect with their primal roots and rely on the Scriptures of the Old and New Testaments, a more universal and exportable Christianity is revealed than the former model of captivity to Western culture. For Bediako, the implications of this possibility are nothing less than the remaking of Christian theology: Africans may have saved Christianity.

"In the remaking of theology in our time," Bediako wrote, "the Christian churches and scholars of Africa, and also of the other Christian heartlands in

---

38. Bediako, *Christianity in Africa*, 265.

39. Bediako, "In the Bible," 38.

40. Kwame Bediako, "Africa and Christianity on the Threshold," 307.

41. Bediako, *Christianity in Africa*, 207. Bediako is quoting Andrew Walls, "Structural Problems in Mission Studies," *International Bulletin of Missionary Research* 15, no. 4 (1991): 146. Perhaps Bediako was also thinking of John Mbiti's famous quotation that Western Christians know more about the heretics of the second and third centuries than about contemporary Christians living in the developing world. See Bediako, *Christianity in Africa*, 154ff. Mbiti wrote,

> It is utterly scandalous for so many scholars in older Christendom to know so much about Christian movements in the second and third centuries, when so few of them know so little about Christian movements in areas of the younger churches. We feel deeply affronted and wonder whether it is more meaningful theologically to have academic fellowship with heretics long dead than with the living brethren of the Church today in the so-called Third World.

John Mbiti, "Theological Impotence and the Universality of the Church," *Lutheran World* 21, no. 3 (1974): 259; republished in Gerald Anderson and Thomas Stransky, eds., *Mission Trends 3: Third World Theologies* (New York: Paulist; Grand Rapids: Eerdmans, 1976): 6–18.

42. Bediako, "Whose Religion Is Christianity?," 116.

Latin America, Asia and the Pacific, are called upon to lead the way."[43] The change in role for African Christian theologians – from the earliest stages of seeking an African Christian identity to now leading the way for the remaking of Christian theology worldwide – transformed Bediako's understanding of the African theologian's task. African Christian theological scholarship "is no longer merely for Africa. It is for the world, which means that it cannot narrow its focus on Africa for its inspiration. . . . African theological scholarship can ill afford any short cuts, and it must resist the temptation to succumb to them."[44] Bediako's goal was for the depth and particularity of African theological scholarship to influence theological reflection worldwide. The sources of African theology lay in Africa – not outside of the continent, not in Europe, or elsewhere. Bediako expresses his point passionately: "The point here is the need for African, Asian and Latin American Christian scholars and theologians to also learn to do fundamental theological work and not merely content themselves with quoting the results of other people's work. We have little choice!"[45] The growth of African Christianity and the concurrent process of globalization (and reverse globalization)[46] have offered a new role to Africans within the worldwide Christian community. For the next era in Christian history, African theologians will lead, and others will follow.

African theologians have been deeply invested in the type of future toward which Africans are leading. Katongole hopes for a future that is "qualitatively different from the present."[47] He desires a future "characterized not simply by the numerical growth of the Christian population, nor merely by an abstract concern for African Christian identity, but also by such mundane concerns"[48] as define the lives of many Africans. Maluleke believes that African theologies must take note of the poor of Africa who are "already creating alternative structures to a global economy that excludes them,"[49] and will do the same in theology and ecclesiology if they are excluded. More than Bediako's concern about "responding to the charge of African intellectuals who say that Christianity can never become an adequate frame of reference for the full

43. Bediako, "The Emergence of World Christianity and the Remaking of Theology," *Journal of African Christian Thought* 12, no. 2 (2009): 54.

44. Bediako, "Emergence of World Christianity," 54.

45. Bediako, "In the Bible," 48.

46. Reverse globalization is the term given to the movement of peoples and ideas from the so-called developing or third world to the so-called developed or first world.

47. Katongole, *Future for Africa*, 156.

48. Katongole, 156.

49. Maluleke, "Black and African Theologies," 18.

expression of African ideals of life," according to Maluleke,[50] it is in discerning "Africa's ability to provide answers to its inhabitants' most vexing questions that we find a clue to its deepest intellectual critique of Christianity."[51] Bediako in his understanding of African Christian thought has attempted to respond to both intellectual critiques, from both African non-Christian intellectuals and also from everyday Africans affected by poverty and injustice.

For Bediako, the considerable intellectual adjustment of a non-Western Christianity and the processes of reverse globalization led to a *universalizing in reverse*. The shift to a non-Western Christianity also leads "a reverse process to the prevailing Western-driven globalization . . . [a] process of globalization 'from below.'"[52] Particularly through migration, Africans are leaving Africa and bringing their African Christianity with them to the West.[53] Since the gospel is universal and applies everywhere, the gospel can be translated from Greek and Hebrew and understood in Africa as God speaks in every tongue. In this way, the universal gospel can be translated into particular, contextualized theologies. The gospel is universal; theology is contextual. Then once understood in Africa, the implications for the meaning of Christianity worldwide can be universalized as a non-Western religion.

Bediako used Revelation 7:9 to justify the universal applicability of the Christian faith: "After this I looked, and there was a great multitude that no one could count, from every nation, from all tribes and peoples and languages, standing before the throne and before the Lamb, robed in white, with palm branches in their hands." He continued, "though Christianity has always been universal in principle, it can be seen to have become universal in practice only in recent history in fact. Now this, of course, is a fact that is not only unique among the world's religions, it is a new feature for the Christian faith itself. One must not underestimate, therefore, what the outworking of a global,

---

50. Maluleke, 6.

51. Maluleke, 16.

52. Bediako, "Africa and Christianity on the Threshold," 314.

53. See Mark Gornik, *Word Made Global: Stories of African Christianity in New York City* (Grand Rapids: Eerdmans, 2011); Jacob K. Olupona and Regina Gemignani, *African Immigrant Religions in America* (New York: New York University Press, 2007); Afe Adogame, *The African Christian Diaspora: New Currents and Emerging Trends in World Christianity* (New York: Bloomsbury Academic, 2013); Afe Adogame, ed., *The Public Face of African New Religious Movements in Diaspora* (New York: Routledge, 2016); and Soong-Chan Rah, *The Next Evangelicalism: Freeing the Church from Western Cultural Captivity* (Grand Rapids: InterVarsity, 2009). In postcolonial poetry, Louise Bennett has described this phenomenon in her 1966 poem, "Colonization in Reverse." Louise Bennett, *Selected Poems* (Kingston, Jamaica: Sangster's Book Stores, 1982), 107.

Christian identity might involve."[54] Bediako later moved beyond only trying to establish and articulate an African Christian identity and toward a global, Christian identity. Yet it must be noted that even a global Christianity identity is not abstract, somehow apart from its host culture. Instead, as always, this universalizing from the bottom-up, or at least from Africa to the world, *must* be particular.

A Theological Reorientation

According to Bediako, new theologies need to emerge from Africa because new theological answers are needed to contemporary questions and the West is incapable of offering much helpful insight.[55] Bediako states:

> It is obvious that the kind of theological re-orientation that is needed cannot be done in the West, nor by Western churches and institutions. The reason is evident: the West is now not the major theatre of Christian interaction. Indeed, Western culture is becoming increasingly hostile to that interaction. The work has to be done in the major theatres of Christian interaction.[56]

Africa, Asia, and Latin America are the locations of exponential growth of the Christian faith. These locales offer the greatest possibility for new theological insights.

African theologians are not merely interested in different content, but also in "charting a new course in theological method."[57] The new method concerns identity, questions of "old" and "new," continuity and discontinuity, African and Christian. One result of the changed method is that it "forced the theologian to become the *locus* of this struggle for integration through a dialogue, which, if it was to be authentic, was bound to become personal and so infinitely more intense."[58] Bediako's own theology demonstrated his claim of the theologian's

---

54. Kwame Bediako, "Reading Signs of the Kingdom," Stone Lecture No. 1, Princeton Theological Seminary, 20 October 2003.

55. Bediako states, "if it is true that the new configuration of the Christian world has taken Christian theology into areas of life where Western theology has no answers because it has no questions, then it is evident that Western theology may not be of much help to us either. . . . Western Christian theology may have little with which to help Africa and why, rather, the world and the West in particular, may need to learn from Africa and from African experience." Bediako, "In the Bible," 44.

56. Bediako, 47.

57. Bediako, "A Half Century of African Christian Thought," 6.

58. Bediako, 7, emphasis original.

struggle for integration as the locus for theological reflection. His major themes of identity, translatability, history, mother-tongue Scriptures, and contextual theology were all deeply personal.

The theologian became a central site of theological reflection. Instead of the Western tendency of removing theologians from their theologies, the deeply contextual African theology of identity does not separate theologians from their theologies. Bediako described the work of African theologians in the same manner that he described the work of early Greco-Roman theologians, as *"apologia pro vita sua"* (a defense of one's life).[59] Bediako further explained why the path of African theologies differed from the prior, Western approaches: "African theology in the last half century has not developed categories or rubrics of systematic or dogmatic theology. . . . Instead, African Christian thought has followed a sense of direction of its own, and sought its own responses to its own questions."[60] The focus on African identity continually drives African theologians back into local African communities. An African understanding of Christianity freed Bediako from his captivity to Western culture. His hope was that by articulating his understanding of Christianity in Africa, his fellow Africans would also be freed.

This growth of the Christian faith and of theological reflection highlights the sometimes tense relationship between academic theology and so-called lived, or grassroots theologies. The spread of the Christian faith through the Scriptures translated into vernacular languages has encouraged everyday Christians – not just educated pastors and church leaders – to actively engage the Scriptures with their spiritual questions. For his part, Bediako saw, "African academic theology as being challenged to be in close contact with the vernacular apprehension of the Christian faith and with its roots in the continuing realities of the traditional primal world-view."[61] In order to investigate the relationship between academic and grassroots theologies, Bediako turned to Afua Kuma, an "illiterate Christian woman . . . theologian from rural Ghana whose prayers and praises of Jesus remind us that, in the final analysis, the whole of our Christian calling is to worship Jesus the Lord."[62]

Afua Kuma was a farmer and a midwife who composed songs of praise that employed earthly images to convey spiritual insights about the Christian

---

59. Bediako, 7. For more on the use of this description, see Fretheim, *Kwame Bediako and African Christian Scholarship*, 129–32.

60. Bediako, "A Half Century of African Christian Thought," 7.

61. Bediako, *Christianity in Africa*, 86.

62. Bediako, "Cry Jesus!" 9, 18.

faith. Her songs were complied, translated from Twi, and published as *Jesus of the Deep Forest*.[63] Bediako believed that her poetry and songs served as "an illustration of that spirituality which gives a clue to the vibrant Christian presence that we know of, and which forms the true basis of African theology; and which also provides clear evidence that Christianity in Africa is a truly African experience. For this is theology which comes from where the faith lives."[64] Bediako seemed enthralled with Madame Kuma's word pictures. He wrote, "in this striking association of images, the Incarnation and the victory of the Cross are brought together and made meaningful in the defeat of the terrors of the African world, in both the invisible realm . . . and in the visible realm of wild creatures like the elephant which, in rural Ghana, can suddenly attack a village and take away a child."[65]

Bediako was drawn to Afua Kuma's hymns because of how he understood them to be drawing connections between the world of Africa and the world of the Bible. Bediako described the parallel as follows:

> the 'Jesus of the deep forest' is also the Jesus of the Gospels, the miracleworker who does the impossible, who triumphs over the obstacles of nature, who provides food for the hungry and water for the thirsty, who delivers from all manner of ailments and who bestows the wholeness of salvation. What is impossible for us is possible with him.[66]

Not only did Bediako see practical connections between the two worlds, but he saw strong theological connections as well. In his analysis,

> By giving ancestral and royal titles to Jesus, these prayers and praises indicate how deeply Madam Afua Kuma has apprehended the allpervasive Lordship of Jesus, in the ancestral realm of spirit power, and in the realm of the living community under reigning

---

63. Afua Kuma, *Jesus of the Deep Forest*, trans. Jon Kirby (Accra, Ghana: Asempa, 1981). For more see Philip Laryea, "Mother Tongue Theology: Reflections on Images of Jesus in the Poetry of Afua Kuma," *Journal of African Christian Thought* 3, no. 1 (2000): 50–60; Mercy Amba Oduyoye, "Jesus Christ," in *The Cambridge Companion to Feminist Theology*, ed. Susan Frank Parsons (Cambridge: Cambridge University Press, 2002), 151–70; and Richard Fox Young, "Clearing a Path through *Jesus of the Deep Forest*: Intercultural Perspectives on Christian Praise and Public Witness in Afua Kuma's Akan Oral Epic," *Theology Today* 70, no. 1 (2013): 38–45.

64. Bediako, "Cry Jesus!" 9.

65. Bediako, 10.

66. Bediako, 11.

kings. The biblical world is felt to be so close to the African world, that biblical realities take on a remarkable immediacy.[67]

The Christology of Afua Kuma's hymns demonstrated to Bediako "an African response to Jesus"[68] that is authentic and grounded in African spiritualties. Encounters like Afua Kuma where everyday Africans encounter God in Jesus Christ from within their traditional cultures and frameworks are for Bediako, "the only valid basis for a tradition of academic theology."[69]

In spite of Bediako's insistence on universality in theological reflection, he believed that the starting point for academic theology is "spontaneous or grassroots theology."[70] Focusing on grassroots theologies prevents academic theology from becoming "detached from the community of faith . . . [as an insular] conversation . . . among the guild of scholars."[71] Thus academic theologians are not under any burden to construct a theology, but rather "academic theology has the important role of understanding, clarifying and demonstrating the *universal* and *academic* significance of the grassroots theology in the interest of the wider missionary task of encountering the world with the Gospel."[72]

Rethinking Theological Education

Theology needs to be different in Africa than in Europe, and theological education needs to be different as well. Bediako wrote, "we have to courageously embrace the challenge of a revision of theological education itself and be open to working toward new and appropriate methodologies of formation, study and research, away from the intellectual baggage that Enlightenment categories have imposed."[73] Specifically when considering biblical studies, "the historical-critical method of exegesis, a legacy of Enlightenment methodology, which belongs to just a segment of Western intellectual history," needs to be given up because it is a product of Western hegemony, not a model passed down from "the Old Testament prophets, nor our Lord Jesus, nor his apostles."[74]

---

67. Bediako, 14–15.
68. Bediako, 15.
69. Bediako, 16.
70. Bediako, 17.
71. Bediako, 17–18.
72. Bediako, 18, emphasis original.
73. Bediako, "In the Bible," 46.
74. Bediako, 46.

Instead, the Scriptures need to be read in light of the "sacred lore and heritage, indigenous to the southern continents where the majority of the Christians now are," so that Christians may be freed "from this persisting Western hegemony and liberate the living Word of God for our time, so that our theology can declare God's authoritative truth to our communities."[75] It is not sufficient to only translate the words of the Scriptures into local vernacular languages. The exegetical methods that are used and taught must be revised as well according to contextual concerns.

Biblical studies are not alone in being singled out for revision in contemporary theological education. Church history, according to Bediako, could benefit from other "cultural traditions of historiography, in which the past is seen as not dead, but living and relevant for the present and with implications for the future."[76] Such an approach where continuity between the past and the present is emphasized, "can liberate Church History into what it really is – Christian history – the unfolding history of the impact of the living God and his Christ through the gospel upon the world."[77] As Christian theology was remade via African Christian thought, a tension emerged between the remaking of academic theology and the impact (or lack thereof) on everyday Africans. Even as academic theology in Africa has changed over the last decades, the message that is preached in rural Africa and urban slums and townships retains the clear imprint of colonial categories as well as contemporary Western influences, including the prosperity gospel. With a majority of African preachers possessing no theological education, non-academic methods of theological education are required to change the theological (and political) landscape in Africa. By simultaneously appealing to pre-Christendom theological understandings and postmissionary expressions of Christianity, African Christian thought and lived African Christianities can lead the way toward the remaking of Christian theology away from Western-centric norms and toward vernacular Christian understandings.

Further Reading of Kwame Bediako

"Conclusion: The Emergence of World Christianity and the Remaking of Theology." In *Understanding World Christianity: The Vision and Work of Andrew F. Walls*,

---

75. Bediako, 46.
76. Bediako, 46.
77. Bediako, 46.

edited by William R. Burrows, Mark R. Gornik, and Janice A. McLean, 243–56. Maryknoll, NY: Orbis, 2011.

"Cry Jesus! Christian Theology and Presence in Modern Africa," chapter 1, 3–19. In *Jesus and the Gospel in Africa*. Maryknoll, NY: Orbis Books, 2004.

"'In the Bible . . . Africa Walks on Familiar Ground': Why the World Needs Africa." *AICMAR* 6 (2007): 32–50.

"A New Era in Christian History – African Christianity as Representative Christianity: Some Implications for Theological Education and Scholarship." *Journal of African Christian Thought* 9, no. 1 (2006): 3–12.

"The Place of Africa in a Changing World: The Christian Factor," chapter 14, 252–67. In *Christianity in Africa: The Renewal of a Non-Western Religion*. Edinburgh: Edinburgh University Press, 1995.

"'Whose Religion Is Christianity?': Reflections on Opportunities and Challenges in Christian Theological Scholarship: The African Dimension." In *Mission in the Twenty-First Century*, 107–17, notes 210–13. London: Darton, Longman & Todd; Maryknoll, NY: Orbis, 2008. Published previously in *Journal of African Christian Thought* 9, no. 2 (2006): 43–48.

7

Politics

A Theology of "Nondominating Power"

Though Bediako's theology has been described as more gospel and culture than gospel and justice, politically he wrote quite a bit about democracy, liberation, and how to live in a religiously pluralistic society.[1] Bediako and his defenders claim that Bediako was very interested in politics and that his theological convictions had significant political implications. Meanwhile, Bediako was criticized for a perceived lack of meaningful engagement in the everyday realities of the masses. His critics believe that his thought is too academic, too aloof, even too Western, with little impact on the lives of the common people. In some of Bediako's late writings, he discusses the dangers of health-and-wealth prosperity preachers to people's lives. He also began to address the trend of parishioners leaving traditional mission churches, such as Presbyterian, Anglican, and Methodist, in favor of deliverance services where pastors cast out demons and offered prayers for healing and economic provision. Though few would characterize Bediako's theology as liberationist, his fondness for liberation theology demonstrated his desire for theology to reach all people.

Bediako's approach to theology, particularly the political implications of his theology, are mainly focused on educated elites. In this sense, he had a trickle-down approach to political theology: if theologians thought and wrote the right things and churches taught and lived out their theological ideas, then the masses would flourish. Advocates of more bottom-up strategies –

---

1. Dedji, *Reconstruction and Renewal*, 209.

in both political organizing and theological reflection – questioned both the wisdom and effectiveness of Bediako's approach. At the very least, Bediako's political inclinations have been under explored.[2] Politically, Bediako most often addressed Christendom and religious pluralism, including the concomitant problems of both African traditional religions and Islam in Africa. His more focused political proposal was a desacralization of politics leading to democracy that was sharply criticized for neglecting the lived realities of the poor and of local churches.

Religious Pluralism

For Bediako, the lived experiences of African Christians point the way for the global church to exist in a post-Christendom, religiously pluralistic world. Bediako's central contention is that the setting of Christianity in Africa has always been religiously pluralistic.[3] From the beginning "in modern Africa, the Christian churches have had to learn to evangelize, grow and affirm that Jesus Christ is Lord in the midst of other religious options, notably the pervasive spiritualities of both the indigenous primal religions and their world-views, and Islam."[4] Bediako distinguished between the context of religious pluralism and the theological agenda of a Christian identity. He wrote, for "modern African theologians, religious pluralism is their *experience*; Christian identity is the *issue*."[5] The correlation for Bediako is clear: since African theologians live in religiously pluralistic societies, they have chosen to focus on Christian identity as a key theological principle for themselves individually and for their fellow Christians. These learnings from Africa can be instructive for the wider world and for the future of Christianity.

---

2. See Fretheim, *Kwame Bediako and African Christian Scholarship*, 103–8: "Bediako's political convictions and involvements remain under-explored, with theological scholarship failing almost entirely to consider these broader influences and thereby missing important aspects of his scholarship." Fretheim, 104.

3. Bediako states, "Long before pluralism – religious as well as cultural – became a subject of serious discussion in the Western world, many of the Christian communities of Africa had been living, witnessing and learning to survive and grow in the context of religious pluralism." Bediako, *Theology and Identity*, 433.

4. Bediako, "Christianity, Islam, and the Kingdom of God," 3.

5. Bediako, *Christianity in Africa*, 257, emphasis original. Bediako understood early Hellenistic Christian theologians to have had identical experience and issue. See also Bediako, *Theology and Identity*, esp. Introduction. For more on Bediako's understanding of the Hellenistic parallels, see Bediako, "Religion and National Identity," 3.

For many theologians from Europe and North America, their societal contexts are no longer homogeneously Christian but are increasingly pluralistic. This recent development in the West has been normal in Africa for centuries. For Bediako, "the 'normal' African (as other non-Western) experience of religious pluralism as the framework for Christian affirmation, means that 'Christian uniqueness' or distinctiveness need not be lost in the midst of pluralism."[6] Western Christians seeking to articulate the Christian faith in increasingly religiously pluralistic societies can learn from Africans who have never understood Christianity as a religious monopoly. Bediako understood the Christian faith in Africa to have preserved its uniqueness and grown exponentially while not seeking religious hegemony.

For Bediako, "a Christian theology of religious pluralism becomes an exercise in spirituality, in which one affirms a commitment to the ultimacy of Christ, whilst accepting the integrity of other faiths and those who profess them."[7] He understood a Christian theology of religious pluralism to entail dual, simultaneous affirmations: the uniqueness of Jesus Christ and the integrity of other faiths. These affirmations are to be maintained "in Christ-like humility and vulnerability."[8] Since virtually all twenty-first century Christians around the world live in societies with people of other religious faiths or of none, a Christian theology of religious pluralism is a necessity.[9] Bediako saw that Africa has much to contribute to the development of a theology of religious pluralism while "the modern West has less to offer than may be readily recognized, unless it be the lessons from the disaster that was Christendom."[10]

One of the legacies of Christendom in Europe and North America is an inability to clearly articulate Christian identity in post-Christian societies. Reflection on Christian identity experienced theological atrophy without regular challenge or exercise as everyone was assumed to be a Christian already.[11] One implication noted by Bediako is that "the tradition of biblical exegesis established in the West may be limited in its capacity to unearth the dynamics of religious engagement implicit in the biblical records."[12] While

---

6. Bediako, "Significance of Modern African Christianity," 62.

7. Kwame Bediako, "The Unique Christ in the Plurality of Religions," in *The Unique Christ in Our Pluralist World*, ed. Bruce Nichols (Grand Rapids: Baker, 1994), 55.

8. Bediako, "The Unique Christ," 55. See also Bediako, "Christianity, Islam, and the Kingdom of God," 6.

9. Bediako, "Africa and Christianity on the Threshold," 316.

10. Bediako, 316.

11. Bediako, "Biblical Exegesis in the African Context," 19.

12. Bediako, 19.

increasing religious pluralism is causing confusion among many Christians in the West, for African Christians, "pluralism is primarily a lived experience."[13] Further, Bediako contends, "Christian theology has not had the option, generally speaking, of establishing its categories in isolation, as though in a Christendom in which all possible religious alternatives are presumed to be non-existent, or in a secularized environment in which specifically religious claims are held to be no longer decisive."[14]

Africans have been and continue to constantly wrestle with the claims of primal religions and Islam. Bediako's working hypothesis is that "most discussions of inter-religious encounter continue to ignore the primal religions, possibly because they were for so long regarded as 'primitive' with little or nothing to contribute."[15] However in Bediako's view, the encounter with primal religions may hold significant insights for interreligious dialogue.[16] His view is based on his understanding that primal "religions constitute the religious background of the majority of Christians everywhere so far in Christian history, they provide in fact the most favourable environment for learning from the actual accumulated Christian experience of inter-religious encounter."[17]

For millennia, from the Greco-Roman period to contemporary sub-Saharan Africa, Christians have been engaging the beliefs and practices of primal religions. Yet the insights gained from this long history of religious encounters have been mostly neglected by Western European theologians. The result of "this protracted neglect . . . is that Christianity gets locked into a Western Enlightenment framework, with a resulting tendency to reduce inter-religious dialogue to the categories of 'the West and the rest,' or else, of 'West and East.'"[18] These binaries hinder thoughtful dialogue. However in modern Africa, "religious pluralism will not lie outside of theological existence; instead it will have its impact on how Christian distinctiveness itself comes to be defined."[19] Increasingly in Europe and North America, non-Christians are defining what it means for others to be a Christian, rather than the Christian faith defining Christian identity of its own terms.

---

13. Bediako, 20.

14. Bediako, 20.

15. Bediako, "A Half Century of African Christian Thought," 9.

16. See Bediako's claim that the primal imagination cannot be ignored when discussing interreligious dialogue in Bediako, "Biblical Exegesis in the African Context," 20.

17. Bediako, "A Half Century of African Christian Thought," 9.

18. Bediako, 9.

19. Bediako, 10.

The whole approach to religious pluralism and interreligious dialogue in oppositional terms of "us vs. them" in the West is quite different from an African and other non-Western framing. The active presence of non-Christian neighbors, and a deeper attentiveness to the primal imagination, offer many non-Western Christians a more generous and open approach to non-Christians. Bediako believes that this long history of Christian engagement with primal religions also leads to better engagement with Islam. "For it is in Africa," wrote Bediako, "that Christianity and Islam meet each other on something approaching equal footing, and where each has been shaped, to varying degrees, by the primal religions and by the primal imagination."[20]

Islam

Bediako's view of Islam parallels his understanding of African traditional religions. He wrote of his belief that African Christianity "may have a special responsibility in relation to Islam . . . to demonstrate and point to the redemptive paradigm of Christ for all peoples and all religions."[21] Bediako considered both Christianity and Islam to be indigenous African religions and stressed "the capacity of both religious faiths to demonstrate a genuine common humanity."[22] Both Christianity and Islam have positive and negative legacies in Africa. Bediako refers to both as "missionary faiths" where "Africans have won other Africans" for their faith.[23] For Bediako, only Jesus Christ can fully answer human longings. He asked, "Will African Christianity, in its African idioms, be able to present Christ as the fulfillment also of the spiritual quests of African Islam?"[24] Like African traditional religions, for Bediako, Islam is not complete without understanding Jesus Christ as Lord and Savior.

Bediako's evangelical Christocentrism shines through in his engagement with Islam. He claims that "the Christian model for living in a multi-religious world is Jesus Christ himself, crucified and risen, that we can have hope that the truth as revealed in Christ will eventually triumph, not to the destruction of those who hold different views from us, but rather to their salvation."[25] Jesus alone is "the pattern of true humanity." Bediako couched his views with an

---

20. Bediako, "A Half Century of African Christian Thought," 10.
21. Bediako, "Christianity, Islam, and the Kingdom of God," 7.
22. Bediako, 5.
23. Bediako, 3, 4.
24. Bediako, 7.
25. Bediako, 6.

appeal for "humility" and "vulnerability" and acknowledged that the religion of Christianity is flawed, as only Christ himself is the one who saves.[26]

Certainly though Bediako believed that there is no salvation outside of Jesus Christ, Islam is an important and significant African religion. For him, African traditional religions and Islam are both completed or fulfilled in Jesus Christ; without Christ as Lord and Savior, neither religion offers a complete understanding of the truth or of salvation. Bediako wrote, "African theology will have to learn to engage with Islam in ways that do justice to the latter's religious and spiritual depth, while at the same time, developing an apologetic that arises from its own best insights that it is not Christianity."[27] While African traditional religions function as preparation for evangelical Christianity and form the substructure of the Christian faith, Islam is best understood as a rival understanding of divine activity in the world.

As a result, Bediako advocated for Christian mission to and dialogue with Islam.[28] Such dialogue will be strengthened, according to Bediako, if Christians are better prepared and equipped through a greater understanding of primal religions, "to engage more meaningfully and more fruitfully with Islam."[29] Bediako's goal was for Muslims to become Christians, and he believed that a deeper engagement with primal religions might help Christians to better understand and therefore better evangelize their neighbors.

Desacralization of Politics

Bediako understood the political implications of his Christology when he wrote, "A Christology which alters so radically the nature and source of power carries, inevitably, immense implications for politics in our societies."[30] Bediako's ancestor Christology places Jesus Christ as the sole ancestor in African, particularly Akan, societies. This exaltation of Jesus Christ relativizes all other ancestors. For Bediako, the ancestors are a myth and thus have mythical power within society, but not real power. The clear and immediate effect of a "Christology which fundamentally undermines and removes the power of the ancestors over the living" is that it "desacralizes the power of the

---

26. Bediako, 6.

27. Bediako, "A Half Century of African Christian Thought," 10.

28. Kwame Bediako, "Foreword," in John Azumah, *My Neighbor's Faith: Islam Explained for African Christians* (Grand Rapids: Zondervan, 2008), x.

29. Bediako, "African Theology as Challenge," 64.

30. Bediako, "Biblical Christologies," 108.

reigning Chief or King."[31] In traditional Akan cosmology, the ancestors not only sacralize the office of the ruler, but indeed the whole realm of politics becomes sacralized with "no sharp dichotomy between 'secular' and 'sacred' realms of existence."[32]

Bediako saw the growth of the Christian faith in Africa as related to the movement in postcolonial Africa toward modern nation-states. He understood the "Biblical faith [to have] been a desacralising force in the world."[33] Thus if "in the field of politics, a sufficient level of desacralisation was achieved in people's attitudes, it may well explain, at least in part, the fact that in the new independent republics, there was no overt return to the 'ontocratic' pattern of the traditional state."[34] Bediako saw a positive role for Christianity in the political history of twentieth-century Africa. In his view, the Christian faith had expanded "the intellectual understandings of Africans" which in turn "enhanced a new African self-understanding and self-appreciation beyond the immediate traditional circles of kinship and lineage, and so paved the way for the modern expressions of African nationalism which finally challenged and overturned Western rule."[35] In this way the Christian faith, particularly through colonial missionary education, aided Africans in repelling Western colonial rule and influence. Christianity could be of service in the political realm. Bediako cited prominent examples such as the role of the Christian church in "the struggle for democratic pluralism and open government" in Kenya, "against the curtailing of human rights in Ghana," and "against the white ontocracy of apartheid" in South Africa.[36]

Though helpful politically, Christians are never to forget the primary, spiritual calling of their faith. Even amid Bediako's call for African political structures to be desacralized, he still wholeheartedly believed in the spiritual underpinnings of African societies. He states, "if Christianity desacralises, it does not de-spiritualise. The African world continues [sic] a spiritual world; what changes is the configuration of forces. The human environment remains

---

31. Bediako, 108.

32. Bediako, *Christianity in Africa*, 241.

33. Bediako, *Christianity in Africa*, 181. See also 243: "Christianity has been a desacralizing force in world history."

34. Bediako, 181. Bediako uses "ontocratic" to describe the flawed structuring of human society based on human biological traits, such as apartheid in South Africa or much European colonial rule in Africa.

35. Bediako, 234.

36. Bediako, 248.

the same, but the answers to its puzzles are different."[37] Thus all of life – physical, economic, political – is spiritual. Theology matters, and all of Bediako's politics are inherently theological. He always argued for the importance of Africa in *theological* discussions and for contemporary thought.

Thus Bediako was not unaware of the role of power in the world, but instead he sought to define power christologically, not temporally. He describes his understanding as follows: "Without such a conception of power as Jesus held, taught, and demonstrated by the Cross, the hope of achieving a real sharing of political power in any society will remain elusive."[38] The power that Bediako describes differs from how power had been understood by either traditional African societies or colonizing countries. For him, "Jesus' way of dealing with political power represents the perfect sacralization of all worldly power."[39] Jesus Christ is the only source of true power. All human power is from God in Christ. All authority "belongs to and derives from the transcendent realm . . . Authority truly belongs only to God."[40] Bediako held an intense skepticism toward politicians and world power. He wrote, "Politicians who presume to hold power in the world may claim events as vindicating their policies. And yet, from the standpoint of the Gospel, there is no doubt where the deeper insight lies. There is probably no more palpable demonstration that the Christianity of Jesus is indeed the religion of the poor of the earth."[41] Worldly power is not the same as the power of the gospel.

Authority does not reside with the sacral ruler, the sacral king, or even the human spirits of the ancestors. Instead "the Cross desacralises *all* the powers, institutions and structures that rule human existence and history – family, nation, social class, race, law, politics, economy, religion, culture, tradition, custom, ancestors – stripping them all of any pretensions to ultimacy."[42] Bediako turns to Jesus Christ to understand and describe what power is:

> Jesus' way was one of engagement and involvement through a new
> way of overcoming, arising from a unique concept of power – the
> power of forgiveness over retaliation, of suffering over violence, of
> love over hostility, of humble service over domination. Jesus won

---

37. Bediako, "Christ in Africa: Some Reflections," 456; cited in Bediako, *Christianity in Africa*, 246.

38. Bediako, "Jesus in African Culture," 29.

39. Bediako, *Christianity in Africa*, 247.

40. Bediako, 244.

41. Bediako, 148.

42. Bediako, 245.

his way to preeminence and glory, not by exalting himself, but by humbling himself, to the point of dying a shameful death. In other words, his conception of power was that of nondominating power.[43]

Nondominating power is the opposite of Christendom power. Bediako sought to envision how Jesus's "unique concept of power" could and should impact how Christians live and seek to act within society. For Christians, authority and the power that comes with it arises by following Jesus's way of forgiveness, suffering, love, and humility.

Ironically for Bediako, Jesus's way makes power less holy, not more holy. He wrote that it is "through an African reading of the Scriptures, particularly in African languages, and by paying attention to the resonances of the Biblical categories into the African primal world-view, that the desacralising impact of the Gospel is experienced afresh."[44] The close interconnection between the spiritual and the earthly, including the political, in African cosmology creates an easy route for sacralizing power.

"In many countries of Africa," wrote Bediako, "pre-colonial political systems tended toward ontocracy, as traditional religious and cultural norms were inclined to sacralize power and authority. In that sense, it is possible to trace the traditional religious roots of some of the problems of post-independence political authoritarianism in Africa."[45] The sacralizing of power in African cosmology contributed to the rise of dictators in postcolonial Africa, according to Bediako. Katongole praised the "far reaching political consequences" of Bediako's case for this spiritual process of the desacralization of political power to check "the dictatorial and absolutist claims that seems to be inherent within African politics."[46] By undercutting spiritual, religious, and cultural justifications for absolute monarchies and dictatorships, Bediako believed that "Jesus de-sacralized all worldly power, relativizing its inherent tendency towards absolutization and its pretensions to ultimacy."[47] In this way, the Christian faith prepared the way for democracy in Africa.

---

43. Kwame Bediako, "Unmasking the Powers – Christianity, Authority and Desacralisation in Modern African Politics," in *Christianity and Democracy in Global Context*, ed. John Witte (Boulder: Westview, 1993), 217.

44. Bediako, *Christianity in Africa*, 245.

45. Bediako, "Africa and Christianity on the Threshold," 321.

46. Katongole, *Future for Africa*, 181.

47. Bediako, "Africa and Christianity on the Threshold," 321.

Bediako's political hopes lay in the spread of democracy in Africa. By offering a "Christian theology of power as non-dominating, [that] liberates politicians and rulers to be humans among fellow-humans, and ennobles politics and the business of government into the business of God and the service of God in the service of fellow-humans," Bediako sought to describe "the only genuine and abiding foundation for any serious quest in Africa for a sustainable culture of freedom and justice in a genuine democracy."[48] He was particularly encouraged by "efforts aimed at linking the mainsprings of responsible Christian political action with the political vision of the kingdom of God and the political option of Jesus as recorded in the Gospels" that he observed during Ghana's presidential and parliamentary elections in 2000.[49]

African Christianity and Democracy

Much like his understanding of Christianity, Bediako did not believe that democracy is indigenous to the West. In his view, democracy emerged from Christian political ideas. And Christianity, after all, is a non-Western religion, an indigenous African religion. Therefore, Christianity led to political freedom for Africans.

In Bediako's view, it is possible "to recognize the achievement of African churches in the democratization of Africa in the 1980s and 1990s as a genuinely religious achievement, linked with 'the mind of Jesus' in the African churches."[50] True democracy requires nondominating power: "without such a conception of power as Jesus held, taught and demonstrated by the Cross, the hope for a sustained democratic culture in modern African politics could prove elusive."[51] In large part, Bediako was interested in power because of his belief that the "struggle for African democracy must address . . . African concepts of authority and power."[52] The life of a Christian is inherently political. Due to the interconnection between the spiritual and the material, human beliefs affect human actions and human societies. As Bediako wrote, "For Christians

---

48. Bediako, "Unmasking the Powers," 221.

49. Kwame Bediako, "Christian Witness in the Public Sphere: Some Lessons and Residual Challenges from the Recent Political History of Ghana," in *The Changing Face of Christianity: Africa, the West, and the World*, ed. Lamin Sanneh and Joel A. Carpenter (New York: Oxford University Press, 2005), 124.

50. Bediako, "Africa and Christianity on the Threshold," 321.

51. Bediako, 321–22.

52. Bediako, "Unmasking the Powers," 211.

to not only believe in Jesus, but also imitate Jesus, is to be engaged in 'power-encounter.'"[53]

Bediako is clear both about the limitations of democracy and the possible contributions of Christianity to more democratic societies. For Bediako, democracy is not the goal: "As the end of human existence is the Biblical vision of *shalom* in the Kingdom of God, the arrival of democracy is not the coming of the Kingdom."[54] Indeed, democracy is not the kingdom of God, but Christianity can help to aid African societies. Bediako wrote: "It is evident that if African politics in the future is to manifest greater tolerance of dissent and to accept a wider pluralism, that is, to exhibit some of the cardinal assumptions of true democratic culture, then African societies are going to need to put in place new conceptions of political authority and power. In this, Christianity in Africa may have a unique role."[55] Bediako viewed Christianity's political role within Africa as essential for African societies. Though this role is perhaps more subtle than the prophetic and confrontational role of theologians in South Africa and elsewhere, Bediako did not want to minimize the importance of the church and Christianity. In fact, Bediako resented what he saw as a false dichotomy between the political, "black" theology of South Africa and the cultural, "African" theology of the rest of the continent.[56]

Black Theology vs. African Theology

For Bediako, black theology and African theology "are mutually engaged in a 'theology of reconstruction' to address the complex realities of African existence."[57] He understood black theology to be a theology of liberation that was birthed in response to the particular circumstances of inequality and oppression in South Africa. He understood so-called African theology as "the theological exploration into the indigenous cultures of African peoples, with particular stress on their pre-Christian (and also pre-Islamic) religious traditions."[58] Bediako's claim is that political independence in Africa south of the Sahara desert and north of the Limpopo river "took away a direct experience of the socio-political pressures" felt in South Africa, and instead

---

53. Bediako, 229.
54. Bediako, *Christianity in Africa*, 249; emphasis original.
55. Bediako, "Unmasking the Powers," 215.
56. Bediako, "Africa and Christianity on the Threshold," 312.
57. Bediako, 312.
58. Bediako, "Understanding African Theology," 49.

"the broad aim was to achieve integration between the African pre-Christian religious experience and African Christian commitment in ways that would ensure the integrity of African Christian identity and selfhood."[59] He agreed with Desmond Tutu's assessment that black theology and African theology are not mutually exclusive but rather that black theology fits within the wider and broader category of African theology.[60]

Many, but not all, of the harshest critics of Bediako's politics are South African theologians who either espouse black theology or are very familiar with it. Tinyiko Maluleke identifies in Bediako's thought an "unease with the agenda of political liberation"[61] and believed that Bediako's optimism blinded him from seeing the challenges that Africans face. Anthony Balcomb notes the "serious omission" in Bediako's theology of any evidence that he was "seriously struggling . . . with issues of economics in Africa."[62] Maluleke expanded that analysis to include the church as well: "In his fascination with African Christianity as a surprise story, Bediako seems to gloss over the many tremendous problems within and between African churches."[63] Taking his criticism further, Maluleke observes in Bediako, "an astonishing disinterest in the kinds of 'political' issues raised by such African women theologians as his own compatriot Mercy Oduyoye."[64] Bediako's omission of the topics of gender and sexuality extended to little discussion about the place of women in African society or the AIDS/HIV epidemic.[65] While Bediako did mention these topics occasionally, he generally seemed to feel that others should address them directly. Isabel Phiri and Sarojini Nadar "lament the absence of dialogue with the concerns of African women theologians in Bediako's work."[66] This absence led them to believe that Bediako "had not read seriously the pioneering

---

59. Bediako, 49.

60. Bediako, 49.

61. Tinyiko Sam Maluleke, "The Rediscovery of the Agency of Africans: An Emerging Paradigm of Post-Cold War and Post-Apartheid Black and African Theology," in *African Theology Today*, ed. Emmanuel Katongole (Scranton, PA: University of Scranton Press, 2002), 157.

62. Anthony Balcomb, "Faith or Suspicion?: Theological Dialogue North and South of the Limpopo with Special Reference to the Theologies of Kwame Bediako and Andrew Walls," *Journal of Theology for Southern Africa* 100 (March 1998): 14.

63. Maluleke, "In Search of," 215.

64. Maluleke, "Rediscovery of the Agency," 157.

65. Ezra Chitando, *Living with Hope: African Churches and HIV/AIDS 1* (Geneva: WCC Publications, 2007), 25.

66. Isabel Apawo Phiri and Sarojini Nadar, "'Going through the Fire with Eyes Wide Open': African Women's Perspectives on Indigenous Knowledge, Patriarchy and Sexuality," *Journal for the Study of Religion* 22, no. 2 (2009): 6.

work of African women theologians who had already begun the process of finding indigenous knowledge to critique patriarchy."[67] Nadar and Phiri critique Bediako for his sins of omission – expecting more from the leading African theologian of his generation.

These critiques open serious questions about the impact of Bediako's theology for everyday Africans. Valentin Dedji of Benin feared that "Bediako's proposed agenda [is] at risk of being too 'traditional' and therefore lacking enough commitment to the fate of millions of Africans for whom the urgent questions are not those of 'Gospel and culture,' but of 'Gospel and justice.'"[68] Balcomb remained deeply concerned that "The issues of justice and equality are not apparent, *per se*, in Bediako's theology."[69] His only conjecture is "that the reason for this is not because Bediako does not see them as important but that they are normally associated with humanist (*qua* Enlightenment) thinking."[70] While Balcomb's reasoning might explain why Bediako avoided humanist terminology, his lack of engagement with Oduyoye's work or that of other female theologians, including the Circle of Concerned African Women, is troubling. Bediako's writings demonstrated little concern for the contributions of woman theologians, aside from Madam Afua Kuma, or for so-called women's concerns including "such mundane concerns of how Christians draw water, plant cabbages, dig pit latrines, raise babies, educate children, etc."[71] For Katongole, these concrete issues must be addressed by the local churches. To address these concrete issues, he wrote, "the notion and reality of the church has to be central to the theological project."[72] However, Bediako's "descriptions of the challenges facing African Christians are lacking to the extent that the nature and reality of the church is obscured."[73] Without reflection on the church, these concrete challenges will not be addressed by African Christianity.

Katongole believes that "Bediako's work provides a very good case study of this failure [to theologically engage the church in Africa]. But in order to understand how he concretely fails to face this challenge and even

---

67. Phiri and Nadar, "Going through the Fire," 7.

68. Dedji, *Reconstruction and Renewal*, 209.

69. Anthony O. Balcomb, "Narrative, Epistemological Crisis and Reconstruction – My Story with Special Reference to the Work of Kwame Bediako," *Scriptura* 97 (2008): 58, emphasis original.

70. Balcomb, "Narrative, Epistemological Crisis and Reconstruction," *Scriptura* 97 (2008): 58.

71. Katongole, *Future for Africa*, 156.

72. Katongole, 156.

73. Katongole, xvii.

avoids it, we need to look at the narrative through which Bediako reads the prospects of African Christianity."[74] As a result of Bediako's seeming lack of interest in mundane concerns or in the "rough and messy ground of tensions, contradictions, and challenges facing African Christians in their concrete existence . . . [poverty, AIDS, political dictatorship, etc.] in his narrative of Christianity in Africa,"[75] Katongole believes that Bediako possessed "a disembodied notion of African Christian identity."[76]

Contrary to many of the criticisms expressed above, Bediako stressed the importance and relevance of contextualizing: "Reading the Bible in the Two-Thirds World context of poverty, powerlessness and religious pluralism is probably the single most important characteristic of this new theology."[77] By "appropriating the Scriptures and the Gospel in context," this new theology acquires fresh insights including "the discovery that the Gospel is good news to . . . the materially poor, socially oppressed and underprivileged."[78] This contextual reading of Scripture among and with the poorest of the poor joins with other strands of liberation theology as a fundamental challenge to the status quo of much Western theology, mission, and ecclesiology.

Bediako saw liberation theology as *the new method* of theological reflection based on the "southward shift of the Church." For their theological expression to be authentic, theologians in and from the developing world must work toward economic and political liberation.[79] Bediako explicitly noted the call for theology to be liberatory based on the needs of the African context: "In the Third World reality of poverty, powerlessness and religious pluralism, such a commitment ties theological activity inextricably into the service of liberation."[80] Bediako's emphasis on grassroots theologies demonstrates his inclination toward doing theology from below, an affinity that he shared with liberation theology.

---

74. Katongole, 156.

75. Katongole, 159.

76. Katongole, 156.

77. Bediako, *Christianity in Africa*, 144.

78. Bediako, 144.

79. Bediako, 163.

80. Bediako, 160.

Conclusion

Bediako's understanding of politics was criticized by a pair of Nigerian theologians who believed that his emphasis on African history and identity neglected a sufficient engagement with the historical church. Roman Catholic theologian Paulinus Ikechukwu Odozor stated that Bediako's "commitment to an evangelical form of Christianity . . . seems to show very little regard for the reality of the church after Augustine."[81] Matthew Michael agreed, writing this "flaw reveals a notable lacunae in the thought of Bediako which fails to knit together his several theological reflections into a coherent Christian identity that refuses to be trapped in the pre-Christian past but opens its doors to the possibilities of the future world in shaping the missions identity of the African church."[82] Bediako might agree with these critics that he underemphasizes the history of the Western church in his theology. Yet, this omission is not an oversight. Instead of a criticism, he might consider their comments to be compliments. Bediako sought an understanding of the church and of politics that was distinctively African – and not indebted to Europe or the United States. Politics did not need to rely on the sacredness of African traditional religions, nor define itself over and against the West. Bediako's political vision mirrored his theological vision: authentic African politics based on African values and informed by African Christian thought. African Christian churches are called to use their power not to dominate (as the colonial powers did) but to serve. Through service, African Christians and African churches can work toward the flourishing of all Africans and all people.

Further Reading of Kwame Bediako

"Africa and Christianity on the Threshold of the Third Millennium: The Religious Dimension." *African Affairs* 99 (2000): 303–23.

"Christianity, Islam, and the Kingdom of God: Rethinking Their Relationship from an African Perspective." *Journal of African Christian Thought* 7, no. 2 (2004): 3–7.

"Christian Religion and African Social Norms: Authority, Desacralization, and Democracy," chapter 13, 234–51. In *Christianity in Africa: The Renewal of a Non-Western Religion*. Edinburgh: Edinburgh University Press, 1995.

---

81. Paulinus Ikechukwu Odozor, *Morality Truly Christian, Truly African: Foundational, Methodological, and Theological Considerations* (South Bend, IN: University of Notre Dame Press, 2014), 23.

82. Matthew Michael, "African Theology and the Paradox of Missions: Three Intellectual Responses to the Modern Missions Crisis of the African Church," *Transformation: An International Journal of Holistic Mission Studies* 31, no. 2 (2014): 86.

"Christian Witness in the Public Sphere: Some Lessons and Residual Challenges from the Recent Political History of Ghana." In *The Changing Face of Christianity: Africa, the West, and the World*, edited by Lamin Sanneh and Joel A. Carpenter, 117–32. New York: Oxford University Press, 2005.

"How Is Jesus Christ Lord?: Evangelical Christian Apologetics amid African Religious Pluralism," chapter 3, 34–45. In *Jesus and the Gospel in Africa*. Maryknoll, NY: Orbis, 2004.

"Unmasking the Powers – Christianity, Authority and Desacralisation in Modern African Politics." In *Christianity and Democracy in Global Context*, edited by John Witte, 207–30. Boulder, CO: Westview, 1993.

Conclusion

Challenges to Western and African Theologies

In 2007, in his last public lecture, Bediako asked and then answered the question: "What, then, might the 'remaking' of theology involve in an era of post-Western World Christianity?"[1] Bediako noted how the massive growth of Christianity in the global South has changed the Christian world. This recognition of the shift in the center of gravity presented an opportunity within world Christianity.

All encounters with new cultures produce new theological insights. As the Christian church in the Africa of the late twentieth century resulted from the colonial missionary encounter between the gospel of Jesus Christ and traditional African cultures in the nineteenth and early twentieth centuries, new insights about Jesus Christ also emerged. Bediako challenged Western theologians to articulate why they should read and take seriously an African theologian. He wrote, "Christian history shows that as Christian faith engages with new cultures, new insights about Jesus Christ also emerge."[2] These insights have been incorporated into African Christian thought.

The gospel and culture encounter in Africa resulted in new insights about Jesus Christ, and Christians in Europe and North America can learn these new insights from Africans. For Bediako, Africa matters theologically because Christianity matters historically and in the present, in part, because Africa is massively Christian.[3] Africans may be like young people in a local congregation, if the churches of Africa are considered as younger than churches in Europe. The African churches are not to be understood as merely the *future* of the church, but they *are* the church *now*. Just as older generations can learn by listening to the youth among them, Western Christians must sit at the feet

---

1. Bediako, "Conclusion: The Emergence of World Christianity," 251.
2. Bediako, "Christianity, Islam and the Kingdom of God," 6.
3. See especially Bediako, "Africa and Christianity on the Threshold."

of Christians from the developing world, particularly from Africa, to learn about the Christian faith. In the learning, theological assumptions and beliefs will be remade in the process.

Western theology has been defined and shaped by a European understanding of race. This understanding has centered whiteness and defined all nonwhite peoples and their belief systems as "other" and lesser. Part of the path of growth for white Christians is to (re-)discover the insights of non-Western theologians such as Bediako. Immersing oneself within another's theological thought challenges stereotypes, broadens understandings, and opens up new understandings of who God is and of God's work in the world.

Bediako is clear in his early writings that "western Christians are called upon to engage in self-criticism and a critical scrutiny of their own cultures in the light of the Word of God. The fact is that none of us can read the Scriptures without cultural blinkers of some sort."[4] More broadly, Bediako's insight can be seen in how different "types" of theology are named. There are womanist theologies, Latinx theologies, and indigenous theologies, just to name a few; yet when the terms "theology" or "Christian theology" are used without any other modifiers, the implication is often that one is talking about Western theology. The further implication is that this unmodified theology attempts to be without context, or perhaps is a pure theology that dropped fully formed from the sky. It is "simply imaginary" to claim that there is "a pure Gospel devoid of cultural embodiment,"[5] yet many who hold Western theological views behave as if they are in an echo chamber, unable to hear other voices, simply repeating the same things over and over again.

Bediako's self-appointed task was to name the cultural blinkers that Westerners (and Africans like Byang Kato who wholly embrace Western theologies) unconsciously wear. His understanding of the remaking of Christian theology contained the need to unlearn harmful habits and behaviors while also constructing a way forward. His Christian thought explicitly rejects the claims and assumptions of Christendom. In his book *Theology and Identity*, Bediako jumps from the end of the fourth century to the middle of the twentieth century because he disdained the corrupting impact of yoking political power and the Christian faith upon Christian theology. He saw little value in Western theology, for in the words of his widow, "Western theology is

---

4. Bediako, "[Response to] David Hesselgrave," 13.
5. Bediako, "Willowbank Consultation," 28.

Western theology."[6] Theology in the West has been corrupted by Christendom and the Enlightenment and left hollow.

All told, Bediako was convinced that Western Christianity is not faithful to the gospel, but is actually a projection of Western culture. For him, the West has traded the good news of the gospel for a poor substitute. Instead of being founded on the unchanging gospel of Jesus Christ, Western churches have placed their confidence in the shifting sands of culture. At first, that culture was territorial Christianity or Christendom. Then Western theology was given over to Enlightenment rationalism. Historically, Bediako saw a tremendous amount of Western attention devoted to combating syncretism in churches and theologies of the developing world, but "an insufficient alertness to similar phenomena threatening the churches of the West."[7] Bediako's view of Western theology is that it is syncretistic with Western culture and distorts the gospel. Therefore translating this distorted gospel is not enough for churches in the global South. These churches must go further. African churches must seek alternative sources to shape an African Christian identity. For Bediako, the gospel of Jesus Christ does not change, but its cultural form must change as the gospel is translated from one culture to the next. Bediako believed these sources already reside within the heritage of African religions, especially through a recovery of the primal imagination.

Bediako constructed his theology on a non-Western, post-Christendom foundation.[8] Bediako sought to use the African past for the sake of African Christian thought in the present in his theology of négritude.[9] This act of retrieval, *sankofa* for the Akan, kept his focus firmly facing forward while reaching back for insights and building blocks that he found useful. Western Christians cannot blindly adopt Bediako's theology, but aspects of his theological method may be embraced and imitated. Bediako employed a christological lens to interpret biblical texts in order to address questions being asked in his context. For many white Western Christians, theology has come in one of two ways: either handed down from European ancestors who reconceived religion and religious institutions following the Reformations and counter-Reformations of the sixteenth century, or through cultural osmosis

---

6. Gillian Mary Bediako, personal interview, 1 June 2012, Akrofi-Christaller Institute, Akropong-Akuapem, Ghana.

7. Bediako, "Willowbank Consultation," 26.

8. The psychoanalyst Maurice Apprey, a friend of Bediako's at the Mfantsipim school, referred to him as an original, or "autochthonous thinker." Personal interview, 5 November 2012, Charlottesville, VA.

9. Hartman, "Act of Theological Négritude."

as part of Western cultures that have been assumed to be Christian. The latter method – theology received through cultural osmosis – is primarily passive, and people seek to make it contemporary by reacting to current questions by looking within themselves and the culture. The former method – theology received by tradition – remains primarily focused on the questions asked by the European reformations: questions about sin, atonement, salvation, and redemption. Offering sixteenth century answers to twenty-first century questions leads to a disconnect between theological doctrine and everyday life and to theologies that are not contextual.[10]

Bediako offered clear critiques and challenges for Western Christians. From the impact of Christendom, to an over intellectualizing of Christian thought in the Protestant Reformation, to failing to resist Enlightenment ideals, to the horrors of colonization, to an unqualified embrace of capitalism, Western (colonial) Christianity is fatally flawed. On the other hand, Bediako believed that African theology is characteristic and representative of the twenty-first century.[11] The gift of African Christian thought to the rest of the world is the possibility of a Christianity that is not infected by the ills of racism, whiteness, and privilege that afflict Western theologies. By no means have Africans, or Bediako himself, understood the Bible or Christian theology perfectly. However, Bediako sought to offer a different narrative, an African one, to challenge the dominant Western narrative of the Christian faith.

Bediako's Diagnosis of and Prescription for Western Christian Thought

Bediako diagnosed three major problems within the Christianity that emerged from Europe. He also offered a prescription for what ails Western theology and used aspects of African Christian thought to name aspects of Western theology so that Western Christians could emulate African Christians. Some of this "medicine" might be difficult for Western Christians to swallow. Yet in Bediako's perspective, Western theology is terminally ill and requires radical treatment if the Christian faith is to survive, much less flourish in the West.

---

10. For more on how Bediako's theolgy might contribute to the future of theological reflection, see Hartman, *Theology After Colonization*.

11. See Kwame Bediako, "African Theology as a Challenge to Western Theology," in *Christian Identity in Cross-Cultural Perspective*, ed. Martien E. Brinkman and Dirk van Keulen (Meinema: Zoetermeer, 2003), 57.

Syncretistic Western theology has no answer for religious pluralism

For Bediako, Western thinking people are syncretistic in their theology and do not know it. The context of the creation of what came to be called Western theology did not necessitate asking and answering questions of religious diversity. The methods used to evangelize Europe – the conquest and forced conversions of indigenous cultures – led to a prevailing theology of the conquering. The defining characteristic of Western theology became an inherent insistence on a singular point of view.

Bediako's prescription is that Western Christians must acknowledge and name their cultural blinkers in order to begin the process of disambiguating the gospel of Jesus Christ from Western culture. African Christian thought positively has to offer the ability to address contemporary concerns and questions. In Bediako's view, many Western theologians are not asking any questions about, and therefore have no answers for, contemporary issues and topics.[12] Western theology was conceived as the theological challenges of religious pluralism were being vanquished: Christianity had achieved hegemonic power. Thus, these Western theologians have struggled to engage questions of religious pluralism because the very question of religious diversity has been outside of the Western theological framework. Because of this, some Western theologians have no answers for religious pluralism because they do not consider the questions.

Bediako wanted to recover the spiritual dimension of theology so as to provide a confident basis for courageous Christian witness amid religious pluralism. For Bediako, the recession of the church in the West is symptomatic of the sickened condition of Western theological thought. The context of Christianity in the West has changed with the end of territorial Christianity, or Christendom. Western theology emerged from this yoking of Christian faith and political power. For Bediako, this coupling was fatal for the ability of the adherents of Western theology to express the gospel of Jesus Christ and prevents them from adapting to the contemporary challenges of secularization and globalization. Instead of religiously homogeneous societies, as had existed in Europe under Christendom, "Now virtually all Christians the world over live in pluralistic societies, comprising persons of diverse religious faiths or of [no faith]."[13] In response to this changed religious context, according to Bediako, "the modern West has less to offer than may be readily recognized."[14]

---

12. Bediako, "African Theology as a Challenge to Western Theology," 57.

13. Bediako, "Conclusion: The Emergence of World Christianity," 252.

14. Bediako, 252.

This wholesale rejection of Christendom calls for Christianity to be separate from political power and for governments to be treated with distance and a degree of skepticism. Religiously, the rejection of Christendom assumptions allows Christians to expect – not to be surprised by – religious diversities and religious pluralism.

Under Christendom, "Western Christian thought lacked the regular challenge to establish its conceptual categories in relation to alternative religious claims."[15] From Bediako's perspective as an *African* Christian who grew up with Muslims, Christians, and practitioners of traditional African religions, he knew that, "How persons in such situations may live in harmony and contribute to a common human intellectual space has become a crucial testing of the public theology of every religious faith."[16] Western Christian thought has failed this test as Western societies have engendered both deep religious polarization and the diminishing of religious conviction. The context of religious pluralism has exposed this fatal flaw of Western Christian thought. But religious pluralism offers the opportunity for authentic Christian witness amid diverse articulation of the Christian faith. In this way, we may view the end of Christendom positively, for it has exposed the yoking of Christianity and political power as a false gospel and offers hope for a true gospel to rise in its place.

Too much Enlightenment philosophy; not enough living church

The lack of an external challenge from non-Christian religions is only part of the problem for Western Christian thought. In addition, "the secularized environment that followed the Enlightenment has tended to suggest that specifically religious claims are no longer decisive."[17] The uncritical adoption of significant assumptions from Enlightenment thinking into Western theology has hindered theological understanding. The corresponding prescription is deceptively simple: theologians must seek to avoid Enlightenment ideals that emphasize reason over revelation, the autonomous individual self over community and collective consciousness, and the present, so-called modernity over the past and tradition. The crux of the problem, as Bediako succinctly states it, is this: "The Western Christian theology that emerged from that bruising struggle was Enlightenment theology, a Christian theology shaved

---

15. Bediako, 252.
16. Bediako, 252.
17. Bediako, 252.

down to fit the Enlightenment world-view."[18] One of the major losses of this capitulation to Enlightenment thought is that there is then little space in Western theology for the transcendent to impact everyday human existence. Because of this issue, Western theology is not big enough for Africa and the deep connections of Africans to the spiritual universe. Nor is Western theology big enough for the global North.[19]

The prescription for avoiding Enlightenment ideals is to embrace multiplicity, ambiguity, difference, emotion, and experience. African Christian thought emphasizes the centrality of faith and religion in society and everyday life. Throughout Africa words of divine blessing are invoked, and God is praised on a regular basis. The cultural assumption is often that God is active in the world. While the divine name might be debated – Jesus, Allah, or *Nyame*, among others – the shared conviction is that God is intimately involved with humanity. This belief is directly related to the communal understanding that what is best for all is best for any individual. Bediako fiercely resisted the Western tendency toward individualism and the privatization of belief claims, while also insisting that every individual must positively respond to God in Jesus Christ in order to become Christian.[20]

The living church doing theology is essential for the remaking of theology. Bediako's diagnosis focuses on the embrace of Enlightenment rationalism as a large part of the Western problem. Instead, his call is to focus on the lived experience of Christians and their churches to ascertain what they actually believe – a focus on actions rather than ideals. Bediako calls this approach grassroots theology, better known as theology from below. Instead of a top-down, idea-heavy, rational theological system for every Christian to learn propositional truths, the prescription here is to listen to the story of God as understood and lived out in the lives of God's people. Bediako's bottom-up approach emphasizes reading of Scripture as an oral text passed from one generation to the next, not an answer book or a how-to manual. Bediako seeks to avoid Enlightenment ideals by valuing indigenous traditions and spiritualities.

---

18. Bediako, 253.

19. For a similar claim, see J. B. Phillips, *Your God Is Too Small* (New York: Macmillan, 1953).

20. As Kwabena Asamoah-Gyadu notes, "There may well be others, but [Bediako] is the only African evangelical theologian and preacher that I have personally witnessed calling for people to come forward to offer their lives to Jesus Christ in a Billy-Graham-style altar call." J. Kwabena Asamoah-Gyadu, "Kwame Bediako and the Eternal Christological Question," in *Seeing New Facets of the Diamond, Christianity as a Universal Faith: Essays in Honour of Kwame Bediako*, ed. Gillian Mary Bediako, Benhardt Y. Quarshie, and J. Kwabena Asamoah-Gyadu (Akropong-Akuapem, Ghana: Regnum Africa, 2014), 51.

Missing the primal substructure; need to recover spirituality

Western theology is limited because it has lost contact with the primal imagination. The prescription is for remade Christian theologies that value indigenous traditions and spiritualities, especially the primal imagination. Bediako saw a parallel between using African traditional religions and primal spiritualties as preparation and a foundational substructure for African Christian thought and Christianities based in primal spiritualities in other parts of the world. Western Christian thought lacks the explicit embrace of the primal imagination and its foundation role in theological reflection that are practiced in African Christian thought. Bediako repeatedly emphasized that the primal imagination is the "substructure" of African Christian thought. His clear implication is that Western theology needs to rediscover the primal *Western* imagination. Any true Christianity must be built upon an understanding and appreciation of the primal imagination beneath every culture. Bediako did not propose how Westerners could rediscover the primal imagination that had been erased, and he certainly was no advocate of neo-paganism. Yet without connecting to its primal imagination, Western theology remains inherently a projection of Western (white) culture.

Western cultural ideals have been extremely effective at eradicating difference and dissent. Very little remains of the European primal imagination aside from the names for the days of the week and the vestiges of pagan rituals, such as decorating an evergreen tree at Christmas time. In the United States, indigenous spiritualties were killed, conquered, and cordoned off on reservations for Native Americans. Following Bediako's insights, the contemporary increases in the worship of Gaia the Earth goddess or other forms of neo-paganism, as well as Christians interested in Celtic Christianity, are evidence of the human yearning for primal spiritualties. Indeed, much of the increase in the West of individuals who consider themselves spiritual but not religious (SBNR) has its roots in the yearning for primal spiritualities. Bediako's thought calls for rediscovering primal spiritualities within Christianity, not a rejection or condemnation of the primal.

The remaking of Christian theologies requires the recovery of spirituality in theology. Bediako advocated restoring the ancient Christian unity of theology and spirituality through the primal imagination.[21] Not only do hyperrationalized Enlightenment ideals squeeze out the transcendent, these ideals also are highly skeptical of the spiritual world over against the physical world.

---

21. Bediako, *Christianity in Africa*, 105.

Based on Bediako's diagnosis of the ills of Western theology and his prescription for the remaking of theology, his thought can helpfully impact Western Christians. Bediako sought to use his understandings of African Christianity to assist Western Christians in identifying the cultural blind spots in their faith understandings. Undergirding all three of these parts of the prescription is this key point: The only way for Western Christians to become less Western in their theologizing is to learn from theologies of the global South through conversation and collaboration. Or to paraphrase Kenyan theologian John Mbiti from nearly a half century ago: "We have eaten and drunken theology with you Westerners. Western theology has inhabited our [African] subconscious. When will you make us part of your subconscious process when theologizing? When will you eat theology with us?"[22]

Bediako's work exposes how syncretistic Western theology can be while also offering concrete suggestions for the future of Western theology. For students who believe that their theology is self-evident, or without context, Bediako's work names some of the cultural blinders endemic to Western theology. Rather than an alternative theological proposal, Bediako offers a mirror: his writings expand the ways that Western cultural understandings are consciously confused with the gospel of Jesus Christ.

For Western Christians, the task of naming and beginning to dismantle their cultural blinkers is perhaps the most challenging. The responsibility here is for Christians – particularly white Christians like me in North America and Europe – to become aware of the air we breathe theologically. In the same way that fish seem blissfully unaware of the water they swim in, many Western Christians are quite comfortable within Western theology. In short, it is all they have ever known. Many are unaware of any other options or of all the assumptions from Christendom, from the Enlightenment, of notions of progress, etc. that are inherent in their beliefs. Like a fish out of water suddenly realizing what water is and its necessity for marine life, Western Christians need to realize that the water we swim in, the air we breathe, is polluted with Western assumptions. As these assumptions went unchallenged, they led to perceptions of superiority and of dominance that led to the horrors of colonialism, slavery, and apartheid. The prescription here is for Western Christians to listen to those outside the West to hear about the underside of Western theology and its stark limitations. We must listen to and learn from African Christians. And then

---

22. John Mbiti, "Theological Impotence and the Universality of the Church," in *Mission Trends No. 3: Third World Theologies*, ed. Gerald Anderson and Thomas Stransky (Grand Rapids: Eerdmans, 1976), 16–17.

we must do the very difficult work of stripping away assumptions steeped in power and privilege that have shaped Western readings of Scripture and the task of assembling *systematic* theologies.

Bediako and Western Christians

There are some real hurdles for Western Christians seeking to embrace Bediako's ideas and perspectives. The difficulty implicit in Bediako's writings for many Western Christians is his frequent and repeated uses of male language for God. Bediako only used male pronouns to speak of God. In a paragraph late in his life, Bediako notes the helpfulness of indigenous African languages using nonsexist God talk. Yet while noting this insight, he also passed off the question of gendered language for God as a women's issue, saying that it "could be revealing if this characteristic of African languages were to be more fully explored in African women's theology."[23] Issues of gender did not feature prominently in Bediako's writings, neither when thinking about God nor when speaking about humanity. His writings did not address questions of sexuality either, aside from considerations of the traditional African practice of polygamy (especially Western responses to polygamy) and his own condemnations of homosexuality, particularly in the West.[24]

A theological impediment that some Western Christians might have with Bediako is his radical, unrelenting, unapologetic Christocentrism. Bediako described himself as "African evangelical Christian of the twentieth century."[25] While seeking to expand Christians' self-understanding away from being a thoroughly Western religion, Bediako wholly embraced the label evangelical. He clung to the centrality of Jesus Christ, the authority of the Scriptures in the Old and New Testaments, and the necessity to share the good news of the gospel of Jesus Christ with others. At times Bediako's, unnuanced, unreflective

---

23. Bediako, "Whose Religion Is Christianity?," 116.

24. Bediako addressed questions about homosexuality on three occasions in his writings. In *Christianity in Africa*, he referred to "the modern problem of homosexuality within the Western church and how to deal with it." Bediako, *Christianity in Africa*, 183. Second, he compared promiscuity and homosexuality: "African 'promiscuity' comes to the forefront, while Western homosexuality falls into the background of attention." Kwame Bediako, "Theological Reflections," in *Serving with the Poor in Africa*, ed. Yamamori et. al. (Monrovia: MARC, 1996), 182. Third, he accused Westerners of distorting Scripture because of the impact of secularization: "Through secularisation, the West has cut off the transcendent and this includes distorting Scripture by the justification of ethical aberrations such as homosexuality." Bediako, "Scripture as the Hermeneutics," 10.

25. Bediako, "How Is Jesus Christ Lord? Evangelical Christian Apologetics amid African Religious Pluralism," in *Jesus and the Gospel in Africa*, 34.

Christocentrism seems to prevent a robust understanding of the Trinity or dialogue about religious pluralism.

Bediako's Christocentrism is consistent with his views that the other African religions are incomplete. For Bediako, African traditional religions are evangelical preparation for Christianity with primal religions as the substructure of African Christianity. African traditional religions have limited integrity in their own right; their value comes from preparing Africans to become African Christians. Islam, which Bediako saw as a modern rival to Christianity in Africa, he viewed as less helpful at preparing Africans to become Christians, but as offering a number of interesting insights about humanity while remaining unable to fulfill all its promises or to grant its followers access to the afterlife. Bediako's Christocentrism and emphasis on salvation occurring only by Jesus Christ inhibits some Western Christians from turning to Bediako in conversations about religious pluralism. For Bediako, salvation is only in and through Jesus Christ, though Christ might use unexpected means outside of the Christian religion to draw persons to himself.

Christologically, Bediako had a tendency to emphasize Jesus's divinity more than Jesus's humanity. Particularly in "Jesus in African Culture: A Ghanaian Perspective," Bediako relies on the divinity of Jesus Christ in order to stress the universality of Christ as the Great Ancestor of all. In order to answer the question of how Africans can relate to Jesus who is not of their clan, Bediako emphasizes how Jesus's divinity makes him the *universal* Savior of all humankind and in doing so downplays Jesus's Jewishness.[26] Because of the racial and cultural distance between Africans and Jesus of Nazareth, Bediako seemingly could not emphasize Jesus's humanity while also developing an indigenous African Christianity.

A further obstacle for some Westerners and some Africans is Bediako's negative view of Pentecostalism. As the fastest growing segment of world Christianity, Pentecostal and charismatic Christians form an important part of the Christian population, especially in the developing world. On the few occasions that Bediako wrote about Pentecostal and charismatic Christians, he was quite critical of the "prosperity movement."[27] Certainly, Bediako's theological bias was in favor of the so-called mission churches: Presbyterians, Methodists, Anglicans, and Roman Catholics. Though I would think that the indigenous interpretations of many Pentecostal and charismatic churches

---

26. Bediako, "Jesus in African Culture," 24.

27. See Kwame Bediako, "Gospel and Culture: Some Insights," *Journal of African Christian Thought* 2, no. 2 (December 1999): 10; Bediako, "Whose Religion Is Christianity?," 116–17.

would appeal to Bediako, he was deeply concerned about their focus on health and wealth as the central tenets of the so-called prosperity gospel which he believed was not faithful to biblical interpretation.

A Theological Revolution

In short, Bediako proposed a theological revolution. The Western world, Europe and North America, is not the center of the theological universe. In fact, the theological universe does not have a permanent center.[28] In the twenty-first century, an understanding of world Christianity with multiple centers has been inaugurated. The former European center now is at the periphery of contemporary Christian theological reflection. The former peripheries of the Christian faith, the so-called developing world, host the most creative, innovative, and thoughtful theological centers in the world. In a most unexpected reversal, the center has become the periphery, and the periphery has become the new centers. Bediako has offered a theology for this world turned upside down.

For African Christians, Bediako understood his work as a beginning of a process, not the end. His call to his fellow Africans was to take up the work of theological revolution; a turning away from Western understandings of Christianity toward African understandings. The outline was to call upon Scripture, African traditions, the lived experiences of Africans, and African logics and reasoning as theological sources. His theological norm was the articulation of an indigenous, authentic African Christianity. He foresaw the difficult yet important work ahead:

> This requires us to bend our energies in the direction of the evangelisation of our cultures, to seek the conversion of our cultural heritage (with all that this requires in a recovery of our languages as the medium of reflection on, and communication of, the gospel). It is going to require from us the same spiritual discipline, intellectual rigour and dedicated selflessness that have been required of our predecessors and ancestors in the faith from biblical times and throughout Christian history. The rest of the world will learn from how we respond, as African Christians, to our challenges.[29]

---

28. This was Jenkins' mistake – seeking to replace the end of Christendom with a *next* Christendom. Bediako, "Conclusion: The Emergence of World Christianity," 247.

29. Bediako, 30.

For Bediako, Africans might save Christianity itself by uncoupling Christian theology from Western thought and culture.

One key step in this process of disentanglement is acknowledging that there is no such thing as "pure" theology. Theology is always culturally inflected, always contextual. Part of Bediako's contribution is to celebrate the gift of the impact of context upon theological reflection rather than lamenting the cultural impact, or worse pretending that – somehow – theology exists outside of culture. He sought continuities between African culture and the gospel of Jesus Christ in the Scripture of the Old and New Testaments. Certainly he encountered discontinuities where aspects of traditional African cultures needed to be rejected in light of the Scriptures, yet his emphasis lay in building bridges and accepting as much as possible. Bediako valued the primal imagination as the substructure of Christianity – a substructure that he believed had been lost in Western culture. For Bediako, the primal lies deeper than every culture, so that no single culture, not an African culture nor a European one, can serve as the foundation for the Christian faith.

Cultural context may inflect theology, but not ground it. Christian theology comes from Christ alone as revealed to humanity in the Bible. The process of divine revelation has always employed cultural media, including human languages. The medium of revelation is the message of the Christian faith. God came in the flesh as the human being, Jesus of Nazareth. God's mode of revelation as a solitary, Jewish, male human being has defined how God has been received and understood ever since. Theology, for Bediako – and he would say for all of us – is earthly, not heady, growing from the everyday lives of Christians. Though he never said so directly, Bediako would define theology as biblical reflection upon the insights of everyday Christians.

The rejection of anything like a "pure theology" short circuits any attempts at regional hierarchies between theologians. There becomes no basis for claiming that Western theologies are better than African or Latin American or Asian theologies, or that white thought is better than black or brown. People from each cultural context are called to offer their own understandings of the triune God, of the revelation of God, and of God's word. There is no expectation that everyone will agree; rather in sharing the multiple understandings and interpretations with one another, everyone's understanding might be enriched. The shared goal is for everyone, no matter their culture or ethnicity, to live in the way of Jesus wherever they are. For his part, Bediako offered a Christ-centered, contextually African theology. The task he outlines for today's Christians is to be local, indigenous theologians – in dialogue with Scripture, the saints who have interpreted Scripture before us, and our sisters and brothers in Christ around the world. We cannot simply assume or absorb Bediako's theology. Each of us is required to make theological decisions in our own context. We cannot wholly and uncritically swallow Calvin's or Wesley's or Barth's or Bediako's theology. We can learn from Bediako's theology – both from his methods and his conclusions.

An African schooled in Western thought, Bediako came of age as Ghana celebrated its independence. As an adolescent, he rejected Christianity and declared himself an avowed atheist who debated Christians on the implausibility of their faith. Later as a graduate student living in France, he experienced a dramatic and unexpected conversion to Christianity that led him to embrace an African understanding of Christian thought. He turned this embrace into a full-fledged exposition of Christianity as a non-Western religion. In doing so, he pioneered an understanding of the Christian faith as a truly world faith, not merely as an European export to a needy world. His thought demonstrates a frequent, repeated, and intentional wrestling with questions of identity, gospel, and culture. His personal biography is engaging, and his fresh theological insights are significant for twenty-first century Christians.

Bediako offered a number of suggestions for how Christians can authentically articulate indigenous, local theologies. The first step builds on his understanding of the primal imagination and African traditional religions as evangelical preparation for Christianity. Each person can begin by embracing their own past as divine preparation for the present. Implicit in Bediako's claims about preparation is strong belief in providence: God is active in and through history. Bediako believed that God is active in each person's life drawing them closer to God.

Bediako is clear that all Christians, including Christian theologians, must devour the Scriptures of the Old and New Testament. In part, this belief comes from his own history in which he read the Bible cover to cover several times immediately following his conversion.[30] When reading the Bible, the task becomes interpreting the texts contextually to discover what the biblical text has to say to one's self, neighbors, and community. The key interpretive step for Bediako is to cling to Jesus Christ while interpreting the Scriptures contextually. The life of Jesus and the ongoing activity of God in Jesus Christ are to form the basis of the Christian faith and all theological reflection.

European and North American Christians must interrogate their own theological assumptions and begin the process of learning from those outside the West. Engaging with Bediako and other non-Western theologians brings

---

30. Bediako and Visser, "Introduction," *Jesus and the Gospel in Africa*, xii.

clarity to contemporary Christians' own theological self-assessments and constructive theological claims and beliefs.

Further Reading of Kwame Bediako

"African Theology as a Challenge to Western Theology." In *Christian Identity in Cross-Cultural Perspective*, edited by Martien E. Brinkman and Dirk van Keulen, 52–67. Meinema: Zoetermeer, 2003.

Christianity in Africa: The Renewal of a Non-Western Religion. Edinburgh: Edinburgh University Press, 1995. Especially chapters 6 and 10.

"Conclusion: The Emergence of World Christianity and the Remaking of Theology." In *Understanding World Christianity: The Vision and Work of Andrew F. Walls*, edited by William R. Burrows, Mark R. Gornik, and Janice A. McLean, 243–56. Maryknoll, NY: Orbis, 2011.

"A Half Century of African Christian Thought: Pointers to Theology and Theological Education in the Next Half Century." *Journal of African Christian Thought* 3, no. 1 (2000): 5–11.

"A New Era in Christian History – African Christianity as Representative Christianity: Some Implications for Theological Education and Scholarship." *Journal of African Christian Thought* 9, no. 1 (2006): 3–12.

"'Whose Religion Is Christianity?': Reflections on Opportunities and Challenges in Christian Theological Scholarship: The African Dimension." In *Mission in the Twenty-First Century*, 107–17 with notes 210–13. Previously published in *Journal of African Christian Thought* 9, no. 2 (2006): 43–48.

Bibliography

Adogame, Afe. *The African Christian Diaspora: New Currents and Emerging Trends in World Christianity.* New York: Bloomsbury Academic, 2013.

————. *The Public Face of African New Religious Movements in Diaspora.* New York: Routledge, 2016.

African Christianity Rising. Directed by James Ault. Northampton, MA: James Ault Productions, 2013.

Aimé Césaire, une voix pour l'histoire. Directed by Euzhan Palcy. Martinique: JMJ Productions, [1994] 2006.

Apprey, Maurice. Personal interview by Tim Hartman. Charlottesville, VA, November 5, 2012.

Asamoah-Gyadu, J. Kwabena. "Bediako of Africa: A Late 20th Century Outstanding Theologian and Teacher." *Mission Studies* 26 (2009): 5–16.

————. "Kwame Bediako and the Eternal Christological Question." In *Seeing New Facets of the Diamond, Christianity as a Universal Faith: Essays in Honour of Kwame Bediako,* edited by Gillian Mary Bediako, Benhardt Y. Quarshie, and J. Kwabena Asamoah-Gyadu, 38–55. Akropong-Akuapem, Ghana: Regnum Africa, 2014.

Ashcroft, Bill, Gareth Griffiths, and Helen Tiffin. *The Empire Writes Back: Theory and Practice in Post-Colonial Literature.* London: Routledge, 1989.

Baëta, C. G. "The Challenge of African Culture to the Church and the Message of the Church to African Culture" in *Christianity and African Culture,* 51–61. Accra: Christian Council of the Gold Coast, 1955.

Balcomb, Anthony O. "Faith or Suspicion?: Theological Dialogue North and South of the Limpopo with Special Reference to the Theologies of Kwame Bediako and Andrew Walls." *Journal of Theology for Southern Africa* 100 (March 1998): 3–19.

————. "Narrative, Epistemological Crisis and Reconstruction: My Story with Special Reference to the Work of Kwame Bediako." *Scriptura* 97 (2008): 47–59.

Bediako, Gillian Mary. Personal Interview by Tim Hartman. Akropong, Ghana, 1 June 2012.

————. *Primal Religion and the Bible: William Robertson Smith and his Heritage.* Sheffield: Sheffield Academic Press, 1997.

Bediako, Kwame. "Africa and Christianity on the Threshold of the Third Millennium: The Religious Dimension." *African Affairs* 99 (2000): 303–23.

————. "African Christian Thought." In *Oxford Companion to Christian Thought,* edited by A. Hastings and A. Mason, 8–10. Oxford: Oxford University Press, 2000.

————. "The African Renaissance and Theological Reconstruction: The Challenge of the Twenty-First Century." *Journal of African Christian Thought* 4, no. 2 (2001): 29–33.

———. "African Theology as a Challenge to Western Theology." In *Christian Identity in Cross-Cultural Perspective*, edited by Martien E. Brinkman and Dirk van Keulen, 52–67. Meinema: Zoetermeer, 2003.

———. "Andrew F. Walls as Mentor." In *Understanding World Christianity: The Vision and Work of Andrew F. Walls*, edited by William R. Burrows, Mark R. Gornik, and Janice A. McLean, 7–10. Maryknoll, NY: Orbis, 2011.

———. "'In the Bible . . . Africa Walks on Familiar Ground': Why the World Needs Africa." *AICMAR* 6 (2007): 32–50.

———. "Biblical Christologies in the Context of African Traditional Religion." In *Sharing Jesus in the Two-Thirds World*, edited by Vinay Samuel and Chris Sugden, 81–121. Grand Rapids: Eerdmans, 1984.

———. "Biblical Exegesis in the African Context: The Factor and Impact of Translated Scriptures." *Journal of African Christian Thought* 6, no. 1 (2003): 15–23.

———. "Brief Statement on a Projected PhD Thesis." 22 March 1978. Unpublished.

———. "Challenges of Ghana's Fourth Republic: A Christian Perspective." The William Ofori-Atta Memorial Lectures, Accra, Ghana, October 7–9, 1992.

———. "Christ in Africa: Some Reflections on the Contribution of Christianity to the African Becoming." In *Proceedings of African Futures: 25th Anniversary Conference Held in the Centre of African Studies, University of Edinburgh, 9–11 December 1987*, edited by Christopher Fyfe and Chris Allen, 447–58. Edinburgh: Centre of African Studies, 1987.

———. "Christian Faith and African Culture: An Exposition of the Epistle to the Hebrews." *Journal of African Christian Thought* 13, no. 1 (2010): 45–57.

———. *Christianity in Africa: The Renewal of a Non-Western Religion*. Edinburgh: Edinburgh University Press, 1995.

———. "Christianity, Islam, and the Kingdom of God: Rethinking Their Relationship from an African Perspective." *Journal of African Christian Thought* 7, no. 2 (2004): 3–7.

———. "Christian Tradition and the African God Revisited: A Process in the Exploration of a Theological Idiom." In *Witnessing to the Living God in Contemporary Africa*, edited by David Gitari and Patrick Benson, 77–97. Nairobi: Uzima, 1986.

———. "Christian Witness in the Public Sphere: Some Lessons and Residual Challenges from the Recent Political History of Ghana." In *The Changing Face of Christianity: Africa, the West, and the World*, edited by Lamin Sanneh and Joel A. Carpenter, 117–32. New York: Oxford University Press, 2005.

———. "Conclusion: The Emergence of World Christianity and the Remaking of Theology." In *Understanding World Christianity: The Vision and Work of Andrew F. Walls*, edited by William R. Burrows, Mark R. Gornik, and Janice A. McLean, 243–56. Maryknoll, NY: Orbis, 2011.

———. "Culture." In *New Dictionary of Theology*, edited by Sinclair Ferguson and David Wright, 183–84. Downers Grove, IL: InterVarsity Press, 1988.

———. "Danquah's Conception of Culture and Its Place in the Renewal and Enhancement of Society." In *Religion, Culture, Language: An Appreciation of the Intellectual Legacy of Dr J. B. Danquah.* J. B. Danquah Memorial Lectures, Series 37, 2–4 February 2004. Accra: Ghana Academy of Arts and Sciences, 2006.

———. "Danquah's Use of Mother Tongue in Intellectual Discourse and Its Relevance in Our Time." In *Religion, Culture, and Language: An Appreciation of the Intellectual Legacy of Dr. J. B. Danquah.* J. B. Danquah Memorial Lectures, Series 37, 2–4 February 2004. Accra: Ghana Academy of Arts and Sciences, 2006.

———. "Death and the Gospel in the Ghanaian Context." *Exchange* 20, no. 2 (1991): 147–49.

———. "The Emergence of World Christianity and the Remaking of Theology." Nagel Institute Public Lecture at Calvin College, 19 July 2007. Later published as "The Emergence of World Christianity and the Remaking of Theology." *Journal of African Christian Thought* 12, no. 2 (2009): 50–55.

———. "'Ethiopia Shall Soon Stretch Out Her Hands to God' (Ps. 68:31): African Christians Living the Faith: A Turning Point in Christian History." In *A New Day Dawning: African Christians Living the Gospel: Essays in Honour of Dr. J. J. (Hans) Visser,* edited by Kwame Bediako, Mechteld Jansen, Jan van Butselaar, and Aart Verburg, 30–40. Zoetermeer: Boekencentrum, 2004.

———. "Forward." In John Azumah. *My Neighbor's Faith: Islam Explained for African Christians,* ix–x. Grand Rapids: Zondervan, 2008.

———. "Gospel and Culture: Some Insights for Our Time from the Experience of the Earliest Christians." *Journal of African Christian Thought* 2, no. 2 (1999): 8–17.

———. "Guest Editorial." *Journal of African Christian Thought* 5, no. 1 (2002): 1–3.

———. "A Half Century of African Christian Thought: Pointers to Theology and Theological Education in the Next Half Century." *Journal of African Christian Thought* 3, no. 1 (2000): 5–11.

———. "The Holy Spirit, the Christian Gospel and Religious Change: The African Evidence for a Christian Theology of Religious Pluralism." In *Essays in Religious Studies for Andrew Walls,* edited by James Thrower, 44–56. Aberdeen: Department of Religious Studies, University of Aberdeen, 1986.

———. "The Impact of the Bible in Africa." Epilogue to Ype Schaaf, *On Their Way Rejoicing – The History and Role of the Bible in Africa,* 243–54. Carlisle: Paternoster, 1995.

———. "Into All the World." In *Jesus 2000,* edited by Richard Bauckham et. al., 222–25. Oxford: Lion, 1989.

———. *Jesus and the Gospel in Africa: History and Experience.* Maryknoll, NY: Orbis Books, 2004 [2000].

———. *Jesus in African Culture: A Ghanaian Perspective.* Accra: Asempa, 1990; reprinted 1992.

———. *Jesus in Africa: The Christian Gospel in African History and Experience.* Oxford: Regnum Africa, 2000.

————. "L'Univers interior de Tchicaya U Tam'si." PhD dissertation, T.E.R., Bordeaux III, 1973.

————. "Memorandum to Christian Service College Council on the Work of the College." 29 May 1978, unpublished archival document.

————. "'Missionaries Did Not Bring Christ to Africa – Christ Brought Them': Why Africa Needs Jesus Christ." *AICMAR* 6 (2007): 17–31.

————. "Négritude et Surréalisme: Essai sur l'oeuvre poétique de Tchicaya U Tam'si." MA thesis, T.E.R., Bordeaux III, 1970.

————. "A New Era in Christian History – African Christianity as Representative Christianity: Some Implications for Theological Education and Scholarship." *Journal of African Christian Thought* 9, no. 1 (2006): 3–12.

————. "New Paradigms on Ecumenical Co-Operation: An African Perspective." *International Review of Mission* (July 1992): 375–79.

————. "Reading Signs of the Kingdom." Stone Lecture No. 1, Princeton Theological Seminary, Princeton, NJ, 20 October 2003.

————. "Recognizing the Primal Religions." Stone Lecture No. 2, Princeton Theological Seminary, Princeton, NJ, 21 October 2003.

————. *Religion, Culture and Language: An Appreciation of the Intellectual Legacy of Dr. J. B. Danquah.* J. B. Danquah Memorial Lectures, Series 37, 2–4 February 2004. Accra: Ghana Academy of Arts and Sciences, 2006.

————. "The Relevance of a Christian Approach to Culture in Africa." In *Christian Education in the African Context: Proceedings of the First Africa Regional Conference of the International Association for the Promotion of Christian Higher Education (IAPCHE), 4–9 March 1991, Harare, Zimbabwe,* 24–35. Grand Rapids: IAPCHE, 1991.

————. "Religion and National Identity: Assessing the Discussion from Cicero to Danquah." Law and Religion Inaugural Lecture, 25 June 1997, 1–18. Accra: Ghana Academy of Arts and Sciences, 2006.

————. "[Response to] David Hesselgrave: Dialogue on Contextualization Continuum." *Gospel in Context* 2, no. 3 (1979): 12–13.

————. "Response to Taber: Is There More than One Way to Do Theology?" *Gospel in Context* 1, no. 1 (1978): 13–14.

————. "Review of *African Theology en Route.*" *Journal of Religion in Africa* 11, no. 2 (1980): 158–59.

————. "Scripture as the Hermeneutic of Culture and Tradition." *Journal of African Christian Thought* 4, no. 1 (2001): 2–11.

————. "The Significance of Modern African Christianity – A Manifesto." *Studies in World Christianity, Edinburgh Review of Theology and Religion* 1, no. 1 (1995): 51–67.

————. "'Their Past Is Also Our Present': Why All Christians Have Need of Ancestors: Making a Case for Africa." *AICMAR* 6 (2007): 1–16.

————. "Theological Reflections." In *Serving with the Poor in Africa*, edited by Tetsunao Yamamori et. al., 181–92. Monrovia, Liberia: MARC, 1996.

————. *Theology and Identity: The Impact of Culture on Christian Thought in the Second Century and Modern Africa*. Oxford: Regnum, 1992.

————. "Thoughts on the Nature of the Project." *Journal of African Christian Thought* 11, no. 2 (2008): 3–4.

————. "Types of African Theology." In *Christianity in Africa in the 1990s*, edited by C. Fyfe and A. Walls, 56–69. Edinburgh: University of Edinburgh, Centre for African Studies.

————. "Understanding African Theology in the Twentieth Century." In *Jesus and the Gospel in Africa*, 49–62. Oxford: Regnum, 2000.

————. "The Unique Christ in the Plurality of Religions." In *The Unique Christ in Our Pluralist World*, edited by Bruce Nichols, 47–56. Grand Rapids: Baker, 1994.

————. "Unmasking the Powers – Christianity, Authority and Desacralisation in Modern African Politics." In *Christianity and Democracy in Global Context*, edited by John Witte, 207–30. Boulder, CO: Westview, 1993.

————. "What Kind of People Should We Be?" Stone Lecture No. 5, Princeton Theological Seminary, Princeton, NJ, 23 October 2003, audio recording.

————. "'Whose Religion Is Christianity?': Reflections on Opportunities and Challenges in Christian Theological Scholarship: The African dimension." In *Mission in the Twenty-First Century: Exploring the Five Marks of Global Mission*, edited by Andrew F. Walls and Cathy Ross, 107–17 with notes 210–13. Maryknoll, NY: Orbis, 2008. Also published in *Journal of African Christian Thought* 9, no. 2 (2006): 43–48.

————. "'Why Has the Summer Ended and We Are Not Saved?': Encountering the Real Challenge of Christian Engagement in Primal Contexts." *Journal of African Christian Thought* 11, no. 2 (2008): 5–8.

————. "The Willowbank Consultation, January 1978 – A Personal Reflection." *Themelios* 5, no. 2 (January 1980): 25–32.

————. "Worship as Vital Participation: Some Personal Reflections on Ministry in the African Church." *Journal of African Christian Thought* 8, no. 2 (2005): 3–7.

Bediako, Kwame, and Gillian Mary Bediako. "'Ebenezer, This Is How Far the Lord Has Helped Us': Reflections on the Institutional Itinerary of the Akrofi-Christaller Memorial Centre for Mission Research & Applied Theology (1974–2005)." Unpublished handbook, Akropong-Akuapem: ACI, 2005.

Bennett, Louise. *Selected Poems*. Kingston, Jamaica: Sangster's Book Stores, 1982.

Brathwaite, Kamau. "History of the Voice." In *Roots: Essays in Caribbean Literature*, 259–304. Ann Arbor: University of Michigan Press, 1993.

Bujo, Bénézet. *African Theology in Its Social Context*. Translated by John O'Donohue. Maryknoll, NY: Orbis, 1992.

"Call to Glory." Funeral program for Kwame Bediako. July 2008.

Césaire, Aimé. *Notebook of a Return to the Native Land*. Translated and edited by Clayton Eshleman and Annette Smith. Middletown, CT: Wesleyan University Press, 2001.

Chitando, Ezra. *Living with Hope: African Churches and HIV/AIDS*. Geneva: WCC Publications, 2007.

Danquah, J. B. *The Akan Doctrine of God: A Fragment of Gold Coast Ethics and Religion*. 1944. Reprint of 1968 2nd ed. New York: Routledge, 2006.

Danso, Yaw. *The Basel Mission in Anum 1863–1918*. Osu, Ghana: Heritage, 2013.

Dedji, Valentin. *Reconstruction and Renewal in African Christian Theology*. Nairobi: Acton, 2003.

Dickson, Kwesi. "A New Introduction." In *The Akan Doctrine of God*, edited by J. B. Danquah, vii–xxvi. New York: Routledge, 1944.

Dinkelaker, Bernhard. *How Is Jesus Christ Lord? Reading Kwame Bediako from a Postcolonial and Intercontextual Perspective*. Bern: Peter Lang, 2017.

Dube, Musa W. "Consuming a Colonial Cultural Bomb: Translating *Badimo* into 'Demons' in the Setswana Bible (Matthew 8:28–34; 15:22; 10:8)." *Journal for the Study of the New Testament* 72 (1999): 33–59.

Ephirim-Donkor, Anthony. *African Religion Defined: A Systematic Study of Ancestor Worship among the Akan*. New York: University Press of America, 2010.

Ezigbo, Victor I. *Re-Imagining African Christologies: Conversing with the Interpretations and Appropriations of Jesus in Contemporary African Christianity*. Eugene, OR: Pickwick, 2010.

Ferguson, James. *Global Shadows: Africa in the Neoliberal World Order*. Durham, NC: Duke University Press, 2006.

Fotland, Roar. "Ancestor Christology in Context: Theological Perspectives of Kwame Bediako." PhD dissertation, University of Bergen, 2005.

Fretheim, Sara. *Kwame Bediako and African Christian Scholarship: Emerging Religious Discourse in Twentieth-Century Ghana*. Eugene, OR: Pickwick, 2018.

"Global Christianity – A Report on the Size and Distribution of the World's Christian Population." Pew Research Center, December 19, 2011. www.pewforum. org/2011/12/19/global-christianity-exec/.

Gornik, Mark. *Word Made Global: Stories of African Christianity in New York City*. Grand Rapids: Eerdmans, 2011.

Gyekye, Kwame. *Essay on African Philosophical Thought: The Akan Conceptual Scheme*. Cambridge: Cambridge University Press, 1987.

Hartman, Tim. "An Act of Theological Négritude: Kwame Bediako on African Christian Identity." In *Religion, Culture and Spirituality in Africa and the African Diaspora*, edited by William Ackah, Jualynne E. Dodson, and R. Drew Smith, 81–95. New York: Routledge, 2018.

———. *Theology after Colonization: Bediako, Barth, and the Future of Theological Reflection*. South Bend, IN: University of Notre Dame Press, 2020.

Idowu, Bolaji. *African Traditional Religion: A Definition*. Maryknoll, NY: Orbis, 1973.

Igboin, Benson Ohihon. "An African Religious Discourse on Names and Identity." *Filosofia Theoretica: Journal of African Philosophy, Culture and Religions* 3, no. 1 (2014): 26–40.

Jenkins, Philip. *The New Faces of Christianity: Believing the Bible in the Global South.* New York: Oxford University Press, 2006.

———. *The Next Christendom: The Coming of Global Christianity.* New York: Oxford University Press, 2002.

Katongole, Emmanuel. *A Future for Africa: Critical Essays in Christian Social Imagination.* Scranton, PA: University of Scranton Press, 2005.

Kaunda, Chammah J., Kennedy O. Owino, and Isabel A. Phiri, "Applicability of Translatability Theory to European Missionary Masculinity Performance in Africa: Contestations and Reflections." *Alternation* Special Edition:14 (2015): 212–30.

Knipp, Thomas R. "Négritude and Negation: The Poetry of Tchicaya U Tam'si." *Books Abroad* 4, no. 3 (Summer 1974): 511–15.

Kuma, Afua. *Jesus of the Deep Forest: Prayers and Praises of Afua Kuma.* Edited by Peter Kwasi Ameyaw, translated by Fr. Jon Kirby. Accra, Ghana: Asempa, 1980.

Laryea, Philip. "Mother Tongue Theology: Reflections on Images of Jesus in the Poetry of Afua Kuma." *Journal of African Christian Thought* 3, no. 1 (2000): 50–60.

Magesa, Laurenti. *Anatomy of Inculturation: Transforming the Church in Africa.* Maryknoll, NY: Orbis, 2004.

Maluleke, Tinyiko Sam. "African Traditional Religions in Christian Mission and Christian Scholarship: Re-Opening a Debate That Never Started." *Religion and Theology* 5, no. 2 (1998): 121–37.

———. "Black and African Theologies in the New World Order: A Time to Drink from Our Own Wells." *Journal of Theology for Southern Africa* 96 (November 1996): 3–19.

———. "Half a Century of African Christian Theologies: Elements of the Emerging Agenda for the Twenty-First Century." *Journal of Theology of Southern Africa* 99 (November 1997): 4–23.

———. "Identity and Integrity in African Theology: A Critical Analysis." *Religion and Theology* 8, no. 1 (2001): 26–41.

———. "The Rediscovery of the Agency of Africans: An Emerging Paradigm of Post-Cold War and Post-Apartheid Black and African Theology." In *African Theology Today*, edited by Emmanuel Katongole, 147–70. Scranton, PA: University of Scranton Press, 2002.

———. "In Search of 'The True Character of African Christian Identity': A Review of the Theology of Kwame Bediako." *Missionalia* 25, no. 1 (August 1997): 210–19.

Mazrui, Ali M. *The African Condition: A Political Diagnosis.* London: Faber & Faber, 1980.

Mbiti, John. *Bible and Theology in African Christianity.* Nairobi: Oxford University Press, 1986.

———. *New Testament Eschatology in an African Background: A Study on the Encounter between New Testament Theology and African Traditional Concepts*. Oxford: Oxford University Press, 1971.

———. "Some Reflections on African Experience of Salvation Today." In *Living Faith and Ultimate Goals*, edited by S. J. Samartha, 108–19. Geneva: World Council of Churches, 1974.

———. "Theological Impotence and the Universality of the Church." In *Mission Trends No. 3: Third World Theologies*, edited by Gerald Anderson and Thomas Stransky, 6–18. Grand Rapids: Eerdmans, 1976.

Michael, Matthew. "African Theology and the Paradox of Missions: Three Intellectual Responses to the Modern Missions Crisis of the African Church." *Transformation: An International Journal of Holistic Mission Studies* 31, no. 2 (2014): 79–98.

Miller, Jon. *Missionary Zeal and Institutional Control: Organizational Contradictions in the Basel Mission on the Gold Coast 1828–1917*. Grand Rapids: Eerdmans, 2003.

Moore, Gerald. "The Politics of Négritude." In *Protest and Conflict in African Literature*, edited by Cosmo Pieterse and Donald Munro, 38–39. London: Heinemann, 1969.

Mugambi, J. N. K. "Ecumenism in African Christianity." In *The Routledge Companion to Christianity in Africa*, edited by Elias Kiffon Bongmba, 232–51. New York: Routledge, 2016.

Ngodji, Martin. "The Applicability of the Translatability and Interpretation Theory of Sanneh and Bediako: The Case of the Evangelical Lutheran Church in Nambia, in Northern Namibia." PhD dissertation, University of Swazulu Natal, Pietermaritzburg, South Africa, 2010.

Ngong, David Tonghou. *The Holy Spirit and Salvation in African Christian Theology: Imagining a More Hopeful Future for Africa*. New York: Peter Lang, 2010.

Odozor, Paulinus Ikechukwu. *Morality Truly Christian, Truly African: Foundational, Methodological, and Theological Considerations*. South Bend, IN: University of Notre Dame Press, 2014.

Oduyoye, Mercy Amba. "Jesus Christ." In *The Cambridge Companion to Feminist Theology*, edited by Susan Frank Parsons, 151–70. Cambridge: Cambridge University Press, 2002.

Okorocha, Cyril. "The Meaning of Salvation: An African Perspective." In *Emerging Voices in Global Christian Theology*, edited by William Dyrness, 59–92. Grand Rapids: Zondervan, 1994.

Olabimtan, Kehinde. "'Is Africa Incurably Religious?' II: A Response to Jan Platvoet and Henk van Rinsum." *Exchange* 32, no. 4 (2003): 322–39.

Olupona Jacob K., and Regina Gemignani. *African Immigrant Religions in America*. New York: New York University Press, 2007.

Omenyo, Cephas. "Ghana, Liberia and Sierra Leone." In *Christianity in Sub-Saharan Africa*, edited by Kenneth Ross, J. Kwabena Asamoah-Gyadu, and Todd Johnson, 201–13. Edinburgh: Edinburgh University Press, 2017.

Opoku, Kofi. "Toward a Holistic View of Salvation." In *Healing for God's World: Remedies from Three Continents*, edited by Kofi Asare Opoku and Yong-Bok Kim, 41–60. New York: Friendship Press, 1991.

Parrinder, Geoffrey. *Religion in Africa.* Harmondsworth: Penguin, 1969.

p'Bitek Okot. *African Religions in Western Scholarship.* Kampala: East African Literature Bureau, 1970.

———. "Intellectual Smugglers in Africa." *East Africa Journal* 8, no. 12 (1971): 7–9.

Phiri, Isabel Apawo, and Sarojini Nadar. "'Going through the Fire with Eyes Wide Open': African Women's Perspectives on Indigenous Knowledge, Patriarchy and Sexuality." *Journal for the Study of Religion* 22, no. 2 (2009): 5–21.

Platvoet, Jan, and Henk van Rinsum. "Is Africa Incurably Religious? Confessing and Contesting an Invention." *Exchange* 32, no. 2 (2003): 123–53.

Quarshie, Benhardt Y. "'Jesus, Pioneer and Perfecter of Faith' (Heb. 12:2): Kwame Bediako's Hebrews-Based Ancestor Christology Revisited." In *Seeing New Facets of the Diamond: Christianity as a Universal Faith, Essays in Honour of Kwame Bediako*, edited by Gillian Mary Bediako, Benhardt Y. Quarshie, J. Kwabena Asamoah-Gyadu, 21–37. Eugene, OR: Wipf & Stock, 2014.

Rah, Soong-Chan. *The Next Evangelicalism: Freeing the Church from Western Cultural Captivity.* Downers Grove, IL: InterVarsity, 2009.

Rein, Susan Erica. "Religiosity in the Poetry of Tchicaya U Tam'si." *Journal of Religion in Africa* 10, no. 3 (1979): 234–49.

Ryan, Patrick. "'Arise, O God!': The Problem of 'Gods' in West Africa." *Journal of Religion in Africa* 11, no. 3 (1980): 161–71.

Sanneh, Lamin. "The Horizontal and the Vertical in Mission: An African Perspective." *International Bulletin of Missionary Research* 7, no. 4 (October 1983): 165–71.

———. *Piety and Power: Muslims and Christians in West Africa.* Maryknoll, NY: Orbis, 1996.

———. *Translating the Message: The Missionary Impact on Culture.* Maryknoll, NY: Orbis, 1989.

———. *West African Christianity.* Maryknoll, NY: Orbis, 1983.

Stanley, Brian. *The World Missionary Conference, Edinburgh 1910.* Grand Rapids: Eerdmans, 2009.

Stinton, Diane B. *Jesus of Africa: Voices of Contemporary African Christology.* Maryknoll, NY: Orbis, 2004.

———. "Jesus Christ, Living Water in Africa Today." In *The Oxford Handbook of Christology*, edited by Francesca Aran Murphy, 425–43. New York: Oxford University Press, 2015.

Tam'si, Tchicaya U. *Tchicaya U Tam'si: Selected Poems.* Translated by Gerald Moore. London: Heinemann, 1970.

Tarus, David Kirwa, and Stephanie Lowery. "African Theologies of Identity and Community: The Contributions of John Mbiti, Jesse Mugambi, Vincent Mulago, and Kwame Bediako." *Open Theology* 3 (2017): 305–20.

Taylor, John. "Rereading Tchicaya U Tam'si." *The Antioch Review* 66, no. 4 (Fall 2008): 784–90.

van den Toren, Benno. "Kwame Bediako's Christology in Its African Evangelical Context." *Exchange* 26, no. 3 (1997): 218–32.

Visser, Hans, and Gillian M. Bediako. "Introduction." In *Jesus and the Gospel in Africa*, xi–xvii. Oxford: Regnum, 2000.

Walls, Andrew F. "The Gospel as Prisoner and Liberator of Culture." In *The Missionary Movement in Christian History: Studies in the Transmission of Faith*, 3–15. Maryknoll, NY: Orbis, 1996.

———. "Kwame Bediako and Christian Scholarship in Africa." *International Bulletin of Missionary Research* 32, no. 4 (2008): 188–93.

———. *The Missionary Movement in Christian History: Studies in the Transmission of Faith*. Maryknoll, NY: Orbis, 1996.

———. "Structural Problems in Mission Studies." *International Bulletin of Missionary Research* 15, no. 4 (1991): 146–55.

West, Gerald O. "African Biblical Hermeneutics and Bible Translation." In *Interacting with Scriptures in Africa*, edited by Jean-Claude Loba-Mkole and Ernst R. Wendland, 3–10. Nairobi: Acton, 2005.

———. "Mapping African Biblical Interpretation: A Tentative Sketch." In *The Bible in Africa: Transactions, Trajectories, and Trends*, edited by Gerald O. West and Musa W. Dube, 29–53. Leiden: Brill, 2000.

———. "The Role of the Bible in African Christianity." In *Anthology of African Christianity*, edited by Isabel Apawo Phiri and Dietrich Werner, 76–88. Oxford: Regnum, 2016.

———. *The Stolen Bible: From Tool of Imperialism to African Icon*. Leiden: Brill, 2016.

Wilder, Gary. *Freedom Time: Negritude, Decolonization, and the Future of the World*. Durham, NC: Duke University Press, 2015.

Young, Richard Fox. "Clearing a Path through *Jesus of the Deep Forest*: Intercultural Perspectives on Christian Praise and Public Witness in Afua Kuma's Akan Oral Epic." *Theology Today* 70, no. 1 (2013): 38–45.

Chronological Listing of Kwame Bediako's Writings

1970

Négritude et Surréalisme: Essai sur l'oeuvre poétique de TCHICAYA U TAM'SI, T.E.R., Bordeaux III, October 1970. Unpublished M.A. Thesis.

1973

L'Univers Interieur de TCHICAYA U TAM'SI. Thèse de 3e cycle, L'université de Bordeaux III, July 1973. Unpublished doctoral thesis.

1978

"Response to Taber: Is There More than One Way to Do Theology?" *Gospel in Context* 1, no. 1 (1978): 13–14.

1979

"[Response to] David Hesselgrave: Dialogue on Contextualization Continuum." *Gospel in Context* 2, no. 3 (1979): 12–13.

1980

"The Willowbank Consultation, January 1978 – A Personal Reflection." *Themelios* 5, no. 2 (January 1980): 25–32.

"Review of *African theology en route*." *Journal of Religion in Africa* 11, no. 2 (1980): 158–59.

"Review of *Toward an African Theology*." *Journal of Religion in Africa* 11, no. 3 (1980): 235–37.

1983

Identity and Integration: An Enquiry into the Nature and Problems of Theological Indigenization in Selected Early Hellenistic and Modern African Christian Writers. PhD Dissertation at University of Aberdeen, July 1983. Published as *Theology and Identity* in 1992.

1984

"Biblical Christologies in the Context of African Traditional Religion." In *Sharing Jesus in the Two-Thirds World*, edited by Vinay Samuel and Chris Sugden, 81–121. Grand Rapids: Eerdmans, 1984.

"Liberation Theology: An Evangelical View from the Third World (Book Review)." *Transformation* 1, no. 1 (Jan-Mar 1984): 28–29.

1985

"The Holy Spirit, the Christian Gospel and Religious Change: The African Evidence for a Christian Theology of Religious Pluralism." In *Essays in Religious Studies for Andrew Walls*, edited by James Thrower, 44–56. Aberdeen: Department of Religious Studies, University of Aberdeen, 1985.

"The Missionary Inheritance." In *Christianity: A World Faith*, edited by Robin Keeley, 303–11. Tring: Lion, 1985.

1986

"Christian Tradition and the African God Revisited: A Process in the Exploration of a Theological Idiom." In *Witnessing to the Living God in Contemporary Africa*, edited by David Gitari and Patrick Benson, 77–97. Nairobi: Uzima Press, 1986.

1987

"Christ in Africa: Some Reflections on the Contribution of Christianity to the African Becoming." In *African Futures: 25th Anniversary Conference Proceedings held in the Centre of African Studies, University of Edinburgh, 9–11 December 1987*, edited by Christopher Fyfe and Chris Allen, 447–58. Edinburgh: Centre of African Studies, 1987.

1988

"African Christian Theology," "Theology of African Independent Churches," "Culture," and "Black Theology." In *New Dictionary of Theology*, edited by Sinclair Ferguson and David Wright. Downers Grove, IL: InterVarsity Press, 1988.

"The Ultimate Vision: New Heaven and New Earth: Bible Study on Revelation 21:1–4." *Mission Studies* 5, no. 2 (1988): 32–38.

1989

"The Roots of African Theology." *International Bulletin of Missionary Research* 13, no. 2 (April 1989): 58–65.

"Into All the World." In *Jesus 2000*, edited by Richard Bauckham et al., 222–25. Oxford: Lion, 1989.

"World Evangelisation, Institutional Evangelicalism and the Future of the Christian World Mission." In *Proclaiming Christ in Christ's Way: Studies in Integral Evangelism*, edited by V. Samuel and A. Hauser, 52–68. Oxford: Regnum, 1989.

1990

Jesus in African Culture: A Ghanaian Perspective. Accra: Asempa, 1990; reprinted 1992. Also in William A. Dyrness, *Emerging Voices in Global Christian Theology*, 93–121. Grand Rapids: Zondervan, 2003; and as chapter 2 in *Jesus and the Gospel in Africa*. Maryknoll, NY: Orbis, 2004.

1991

"Death and the Gospel in the Ghanaian Context." *Exchange* 20, no. 2 (1991): 147–49.
"The Relevance of a Christian Approach to Culture in Africa." In *Christian Education in the African Context: Proceedings of the First Africa Regional Conference of the International Association for the Promotion of Christian Higher Education (IAPCHE), 4–9 March 1991, Harare, Zimbabwe*, 24–35. Grand Rapids: IAPCHE, 1991.

1992

"Challenges of Ghana's Fourth Republic: A Christian Perspective." The William Ofori-Atta Memorial Lectures, 7th–9th October 1992. Accra, 1992.
"New Paradigms on Ecumenical Co-Operation: An African Perspective." *International Review of Mission* (July 1992): 375–79.
Theology and Identity: The Impact of Culture on Christian Thought in the Second Century and Modern Africa. Oxford: Regnum, 1992, reprinted 1999.
Ton Crijnen, "What You Need Is a New Willibrord" (ET). Interview with Kwame Bediako in *Trouw* (22 April 1992).

1993

"Cry Jesus! Christian Theology and Presence in Modern Africa." *Vox Evangelica* 23 (April 1993): 7–25. Reprinted as chapter 1 in *Jesus and the Gospel in Africa*. Maryknoll, NY: Orbis, 2004.
"John Mbiti's Contribution to African Theology." In *Religious Plurality in Africa: Essays in Honour of John S. Mbiti*, edited by Jacob Olupona and Sulayman S. Nyang, 367–90. New York: Mouton de Gruyter, 1993.
"Reflectors Report." *Mission Studies* 10, no. 1–2 (1993): 244–47.
"Unmasking the Powers – Christianity, Authority and Desacralisation in Modern African Politics." In *Christianity and Democracy in Global Context*, edited by John Witte, 207–30. Boulder: Westview, 1993.

1994

"Christ Is Lord!: How Is Jesus Christ Unique in the Midst of Other Faiths?" *Trinity Journal of Church and Theology* (Legon) 14, no. 2 (Dec 1994-Jan 1995): 50–61.

"Understanding African Theology in the Twentieth Century." *Themelios* 20, no. 1 (Oct 1994): 14–19.

"The Unique Christ in the Plurality of Religions." In *The Unique Christ in Our Pluralist World*, edited by Bruce Nichols, 47–56. Grand Rapids: Baker, 1994.

1995

Christianity in Africa: The Renewal of a Non-Western Religion. Duff lectures, Edinburgh, 1989–1992. Edinburgh: Edinburgh University Press; New York: Orbis Books, 1995, reprinted 1997.

"De-sacralisation and Democratisation: Some Theological Reflections on the Role of Christianity in Nation-Building in Modern Africa." *Transformation* 12, no. 1 (Jan-Mar 1995): 1–4.

"The Impact of the Bible in Africa." Epilogue in Ype Schaaf, *On Their Way Rejoicing: The History and Role of the Bible in Africa*, 243–54. Carlisle: Paternoster, 1995.

"The Significance of Modern African Christianity – A Manifesto." *Studies in World Christianity, The Edinburgh Review of Theology and Religion* 1, no. 1 (1995): 51–67.

"Theologie van het grondvlak—Afrika en de toekomst van het Christendom." *Wereld en Zending*, 24 (ste Jaargang, 2, 1995): 27–39. Dutch translation and extract of "Cry Jesus!" (1993).

"What Is the Gospel?" *ATF Bulletin* 1 (1995): 6–7. Originally presented as part of the Asempa Jubilee Lectures, 27–29 September 1995 in Accra, Ghana. Later published as "What Is the Gospel?" *Transformation* 14, no. 1 (Jan/Mar 1997): 1–4.

1996

"Five Theses on the Significance of Modern African Christianity: A Manifesto." *Transformation* 13, no. 1 (Jan/Mar 1996): 20–29. An expanded version of the article published in *Studies in World Christianity, The Edinburgh Review of Theology and Religion* 1, no. 1 (1995): 51–67.

"How Is Jesus Christ Lord?: Aspects of an Evangelical Christian Apologetics in the Context of African Religious Pluralism." *Exchange* 25, no. 1 (1996): 27–42.

"Proclaiming Christ Today: As an African and Evangelical Christian." In *Proclaiming Christ Today*, edited by Huibert van Beek & George Lemopoulos, 30–43. Geneva: WCC, 1996.

"Theological Reflections." In *Serving with the Poor in Africa*, edited by Tetsunao Yamamori et. al., 181–92. Monrovia, Liberia: MARC, 1996.

"Types of African Theology." In *Christianity in Africa in the 1990s*, edited by C. Fyfe and A. Walls, 56–69. Edinburgh: University of Edinburgh, Centre for African Studies, 1996.

"Understanding African Theology in the 20th Century." *Bulletin for Contextual Theology in Southern Africa and Africa* 3, no. 2 (June 1996): 1–11.

1997

"African Theology." In *The Modern Theologians*, 2nd ed., edited by David Ford, 426–44. Oxford: Basil Blackwell, 1997.

"Book Review: *The Christian Churches and the Democratisation of Africa* by Paul Gifford," *African Affairs* 96, no. 384 (July 1997): 468–69.

"Curriculum Development: Acquiring the Right Tools for the Context." *ATF Bulletin* 5 (1997): 6–7.

"The Gospel and the Transformation of the Non-Western World." In *Anglican Life and Witness: A Reader for the Lambeth Conference of Anglican Bishops 1998*, edited by Vinay Samuel and Chris Sugden, 169–80. London: SPCK, 1997. Also chapter 10 in *Christianity in Africa: The Renewal of a Non-Western Religion*. Edinburgh: Edinburgh University Press, 1995.

"Religion and National Identity: Assessing the Discussion from Cicero to Danquah Law and Religion. Inaugural lecture, June 25, 1997." Given at the Ghana Academy of Arts and Sciences, 2006. *Law and Religion*. Accra: Black Mask Ltd., 1997, 1–18.

"What Is the Gospel?" *Transformation* 14, no. 1 (Jan/Mar 1997): 1–4. Originally presented as part of the Asempa Jubilee Lectures, 27–29 September 1995 in Accra, Ghana. See also "What Is the Gospel?" *ATF Bulletin* 1 (1995): 6–7.

1998

"Clement Anderson Akrofi," "Ephraim Amu," "Johannes Christaller," and "William Ofori-Atta." In *Biographical Dictionary of Christian Missions*, edited by G. H. Anderson, 9, 17, 133–134, 504–505. New York: Macmillian, 1998.

"The Church in the African State: Some Biblical Reflections." *Journal of African Christian Thought* 1, no. 2 (1998): 58–60.

"The Doctrine of Christ and the Significance of Vernacular Terminology." *International Bulletin of Missionary Research* 22, no. 3 (July 1998): 110–11. Paper for a graduate seminar, Edinburgh, 1997. First appeared in *Akrofi-Christaller Centre News* (January-July 1998) and later as chapter 6, "One Song in Many Tongues," in *Jesus and the Gospel in Africa*. Maryknoll, NY: Orbis, 2004.

"Facing the Challenge: Africa in World Christianity in the 21st Century: A Vision of the African Christian Future." *Journal of African Christian Thought* 1, no. 1 (1998): 52–57. From a paper given at *Akrofi-Christaller Mission Centre* in September 1997; adapted from "What Is the Gospel?" 1995, 1997.

1999

"Gospel and Culture: Guest Editorial." *Journal of African Christian Thought* 2, no. 2 (1999): 1.

"Gospel and Culture: Some Insights for Our Time from the Experience of the Earliest Christians." *Journal of African Christian Thought* 2, no. 2 (1999): 8–17.

Jezus in de cultuur en geschiedenis van Afrika. Kampen: Uitgeverij Kok Kampen, 1999.

"Translatability and the Cultural Incarnations of the Faith." In *New Directions in Mission and Evangelization 3: Faith and Culture,* edited by James A. Scherer and Stephen B. Bevans, 146–58. Maryknoll, NY: Orbis Books, 1999. Also chapter 7, 109–23, in *Christianity in Africa: The Renewal of a Non-Western Religion.* Edinburgh: Edinburgh University Press, 1995.

2000

"Africa and Christianity on the Threshold of the Third Millennium: The Religious Dimension." *African Affairs* 99 (2000): 303–23.

"African Christian Thought" and "John Mbiti." In *Oxford Companion to Christian Thought,* edited by A. Hastings and A. Mason, 8–10, 418. Oxford: Oxford University Press, 2000.

"A Half Century of African Christian Thought: Pointers to Theology and Theological Education in the Next Half Century." *Journal of African Christian Thought* 3, no. 1 (2000): 5–11.

Jesus in Africa: The Christian Gospel in African History and Experience. Oxford: Regnum Africa, 2000.

2001

"The African Renaissance and Theological Reconstruction: The Challenge of the Twenty-First Century." *Journal of African Christian Thought* 4, no. 2 (2001): 29–33.

The Disciplines of the Spiritual Life and the Dynamics of Pastoral Ministry: A Handbook for Ministers. Akopong-Akuapem: Akrofi-Christaller Memorial Centre, 2001.

Editor. *Kamfo Awurade: A Compilation of Ghanaian Choruses and Popular Hymns in English.* Akropong-Akuapem: Akrofi-Christaller Memorial Centre, 2001.

"Scripture as the Hermeneutics of Culture and Tradition." *Journal of African Christian Thought* 4, no. 1 (2001): 2–11.

2002

"Guest Editorial." *Journal of African Christian Thought* 5, no. 1 (2002): 1–3.

"Editorial." *Journal of African Christian Thought* 5, no. 2 (2002): 1–2.

"Toward a New Theodicy: Africa's Suffering in Redemptive Perspective." *Journal of African Christian Thought* 5, no. 2 (2002): 47–52. Paper given at the third Payton lecture, Fuller Theological Seminary, Pasadena, CA, USA, October 2000.

2003

"African Theology as a Challenge to Western Theology." In *Christian Identity in Cross-Cultural Perspective*, edited by Martien E. Brinkman and Dirk van Keulen, 52–67. Meinema: Zoetermeer, 2003.

"Biblical Exegesis in the African Context: The Factor and Impact of Translated Scriptures." *Journal of African Christian Thought* 6, no. 1 (2003): 15–23.

"The Church and the University: Some Reflections on the Rationale for a Christian Participation in the Public Education in Africa." *ATF Bulletin* 16 (2003): 5–7.

"Festivals." *ATF Bulletin* 15 (2003): 5–7.

2004

"Africa and Christian Identity: Recovering an Ancient Story." *Princeton Seminary Bulletin*, ns 25, no 2 (2004): 153–61.

"Christianity, Islam, and the Kingdom of God: Rethinking Their Relationship from an African Perspective." *Journal of African Christian Thought* 7, no. 2 (2004): 3–7.

"'Ethiopia Shall Soon Stretch Out Her Hands to God' (Ps. 68:31): African Christians Living the Faith: A Turning Point in Christian History." In *A New Day Dawning: African Christians Living the Gospel: Essays in Honour of Dr. J. J. (Hans) Visser*, edited by Kwame Bediako, Mechteld Jansen, Jan van Butselaar, and Aart Verburg, 30–40. Zoetermeer: Boekencentrum, 2004.

Jesus and the Gospel in Africa: History and Experience. Maryknoll, NY: Orbis Books, 2004. (First published in 2000 in the Theological Reflections from the South Series by Editions Clé and Regnum Africa as part of Regnum Books International, for the International Fellowship of Evangelical Mission Theologians.)

Religion, Culture and Language: An Appreciation of the Intellectual Legacy of Dr. J. B. Danquah. Publication of the J. B. Danquah Memorial Lectures, Series 37, 2–4 February 2004. Accra: Ghana Academy of Arts and Sciences, 2006.

"Review Essay: *Old Testament Research for Africa: A Critical Analysis and Annotated Bibliography of African Old Testament Dissertations, 1967–2000* by Knut Holter." *International Bulletin of Missionary Research* 28, no. 3 (July, 2004): 138.

2005

"Christian Witness in the Public Sphere: Some Lessons and Residual Challenges from the Recent Political History of Ghana." In *The Changing Face of Christianity: Africa, the West, and the World*, edited by Lamin Sanneh and Joel A. Carpenter, 117–32. New York: Oxford University Press, 2005.

"Ebenezer, This Is How Far the Lord Has Helped Us." Reflections on the Institutional Itinerary of the Akrofi-Christaller Memorial Centre for Mission Research and Applied Theology (1974–2005), May 2005, with Mary Bediako. Unpublished.

"Guest Editorial: Lived Christology." *Journal of African Christian Thought* 8, no. 1 (2005): 1–2.

"Worship as Vital Participation: Some Personal Reflections on Ministry in the African Church." *Journal of African Christian Thought* 8, no. 2 (2005): 3–7.

2006
"A New Era in Christian History – African Christianity as Representative Christianity: Some Implications for Theological Education and Scholarship." *Journal of African Christian Thought* 9, no. 1 (2006): 3–12.

"Scripture as the Interpreter of Culture and Tradition." In *Africa Bible Commentary*, edited by Tokunboh Adeyemo, 3–4. Grand Rapids: Zondervan, 2006.

"'Whose Religion Is Christianity?': Reflections on Opportunities and Challenges for Christian Theological Scholarship as Public Discourse – The African Dimension." *Journal of African Christian Thought* 9, no. 2 (2006): 43–48.

2007
"'In the Bible . . . Africa Walks on Familiar Ground': Why the World Needs Africa." *AICMAR Bulletin* 6 (2007): 32–50.

"Bible Studies on Slavery and Freedom," with Gillian Bediako. *Journal of African Christian Thought* 10, no. 1 (2007): 3–8.

"The Emergence of World Christianity and the Remaking of Theology." Nagel Institute Public Lecture at Calvin College, 19 July 2007. Later published in *Journal of African Christian Thought* 12, no. 2 (2009): 50–55.

"'Missionaries Did Not Bring Christ To Africa – Christ Brought Them': Why Africa Needs Jesus Christ." *AICMAR Bulletin* 6 (2007): 17–31.

"'Their Past Is Also Our Present.' Why All Christians Have Need of Ancestors: Making a Case for Africa." *AICMAR Bulletin* 6 (2007): 1–16.

2008
"Foreword." In John Azumah, *My Neighbour's Faith: Islam explained for African Christians*, ix–xi. Grand Rapids: Zondervan, 2008.

"Thoughts on the Nature of the Project." *Journal of African Christian Thought* 11, no. 2 (2008): 3–4.

"'Whose Religion Is Christianity?': Reflections on Opportunities and Challenges in Christian Theological Scholarship: The African Dimension." In *Mission in the Twenty-First Century*, 107–17, 210–13. London: Darton, Longman & Todd; Maryknoll, NY: Orbis, 2008. Published previously in *Journal of African Christian Thought* 9, no. 2 (2006): 43–48.

"Why Has the Summer Ended and We Are Not Saved?" *Journal of African Christian Thought* 11, no. 2 (2008): 5–8.

2009

"The Emergence of World Christianity and the Remaking of Theology." *Journal of African Christian Thought* 12, no. 2 (2009): 50–55.

2010

"Biblical Exegesis in Africa: The Significance of the Translated Scriptures." In *African Theology on the Way: Current Conversations,* edited by Diane Stinton, 12–20. London: SPCK, 2010.

"Christian Faith and African Culture: An Exposition of the Epistle to the Hebrews." *Journal of African Christian Thought* 13, no. 1 (2010): 45–57.

2011

"Andrew F. Walls as Mentor" and "Conclusion: The Emergence of World Christianity and the Remaking of Theology." In *Understanding World Christianity: The Vision and Work of Andrew F. Walls,* edited by William R. Burrows, Mark R. Gornik, and Janice A. McLean, 7–10, 243–56. Maryknoll, NY: Orbis, 2011.

2014

"Biblical Perspectives on Christian Leadership in the Ghanaian Context." *Journal of African Christian Thought* 17, no. 2 (2014): 10–15.

Index

 Langham

Langham Literature and its imprints are a ministry of Langham Partnership.

Langham Partnership is a global fellowship working in pursuit of the vision God entrusted to its founder John Stott –

> *to facilitate the growth of the church in maturity and Christ-likeness through raising the standards of biblical preaching and teaching.*

Our vision is to see churches in the Majority World equipped for mission and growing to maturity in Christ through the ministry of pastors and leaders who believe, teach and live by the word of God.

Our mission is to strengthen the ministry of the word of God through:
- nurturing national movements for biblical preaching
- fostering the creation and distribution of evangelical literature
- enhancing evangelical theological education

especially in countries where churches are under-resourced.

Our ministry

Langham Preaching partners with national leaders to nurture indigenous biblical preaching movements for pastors and lay preachers all around the world. With the support of a team of trainers from many countries, a multi-level programme of seminars provides practical training, and is followed by a programme for training local facilitators. Local preachers' groups and national and regional networks ensure continuity and ongoing development, seeking to build vigorous movements committed to Bible exposition.

Langham Literature provides Majority World preachers, scholars and seminary libraries with evangelical books and electronic resources through publishing and distribution, grants and discounts. The programme also fosters the creation of indigenous evangelical books in many languages, through writer's grants, strengthening local evangelical publishing houses, and investment in major regional literature projects, such as one volume Bible commentaries like *The Africa Bible Commentary* and *The South Asia Bible Commentary*.

Langham Scholars provides financial support for evangelical doctoral students from the Majority World so that, when they return home, they may train pastors and other Christian leaders with sound, biblical and theological teaching. This programme equips those who equip others. Langham Scholars also works in partnership with Majority World seminaries in strengthening evangelical theological education. A growing number of Langham Scholars study in high quality doctoral programmes in the Majority World itself. As well as teaching the next generation of pastors, graduated Langham Scholars exercise significant influence through their writing and leadership.

To learn more about Langham Partnership and the work we do visit **langham.org**

Lightning Source UK Ltd.
Milton Keynes UK
UKHW020950161221
395721UK00009B/2090